FERENCZI AND HIS WORLD

The History of Psychoanalysis Series

Professor Brett Kahr and Professor Peter L. Rudnytsky (Series Editors)

Published and distributed by Karnac Books

Other titles in the Series

Her Hour Come Round at Last: A Garland for Nina Coltart
edited by Peter L. Rudnytsky and Gillian Preston

Rescuing Psychoanalysis from Freud and Other Essays in Re-Vision
by Peter L. Rudnytsky

FERENCZI AND HIS WORLD

Rekindling the Spirit of the Budapest School

edited by

*Judit Szekacs-Weisz
and Tom Keve*

KARNAC

First published in 2012 by
Karnac Books Ltd
118 Finchley Road, London NW3 5HT

British Library Cataloguing in Publication Data

A C.I.P. for this book is available from the British Library

ISBN 978 1 78049 020 5

Edited, designed and produced by The Studio Publishing Services Ltd
www.publishingservicesuk.co.uk
e-mail: studio@publishingservicesuk.co.uk

Printed in Great Britain

www.karnacbooks.com

CONTENTS

ACKNOWLEDGEMENTS   vii

ABOUT THE EDITORS AND CONTRIBUTORS   ix

SERIES EDITOR'S FOREWORD by Peter L. Rudnytsky   xiii

INTRODUCTION by Judit Szekacs-Weisz   xxi

CHAPTER ONE
Ferenczi remembered   1
  Tom Keve

CHAPTER TWO
Sandor Ferenczi the man   31
  Imre Hermann

CHAPTER THREE
Some social and political issues related to Ferenczi   39
and the Hungarian school
  Ferenc Erős

CHAPTER FOUR
Ferenczi in context   55
  Edith Kurzweil

CHAPTER FIVE
Ferenczi now and then: an introduction to his world   69
  André Haynal

CHAPTER SIX
Healing boredom: Ferenczi and his circle of literary friends   87
  Michelle Moreau-Ricaud

CHAPTER SEVEN
Ferenczi and Ortvay: two boys from Miskolc   97
  Tom Keve

CHAPTER EIGHT
Ferenczi and trauma: a perilous journey to the labyrinth   111
  György Hidas

CHAPTER NINE
Regression post-Ferenczi   129
  Harold Stewart

CHAPTER TEN
Imre Hermann: researching psyche and space   139
  Sára Klaniczay

CHAPTER ELEVEN
Physics, metaphysics, and psychoanalysis   157
  Tom Keve

INDEX   179

ACKNOWLEDGEMENTS

It is a pleasure to thank all the authors for their excellent and insightful contributions and for their patience through the several years that it has taken to refine this volume. The continued support and helpful, critical comments of Professor Ferenc Erős is gratefully acknowledged. Mrs Anna Kovács and Ildikó Kovács aided us with research and careful copy-editing, while Mr Mark Baczoni kindly translated several Ferenczi obituaries from the Hungarian original for Chapter Two. The professional and personal support of Kathleen Kelley-Lainé over the years is also greatly valued and much appreciated by both of us.

We thank Mr Ivan Ward for his good-natured support over the years and for the facilities of the Freud Museum, of which we availed ourselves. Thanks are also due to Ken Robinson and the Archives of the British Psychoanalytical Society and Institute of Psychoanalysis for access and permission to reproduce correspondence (and photographs). We are happy to thank Her Excellency, Mrs Katalin Bogyay, Hungary's ambassador to UNESCO, for continued interest and support of our projects and for her belief that social sciences and psychoanalytic ideas are a valuable part of a nation's culture.

Last, but certainly not least, we are very pleased to acknowledge helpful advice of our Series Editors, Professors Peter Rudnytsky and Brett Kahr, and are grateful to them and to Mr Oliver Rathbone of Karnac Books for inclusion in their History of Psychoanalysis series.

Judit Szekacs-Weisz and Tom Keve
Imago International, London, June 2011

ABOUT THE EDITORS AND CONTRIBUTORS

Ferenc Erős (1946) studied psychology and literature at the ELTE University in Budapest, and graduated in 1969. He obtained his PhD in 1986, and he has been Doctor of the Hungarian Academy of Sciences (DSc) since 2002. Currently, he is Professor of Social Psychology at the Faculty of Humanities of the University of Pécs, where he has directed a doctoral programme in psychoanalytic studies since 1997. Simultaneously, he directs a social psychological research unit at the Research Institute of Psychology of the Hungarian Academy of Sciences in Budapest. In the academic year 2010–2011, he was senior fellow at the Collegium Budapest, Institute for Advanced Studies. The focus of his present research includes the social and cultural history of psychoanalysis in Central Europe, psychoanalytic theory and its application to social issues, the problem of trauma, and cultural memory. He edited the Hungarian translation of the Freud–Ferenczi correspondence, and he published—in collaboration with Judit Szekacs—the correspondence between Sandor Ferenczi and Ernest Jones. He is author of several scientific books and articles in his areas of research.

André Haynal is Honorary Professor of the University of Geneva (Switzerland) and former Visiting Professor at Stanford University

(CA). Former President of the Swiss Psychoanalytic Society and a former Vice-President of the European Psychoanalytic Federation, he is the author of eleven books (originally in French) and many publications: among others, *Depression and Creativity*; *The Technique at Issue: Controversies in Psychoanalysis, from Freud and Ferenczi to Michael Balint*; *Disappearing and Reviving: Sandor Ferenczi in the History of Psychoanalysis*, and is a scientific supervising editor of the *Freud–Ferenczi Correspondence*.

Imre Hermann (3.11.1889, Budapest–24.02.1984, Budapest), Hungarian neurologist and psychoanalyst. He received his doctorate in medicine in 1913. In 1919, he became a member of the Hungarian Psychoanalytical Society. In 1925, he was secretary, 1936 to 1944, vice president, and after 1945, president of the Hungarian Society. In addition to psychoanalysis, he was interested in, among other things, logic, mathematics, experimental psychology, philosophy, and ethology. His concept of the "clinging instinct" became especially well known. He was an outstanding representative of the Budapest School of psychoanalysis, one of Sandor Ferenczi's students and later his peer, and himself a master to numerous Hungarian analysts. He had the rare opportunity—and capacity—to shape the thinking of three generations of psychoanalysts.

György Hidas (1925), psychiatrist and training analyst is one of the central figures of the renewal of post-war psychoanalysis in Hungary and the recreation of the Hungarian Psychoanalytical Society. Founder member and President of the Sandor Ferenczi Society (1988–1998), he is the author of a wide scope of more than seventy publications, ranging from the history of psychoanalysis (with a special focus on Sandor Ferenczi's life and work, his trauma theory and place and role in the international movement of his time) to more general clinical and technical issues. Lately, he developed a method for working through aspects of the prenatal relationship in the mother–baby dyad. He remains a most respected teacher and therapist of different generations.

Tom Keve studied physics at Manchester University, has a PhD in Crystallography from Imperial College, London, and is a Fellow of the Institute of Physics. Since retiring from an active career in scientific research and industry, he has become an author, with a special interest in the history of science and the history of psychoanalysis. His book, *Triad: The Physicists, The Analysts, The Kabbalists* (in its French translation, *Trois explications du monde*) was shortlisted for the 2010 European Book Prize. He is co-founder and secretary of Imago International.

Sára Klaniczay, psychologist and training analyst, member of the IPA and of the Training Committee of the Hungarian Psychoanalytic Association. Unusually for an analyst, she has a degree in mathematics and has worked as a science teacher, taking a special interest in problem children, before turning to psychology and psychoanalysis. Her mentors were, in mathematics, Péter Rózsa, in developmental psychology, Anna Gleiman, in diagnostics, Ferenc Mérei and Péter Popper. She received her psychoanalytical training from Imre Hermann and child analysis from Lillian Rotter. For many years she worked in the Faludi Street Outpatient's Clinic for Child Psychotherapy with Julia György. Subsequently, she lectured at the College for Teachers of Handicapped Children, and now takes part in the postgraduate training course of Debrecen University, teaching child psychotherapy. Dr Klaniczay has published fifty-six articles and four books, entitled: *Cases from the Field of Child Psychotherapy* (1992), *Space and Psyche: Thoughts about Healing and Creation* (2000), *On Childhood Stuttering* (2001); *Roomy Space* (2006).

Edith Kurzweil, a sociologist, is the former editor of *Partisan Review* and university Professor of Humanities and Social Science, Emeritus, Adelphi University. Her books include *The Age of Structuralism: Levi-Strauss to Foucault* (1980); *Freudians and Feminists* (1995); *The Freudians* (1989); *Nazi Laws and Jewish Lives*. She has written, among others, for *The Psychoanalytic Review, American Sociological Review, Commentary, Psychoanalytic Books, Psychology Today, Partisan Review,* and *The New York Sun*. In 2003, she received the Medal for National Endowment of Humanities. Her memoir, *Full Circle* (2007), was published by Transaction.

Michelle Moreau-Ricaud is a psychoanalyst, Doctor of Psychology, Member and Analytical Secretary of the Quatrième Groupe OPLF, Research Associate of the Centre de Recherche Psychanalyse et Médecine (Université Paris Diderot). She is also the scientific secretary of the Association Internationale d'Histoire de la Psychanalyse, a

Member of the Société Médicale Balint and the President of the Sandor Ferenczi House, Paris.

Harold Stewart, a trusted and respected personification of the independent spirit of British psychoanalysis, brought original thinking and commonsense humanity to the practice of his profession. Born in London, trained at UCL and UCSH, in 1947, a year after qualifying in medicine he entered the NHS at its inception. He was drawn first towards hypnotherapy, then to psychoanalysis, as a more sensitive, productive and far-reaching method of exploring and understanding the patient's experience. He was consultant psychiatrist at the Paddington Centre for Psychotherapy and consultant psychotherapist at the Tavistock Clinic until his retirement in 1989. His many publications include two books, *Psychic Experience and Problems of Technique* (1992) and *Michael Balint, Object Relations Pure and Applied* (1996). Dr Stewart died on 25 June 2005. His contribution to the present volume was one of his last publications.

Judit Szekacs-Weisz, PhD, is a bilingual psychoanalyst and psychotherapist, a member of the Group of Independent Psychoanalysts, and training analyst of the Hungarian Psychoanalytical Society. Born and educated (mostly) in Budapest, she has absorbed the ideas and way of thinking of Ferenczi, the Balints, Hermann, and Rajka, as an integral part of a "professional mother tongue". The experience of living and working in a totalitarian regime sensitised her to the social and individual aspects of trauma, identity formation, and strategies of survival. She was a founding member of the Sandor Ferenczi Society, Budapest. In 1990, she moved to London, where, with a small group of psychoanalysts, therapists, artists, and social scientists, she founded Imago East West, and later the Multilingual Psychotherapy Centre (MLPC), to create a space where diverse experiences of living and changing context and language in different cultures can be explored and creative solutions found. Author of several articles and editor of *Lost Childhood and the Language of Exile* (Freud Museum & Imago East West, 2004), she is President of Imago International.

Peter L. Rudnytsky

If, in the words of Lou Andreas-Salomé recalled by Imre Hermann, in commemorating the centenary of Ferenczi's birth in 1873, "his was not the present but the future", this lovingly edited collection provides abundant evidence that the time of this "most gifted and spiritual of the psychoanalysts" has finally and fully arrived.

As Judit Szekacs-Weisz explains in her Introduction, all the essays she and Tom Keve have brought together were inspired by, or written for, gatherings taking place in London over the past two decades. But this circumstance shaping the genesis of *Ferenczi and His World*, which has led the editors informally to refer to it, together with its forthcoming companion, *Ferenczi in His Time*, as their "London Ferenczi Reader", points to a deeper and more intrinsic connection between "the spirit of the Budapest school" and British psychoanalysis. Not only was Ferenczi named in 1921 the first Honorary Member of the British Psychoanalytical Society, but he was the analyst of Ernest Jones, Melanie Klein, John Rickman, and Michael Balint, and, thereby, became a tutelary spirit also for their numerous analytic descendants. It is, therefore, not surprising that there should be a particular affinity between Ferenczi's prescient contributions and the collective achievements of the British Independent tradition, or that he should be no less ardently beloved by adherents of the relational, interpersonal, and self psychological movements in the USA and, indeed, throughout the world.

Szekacs-Weisz concludes her Introduction by saying that the editors hope "to create an internal thinking space for the reader" of their volume, and, through the emerging "linkages to our experiences", both individually and collectively, to strengthen "our belief in the immense creative potentials of psychoanalysts working together". In furnishing this sketch of this book as it has taken shape in my own "thinking space", I would like to invite other readers to complete the portrait in keeping with their psychic co-ordinates.

After Judit Szekacs-Weisz's Introduction, which includes extracts from hitherto unpublished letters occasioned by Ferenczi's 1927 visit to the UK, the book leads off with a pair of chapters that will be worth their weight in gold to historians of psychoanalysis. In "Ferenczi remembered", co-editor Tom Keve compiles obituaries of Ferenczi, all composed within a year of his death but either largely or altogether unknown to English-speaking readers. The authors are Ignotus (the pen name of Hugo Veigelsberg, editor of the seminal literary journal *Nyugat* ("West") and one of the founders of the Hungarian Psychoanalytic Association), the Hungarian writers Sándor Márai and Frigyes Karinthy, as well as the analytic triad of Balint, Jones, and Rickman. Then, in "Sandor Ferenczi the man", we are treated to the previously cited address delivered by Imre Hermann in 1974, some forty years after the earlier eulogies.

Taken as an ensemble, the tributes to Ferenczi constitute a "composite photograph" that allow his most outstanding qualities to shine through luminously. For Ignotus, Ferenczi taught that "there is only one medicine—the doctor" who could "act on the person as human being" and, thereby, ineffably "heal". Similarly, for Balint, he was "a physician in the finest, richest sense of the word", and "Ferenczi never forgot that psychoanalysis was really discovered by a patient", Anna O. Accordingly, Ferenczi "laid down the principle, above all for his own use, that if a patient is willing to continue the analysis and the work still does not proceed, then it is the physician and his method who are at fault". Jones, needless to say, presents a "classical" view of Ferenczi, singling out the paper "Stages in the development of the sense of reality" (1913) as "the best he ever wrote", while claiming that in the writings of his final period "Ferenczi showed unmistakable signs of mental regression in his attitude toward fundamental problems of psychoanalysis". In so far as Jones' assessment carries the implication that Ferenczi became mentally ill at the end of his life, it is directly refuted by Hermann in his testimonial and is now known to be a canard. On the other hand, it is true that Ferenczi "regressed" in seeking to rehabilitate Breuer and Freud's early emphasis on the role of trauma in pathogenesis, and, although we might wish to dissociate ourselves from Jones' condescending view that Ferenczi's "tremendous significance" is limited to "the earlier development of psychoanalysis", there is no reason to distrust Jones' recollection that *Studies on Hysteria* "remained his favourite among Freud's writings".

Complementing Ferenczi's devotion to healing, another common thread in the tributes is that his work, to quote Balint again, "leads us through every perplexity of the seeker for truth", in which "each subsequent paper is a just but strict and incorruptible criticism of the former". On a less serious note, Ignotus observes that Ferenczi's passion for psychoanalysis made him "single-minded in catching red-handed everyone he happened to be talking to". Hermann independently echoes Balint in highlighting that Ferenczi's "sense of vocation was accompanied by a search for truth", while Jones concurs that his "honesty and loyalty" were so highly developed that they could be described as "ruthless", and "there was a vein of determinedness in his nature which made him never flinch from any path he had decided on, however painful the consequences might be".

In addition to providing a composite photograph of "Ferenczi the man", these invaluable reminiscences also give us a preliminary snapshot of his world. Ignotus, for instance, conjures up what might be regarded as the Budapest counterpart to Freud's "Psychological Wednesday Society" meetings in Vienna when he recounts how he, Ferenczi, the young Sándor Radó (then a lawyer), and others would gather in the studio of the painter Róbert Bérenyi, where they would all animatedly

> discuss Ferenczi's groundbreaking conclusions and observations as the day stretched into night, together with Einstein's theory of relativity, which also poked its head into the world round about the same time, and as the sun came up again, we saw the world differently than we had before.

But if psychoanalysis converged with physics, so did it also (to anti-cipate the title of Tom Keve's essay) with metaphysics when Ignotus would come to Ferenczi's consulting room on a Sunday afternoon and the two men

> sat side by side, in silence, holding hands with our eyes closed, observ-ing our thoughts, and then each scribbling down on a piece of paper what he had thought, what had come to mind, and comparing the two scraps we saw that what had come to my mind was associated by the logic of Freudian dream interpretation with what Ferenczi had thought of . . . and so I believed in the transfer of thoughts.

Should we call this telepathy or a "dialogue of unconsciouses"? It is surely relevant that Rickman's obituary, where he rates Géza Róheim and Melanie Klein as Ferenczi's "two most distinguished pupils", appeared not in an analytic publication, but, rather, in the *Journal of the Society of Psychical Research*. And, although Rickman concurs with Jones in his approbation for "Stages in the development of a sense of reality", it is hard to imagine Jones endorsing Rickman's description of Ferenczi's paper as one of "his most important contributions bear-ing on psychical research", let alone Rickman's commendation of Ferenczi for believing that "to the neurologist the notion of telepathy must be accounted a new belief" and "an important one to study".

If, thus far, I have accorded primacy to Ferenczi's identity as a healer and a seeker after truth, a third quality that stands out in these tributes is his humility. According to Hermann, Ferenczi "never wished to give the impression of being better than others". On the contrary, he adhered to the principle that "the analyst should be kind to his patient even to the point of being humble", whereas, in Ferenczi's view, "Freud's treatment was unfriendly". Since the publi-cation of the *Clinical Diary*, of course, to which Hermann had access, we know that Ferenczi did indeed reluctantly come to see Freud in this negative light. It is, likewise, Ferenczi's profound humility that led him to insist that analysts needed, in Balint's words, to "sacrifice a large amount of medical narcissism" in order to become "the well-meaning, motherly, tender, understanding companion with whom it is possible for the patient to live through the painful events of his early life". And if Ferenczi challenged his fellow healers to surrender their "medical narcissism", should it be surprising that, as Márai remarks, "not one doctor came to his funeral, only his analyst friends", or that

Márai would have celebrated Ferenczi—with an apt allusion to the title of the first novel by his bosom friend Georg Groddeck—as one who "knew more about human life than any of the soul-searchers in Hungary before him", and who might even have been "a poet"?

After the two indispensable liminal chapters containing primary materials on Ferenczi, there follows a series of chapters, all written by leading scholars or clinicians, that take us into the four corners of his world. What might be called the book proper is strongly anchored by Ferenc Erős's synoptic overview of the features that distinguished the two capitals of the Austro-Hungarian monarchy, with the result that "the 'underground' character of psychoanalysis was much clearer in Budapest than in Vienna", and his masterful tracing of the "close connection" between Hungarian psychoanalysis and "the progressivist cultural and spiritual currents of the age". Erős brings out how, as early as "Psychoanalysis and education" (1908), Ferenczi introduced the concept of "surplus repression" that foreshadows the influential formulation of Herbert Marcuse, and he shows more generally the extent to which "the anti-political and anti-authoritarian utopianism of Ferenczi's early writings" anticipates the trenchant social analyses of "Wilhelm Reich, Erich Fromm, and other thinkers of Freudo-Marxism and the Frankfurt School". Above all, in consonance with Balint's stress on Ferenczi's ironic deflation of "medical narcissism," Erős highlights how, "in Fromm's lifelong critique of Freud and of the psychoanalytic movement, Ferenczi is the positive hero who represents a radical challenge to 'the doctor's hidden sadism', that is to say, to the analyst as father-figure", even though, "excluded from the Budapest Medical Association and exiled to the margins of the existing order, Ferenczi apparently abandoned the area of social critique after the First World War".

In my own "internal thinking space", of the ensuing six chapters I would group those by Edith Kurzweil, Michelle Moreau-Ricaud, and Tom Keve into one cluster, and those by André Haynal, György Hidas, and the late Harold Stewart into another. As a sociologist, Kurzweil situates questions posed by the history of psychoanalysis within a "social context", while Moreau-Ricaud revisits Ferenczi's literary ambience evoked in her 1992 French-language anthology, *Cure d'ennui*, an ambiguous phrase that can be rendered as either "boredom therapy" or "healing boredom", and Keve examines the personal and professional links between two "boys from Miskolc", Ferenczi and the distinguished physicist Rudolf Ortvay, born in 1885, twelve years after the psychoanalyst. Whereas the essays by Kurzweil, Moreau-Ricaud, and Keve lead the reader outward, those by Haynal, Hidas, and Stewart lead one into the inner world and grapple with a set of inter-connected issues arising in psychoanalytic theory and clinical practice. Haynal, the dean of contemporary Ferenczians, acknowledges a kinship with Jean Laplanche in proposing a conception of analysis as a process of "mutual seduction"; Hidas underscores the centrality of Ferenczi's investigations of trauma, noting that the Hungarian title of *Thalassa* is *Catastrophes in the Development of Sexual Life*; Stewart extends Balint's reflections on Ferenczi's understanding of regression, a topic of abiding interest to analysts in the British Middle Group.

The final two chapters are *sui generis*, and intriguingly expand the horizons of this book. Sára Klaniczay, who trained with Hermann, expounds the latter's theory of the ethologically grounded clinging instinct, which is paired with its antipode, going-in-search, as well as his work on "the interaction between visual space perception and our emotional life". She promotes the "search for congruency", Hermann's method for understanding psychological phenomena by examining them from the standpoint of a seemingly unrelated field, such as topology, according to which geometric properties are unaf-fected by changes in the size or shape of figures. Klaniczay exempli-fies the ideal of congruency by ranging freely from the ethereal rigours of mathematics to deeply moving personal vignettes, including an encounter with a hospitalised patient who clairvoyantly reassured her at a time when her son's life was hanging in the balance.

In a true *tour de force*, Tom Keve brings the volume to a close with a dazzlingly erudite unfurling of the "web of personal contacts", which is simultaneously one of intellectual affinities, among the most brilliant and creative minds in twentieth-century physics and psycho-analysis. How many scholars of psychoanalysis are aware that "the *really* famous people" invited to Clark University in 1909 were not Freud and Jung, but the Nobel laureates Ernest Rutherford and A. A. Michelson, progenitors, respectively, of quantum physics and the theory of relativity? Most astonishingly, however, Keve demonstrates, with an elegance that will leave positivists shaking their heads, that both physics and psychoanalysis are inseparable from metaphysics or what Ferenczi, in the title of a paper published in 1899, termed "Spiritism". As Niels Bohr responded when asked by a sceptic whether he believed that the horseshoe hanging on the doorframe of his cottage would bring him luck, "Of course not, but I understand it works whether or not you believe!" Suffice it to say that readers of Keve's essay are likely to think twice before emulating Wolfgang Pauli by checking into a hospital room bearing the number 137, which is not only the mathematical value of the letters comprising the Hebrew word *Kabbalah*, but also a very close approximation of "the magic number of physics".

Or, in the words of Sára Klaniczay that illustrate a "general truth", not only of Euclidean geometry but also of psychic life, and which I would choose as my personal epigraph for *Ferenczi and His World*, "In an extremely marginal situation, sometimes one can discover an expanded space".

Professor Peter L. Rudnytsky
Series Co-Editor
Gainesville, Florida

Introduction

Judit Szekacs-Weisz

A central figure of the early psychoanalytical movement and the Budapest School, a dynamic driving force behind the creation of the International Psychoanalytical Association, Honorary Member of the British Society . . . these are just a small sample of the markers of Sandor Ferenczi's life and work. Working from Budapest, the "second capital" of the new science in the early days, Ferenczi devoted his life to the theory, technique, and practice of psychoanalysis.

"He made all analysts his students", wrote Freud about Ferenczi in 1933, and, indeed, the list of such names is very substantial. Ernest Jones, Melanie Klein, Franz Alexander, Sándor Radó, Géza Róheim, John Rickman, Clara Thomson, István Hollós, Imre Hermann, Margaret Mahler, René Spitz, the Balints (of course), Vilma Kovács, Otto Rank . . . just to mention a few analysts of the first generation most closely related to Ferenczi and the Budapest School. His analysands (a term also coined by Ferenczi) and students have taken his ideas, along with themselves, well beyond the borders of Hungary.

Ferenczi died before his sixtieth birthday in 1933. Soon after his death, the development and continuity of the psychoanalytic movement was forcefully interrupted: history interfered. Elaborating the resultant traumatisation will become the psychic task of generations to come.

The project of "rediscovering" Sandor Ferenczi has been an extremely interesting chapter in the recent history of psychoanalysis. The fact that Ferenczi, one of the leading figures of the formative years of psychoanalysis, analyst and teacher of professionals from all over the world, needed to be rediscovered about forty years after his death is a curious story in itself. This story has been researched and told from different perspectives of historical and clinical understanding over the past decades.

After years of silence, the 1980s marked the dawn of a new beginning, opening up the way to recall and reintegrate Ferenczi's image and basic contributions, as well as a few other "lost children" of the early analytical world. These changes also made certain areas of our "forgotten knowledge" rethinkable: concepts regarding the working of body and mind, the development and function of reality testing, the nature of individual and social traumatism, mutuality, technique, methodology, and also the dynamics of societal development.

During the past two decades, Ferenczi Societies have been formed in several countries. There have been conferences, publications, lectures, and workshops devoted to the idea of bringing to life a wide range of his ideas, including the ever-actual and elementary issues of transference and countertransference, his theory of trauma and dynamics of development, and also to achieve a deeper understanding of his surprisingly vivid and contemporary theory of mind.

Ferenczi's links to the UK are many and varied. Having been the analyst of several of the leading figures (and their family members) of the contemporary British world of psychoanalysis, such as Ernest Jones, Melanie Klein, John Rickman, and Michael Balint, he was well known and well respected in Britain during his lifetime.

In 1921, the British Society elected him to Honorary Membership. His papers and books were translated into English soon after they appeared in the original German (or occasionally in Hungarian). He spoke good English, but in his correspondence he used mostly German, while his English-speaking partners replied generally in their native tongue.

Ferenczi was invited to come to London several times. To give the reader a taste of people and bonds, we are going to present you a few extracts from letters in connection with Ferenczi's visit to London, which were discovered in the Archives of the British Psychoanalytical Society in 2004 and are being published here for the first time.

The correspondence surrounding his 1926 visit to the UK shows palpable excitement among his colleagues and pupils living here (among others, Dr Edith Eder, Dr Cole, Marjory Franklin, and William Samuel Inman). The eagerness and competition for "having Ferenczi", even for a few hours, sizzle through the pages. Steady and faithful Rickman orchestrates timetables and itinerary and calms the contenders.

He writes,

13th May, 1927

Dear Inman,

. . . I appear to have been appointed a sort of majordomo, and in this capacity would like to suggest, Sunday, the 12th. If this is convenient I hope you will let me know. He addresses the Medical Section of the British Psychological Society on the 13th, and the British Psycho-Analytical Society on the 15th. I believe that the next week-end, 17th or 18th to 20th, he is booked up with the Joneses.

Inman replies:

27th May, 1927

Dear Rickman,

the way of the organizer seems harder than that of the transgressor. It would appear as if I were messing up your arrangements with or for S.[andor] F.[erenczi] but apart from the question of hospitality I have urgent private reasons for having him as long as possible.

Edith Cole writes,

26th May, 1927

. . . I asked him (Ferenczi) to name a date, when I might offer him + madame Ferenczi hospitality, which has been the custom for the many years I have known the Ferenczi family, to say nothing of being a long standing pupil of the Doctor therefore I should be grateful if you would tell me something of his vacant times as his movements appear to be under your directions.

Reading through these letters, the professional correspondence and other documents of the pioneering years, one cannot help being drawn into the web of personal, and often private connections and associations. Having a taste of the emotional atmosphere of even well known events adds a special flavour to historical research. The linkages cover the whole territory of human existence and reach far and deep. Colleagues discuss new ideas, alliances, and tensions, plans regarding meetings, and also the creation of new groups and institutions. They show enthusiasm in sharing professional experience and discoveries, try to listen to and, more than once, learn from each other.

This volume is a testimony to the extraordinary professional and human relationship that formed between Ferenczi and other leading figures of the history of early psychoanalysis.

Pupils and teachers, colleagues from distant lands belonging to the first and next generations, working, thinking, and arguing with each other. They are the living classics of our profession . . .

London is in the focus of our attention. All the articles included here were written for, or inspired by, meetings, workshops, and conferences in London during the past two decades. The authors of this volume are drawn from the international psychoanalytical community, with a major contribution from Hungarian colleagues. The reader will find articles dealing with linkages between Sandor Ferenczi's work and ideas and the later contributions of the Balints (Michael, Alice, and Enid), of Imre Hermann, Melanie Klein, and Dolto. The professional portraits are drawn against the background of contemporary Europe: history, culture, socio-psychological aspects, and the internal dynamics of the psychoanalytic movement. Their differing capacities and personality traits, the conflicts of their private lives, their professional interests, theoretical disagreements and—last but not least—vicissitudes of the actual group formations within the psychoanalytical movement, all affect the complex relationship between the protagonists.

By reviving the images of a slightly forgotten past, we aim to rekindle not only the spirit of the Budapest School and of Ferenczi himself, but would like to create an internal thinking space for the reader where questioning, understanding, and sharing can happen, linkages to our experiences can be made, and which could be revisited time and again when we are in need of strengthening our belief in the immense creative potentials of psychoanalysts working together.

CHAPTER ONE

Ferenczi remembered[1]

Tom Keve

H ad Vitamin B$_{12}$ been identified and isolated twenty years earlier, Sandor Ferenczi might have survived for many more productive years, instead of passing away at the age of fifty-nine. As it was, Ferenczi died at his home in the early afternoon of Monday 22 May 1933 from complications caused by pernicious anaemia.

The event was reported by the evening newspaper, *Az Est*, as follows:

> A member of the Hungarian medical community of international renown, Dr Sandor Ferenczi, neurologist, founder and president of the Hungarian psychoanalytical Association passed away on Monday at 14.30 hours, in his villa in Lisznyai utca. Sandor Ferenczi had been suffering from severe anaemia for several months. A world famous physician, he would have completed his sixtieth year in July. In the course of his medical career, he came to know Freud, the grand master of psychoanalysis, with whom he formed a long, close friendship. Sandor Ferenczi had written numerous works in the field of psycho-analysis. His books and articles were published in Hungarian, German and English. Twenty years ago, he founded the Hungarian Psycho-analytical Association, which has been active under his presidency

ever since. His funeral will be held this Wednesday afternoon, at 16:00 in the Farkasrét Jewish Cemetery.

A report of the funeral appeared in several journals, including the *Budapesti Hírlap* on 25 May.

> Sandor Ferenczi was buried in the Farkasrét Jewish Cemetery on May 24, 1933 at 4 o'clock in the afternoon. Numerous figures from our medical, literary and artistic establishments were in attendance. Also present were Anna Freud, Martin Freud, Paul Federn and Helene Deutsch. The ceremony was carried out according to the rites of the Jews, with a eulogy given by the Chief Rabbi of Buda. Imre Hermann spoke for the Hungarian Psychoanalytic Association, Paul Federn for the International Psychoanalytical Association while Michael Balint spoke for his many disciples.

Although he had been seriously ill for some time, Ferenczi's death was nevertheless sudden and took his many friends by surprise. A number of those present at the funeral wrote obituaries or articles of remembrance, for the daily press as well as for the psychoanalytic community. The editor-in-chief of the prominent literary magazine *Nyugat*, who was also one of the founding members of the Hungarian Psychoanalytic Association, was unable to attend the funeral. His name was Hugo Veigelsberg (1869–1949), but everybody knew him by his pen-name of Ignotus. His beautifully written piece appeared on the 28th May, just a few days after the interment, in the Budapest daily, *Magyar Hírlap* (Ignotus, 1933).

Eulogy by Ignotus (translated from the Hungarian
original by Mark Baczoni

> Sandor Ferenczi was my friend – and in the hour of his funeral, which I cannot attend, my final salute to his departing soul is to lock myself in my room, face to face with a blank page, I try to write as coolly and calmly about him, and about his discoveries about the human soul, as he once did when he began my analysis; when he had to approach me as a doctor and a scientist, and listen to me opening up. I couldn't stand this commitment at the time, I considered it an affectation from a friend, a pose if you will. Over this difference in views, my analysis ended up breaking down. Which I think in the end gave him a sense of relief – his life was anyway plagued by knowledge of people and

Ignotus, pen name of Hugó Veigelsberg (1869–1949), editor of the Hungarian literary magazine *Nyugat*.

his scientific art, through which he saw everyone in every situation, without their walls to guard them, like Lesage's limping devil saw houses. And despite the fact that he was an analyst, despite the fact that he himself had been analysed, it was in vain that he trained himself to see the natural as just that: he could hardly see it that way, since he was single-minded in catching red-handed everyone he happened to be talking to. This made it hard for him to concentrate on what they were in fact saying, since he was primarily paying attention to what was behind whatever it was that they were saying. Most people, in this way, were 'ruined' for him, and the people that he moreover thoroughly and properly analysed, were lost to him completely. I remained for him, and so I could interest him, like a book he hadn't finished reading . . . it was a sacrifice from Sandor Ferenczi, the scientist and the doctor, in every single case, to produce that objectivity that a scientist must produce faced with the object to be analysed or treated. And I, his friend, who am neither scientist nor doctor, find it perhaps fitting to take on this same responsibility towards him at the hour of our final parting.

He would indeed think this a big sacrifice, since, as worldliness makes the Jesuits the best priests, he was such a great scientist because he was, deep down, like his mentor Freud, the poetic type. Of the three students to whom Freud could entrust his thoughts as if he himself were continuing to think on them, Karl Abraham, Ernest Jones and Sandor Ferenczi, it was Ferenczi who was closest to his master in that he, too, could explore science along the edge of imagination – and like the poet, who tells the truest lies, he dared to assume that every lie is true. If ever there was a Raphael born without hands, it was Ferenczi who was not blessed, unlike Freud, with the art of communication, despite his capacity for it. He would have been very deserving of it – initially this lack gave him terrible pain, and also to his analyst (I don't know who his analyst was), with whom he clearly had great battles over it. But in this sense the process of confronting himself did indeed cure him. Although he fundamentally started out as a writer, from one day to the next, he put aside writing "for beauty" and was happy to write for precision. And so, his most important writings have a mathematical precision about them, like a geometry problem – and they are beautiful after all . . .

The poetic nature and its attractions had a special role in the early development of psychoanalysis, because on the one hand, their subjects being human beings, this predisposition sharpened their eye to little human details which only those experts on human beings, poets, tend to notice; and on the other hand, through the persons of the poets they managed to gain such disciples as took the new belief to the people, and who could thus force it upon the attentions of the established priesthood with the force of the laity and the community of the faithful. After Thomas Mann and Stefan Zweig's studies, university professors and medical weeklies could no longer write in such a carefree and slapdash tone about the new technique of psychological healing as they had done just a little while before. And Ferenczi was particularly great at finding useful phrases from everyday life, and was thus able to win over everyday people to the new science. I was able, in part through my friendship with him, to experience in miniature what became, played large, the history of the spread and triumph of psychoanalysis: the contact between the creative scientists and the intellectuals sitting up and paying attention. After the publication of his first writings, Ferenczi and I would meet every day, he the Freudian and I from the Nyugat circle, at the Városmajor studio and garden of Róbert Berény, who had just then cropped up in the 'Nyolcak' [The Eights] group exhibition. Doctor Halle was also there, a Viennese factory owner and chemist, and the young Doctor Radó, who was a lawyer at the time, but later became a doctor and is today one of the foremost analysts in America. Here we would discuss Ferenczi's groundbreaking conclusions and observations as the day stretched into night, together with Einstein's relativity, which also poked its head into the world round about the same time, and as the sun came up again, we saw the world differently than we had done the day before. Many years later, I can see the two of us sat in his consulting room on a Sunday afternoon when he didn't have patients. We sat side by side, in silence, holding hands with our eyes closed, observing our thoughts, and then each scribbling down on a piece of paper what they had thought, what had come to mind, and, comparing the two scraps we saw that what had come into my mind was associated, by the logic of Freudian dream interpretation, with what Ferenczi had thought of . . . and so I believed in the transfer of thoughts. And what was going on, in a small way, in the Városmajor and on Erzsébet Avenue, must have been going on throughout the world on a far grander scale – and today, as the new physics has engendered a new view of the world, the new analysis has engendered a new view of the person.

Ferenczi's contribution to this new view was to trace back the ancient history of the human soul even further than Freud. Ferenczi's discovery lies in daring to relate back the adult psyche to the infant's, the civilised man's to the apeman's and from these origins, the effects of these origins, to explain its proper nature despite its attempts to hide and its deceptions as well as he diagnosed its illnesses. But man does not begin with man, not even with the caveman, the newborn, the embryo. The embryo, as it develops from a cell into a being, sort of undergoes the process that animals did in developing from single-celled organisms into human beings, and it is impossible, so Ferenczi says, that the memories of this process should not haunt the human psyche. In mammals, like human beings, whose direct ancestors are the reptile and the fish, therefore, there clearly subsist memories in psychological and sexual life of the life of the fish in the sea and the first exploratory forays up rocks. The beginnings of life take us back to the sea: aren't the amniotic fluid and swimming and flying dreams returns of this primeval state? Freud and Rank had already realised that birth, the emergence from the mother's body, scars man with the trauma of a catastrophe for the rest of his life. Isn't perhaps this way of beginning life as an individual a reminder of the catastrophe that afflicted the sea creatures when the sea began to divide around the contours of the earth and their sea-going bodies now had to hug the dry land? And doesn't the memory of this defining catastrophe directly hide in the soul of the animal on dry land to this day? And what about the terrible shock of the ice age, although a much later memory, and subsisting perhaps only in man? . . . I am merely mentioning here what Ferenczi contributed beyond the stricter analytical assumptions and advances in treatment to the psychoanalytical view of the person – some he himself only played with while others he had developed viewpoints for. If psychoanalysis today is not merely a medical craft and conquering of emotional territory, but is some sort of human–natural science upon the foundations of which every other human science must be re-founded, including history, sociology, law, pedagogy, the study of art and religion, then it is Sandor Ferenczi who has the second biggest role to play in all this, after his master.

As someone not in the field, and someone, as I say, who has not even completed analysis, I cannot judge the importance of Ferenczi's medical work. But I can say of him and his enlightenments what is true for all of psychoanalysis: that while it is important for the defence of psychoanalysis that it started in healing and successful healing at that, nonetheless its conclusions and deductions about the soul would stand even if one could not cure with analysis. However much of a benefit it is that we have the electric tram, the telephone, telegraph and the radio, it would not make the principles of electricity any the less true, if we had still not got past the horse and cart. Allow me, although I am merely a layman, not to believe – beyond a point – in a medical craft that one can learn; in other words, let me repeat what I have already said – that there is only one medicine – the doctor. And even the layman could tell that Sandor Ferenczi was just such a medicine-doctor, who could act on the person as human being, and he could therefore – only he knew how – heal. Sandor Ferenczi was a person among people, the essence and lover of his kind. There are one and a half or two billion people on this planet, and many among them are more famous and more heavily decorated than Sandor Ferenczi. And yet we can safely say that with his death, humanity has become more than a one-and-a-half-billionth or two-billionth poorer. Just to dare say this is the kind of bravery that this friend learned from Sandor Ferenczi, and who now tosses it as a final garland onto his coffin . . .

* * *

Sándor Márai (1900–1989), one of the leading writers of pre-Second World War Hungary, is now, in the first decade of the twenty-first century, enjoying new-found fame in the UK. *Embers* was his first novel to appear in English, published in 2000, to be followed by *Memoir of Hungary* in 2001, *Casanova in Bolzano* in 2004, *The Rebels* in

Novelist, Sándor Márai (1900–1989).

2007, and *Esther's Inheritance* in 2008, all of them to much critical acclaim. Márai's *Embers*, adapted by Christopher Hampton, was put on as a very successful play at the Duke of York's Theatre in 2006. Sándor Márai's touching words on the death of his close friend, Ferenczi, appeared in a provincial newspaper.

The Quick and the Dead by Sándor Márai (1933) (translated from the Hungarian original by Mark Baczoni)

I dread opening the papers in the morning, I hate going to the telephone: it seems that not a week goes by any more that someone close to me doesn't die. Beyond a certain age, even if this age be a youthful one if you were to look at a calendar, a person's ties to other people become ever so much finer; everything and everyone slips through the eyes of the sieve. One day, you wake up and notice that on the one hand, you are dreadfully alone, but on the other hand you are also hopelessly embedded in a strange family, which is more real still than an ordinary family. Just a few people, the quick and the dead, who you collided with among the pagan confusion of the world and you knew, without being able to define why, that you were linked to each other. In this alternative family, there is the same sort of hierarchy of relations; there is a father, and a mother, respect, jealousy and squabbles exist there. And yet the point of this small and curious family, not linked by blood, is that you irretrievably belong together. That's said it is not even important that you see your family often; this alternative, more real family, has no need for the intimacy of the nest. The members of this family don't see each other for a year or two, and when they do, they might or might not speak to one another. To my alternative family – and thanks to his extraordinary craft to the alternative families of many others – belonged Sandor Ferenczi.

He died the week after Krúdy's death, on the Monday night, he wasn't even sixty. One fewer in my family . . . there's someone every week now. (There's some sort of dissipation in this month of May; the weather is cold and trembling, unsettling. I write this because man does not live with his brain alone.) The thirtysomethings give long and justified speeches, but I can see that the sixtysomethings do not have a particular resistance to life either. Ferenczi's death affected me in a very primitive way: I didn't believe it. When I replaced the telephone that had given me the news, I pondered a little while and then phoned my informant back – was he sure he hadn't made some mistake? I was thinking about this later, and I realised that Ferenczi's death hurts me and makes me angry; I had this childlike notion that he would have thought of something, he was exempt, that he would die only when he was ready to. As far as I knew, he was not ready yet. (In a roundabout way I found out just how much he was not ready to, and how he despised death, the primitive mechanism of life: he gave strict instructions to a member of his family that if he should happen to die, they shouldn't accept it straightaway, but should give him a vigorous shake . . . That's what he thought of the body – that it was like a quixotic watch which would stop sometimes, and would need to be shaken a bit to get it going again. In this quiet haughtiness, when giving his family a user's guide to his death, lies the whole man, with nothing left out.)

That's why his death hurt me. Maybe they just didn't shake him well enough.

Ferenczi belongs to the firmament of great Hungarian figures of this century, in at least the same way that his friend and master, Freud, belongs to the constellation of great 20th-century thinkers. Whether analysis is a form of therapy, or not, is difficult to decide now. At the moment, I think it is more of an art than a form of therapy. When Tolstoy wrote *War and Peace*, it became fairly unlikely that he would write anything very silly in the future; but it did not mean that his next work would undoubtedly be a masterpiece, as indeed it was not, and it was not until *The Death of Ivan Ilyich* that he managed to craft something approaching it. This is sort of how I see the practical chances of analysis: one or two successful cases are masterpieces, there are one or two geniuses working in the field. Freud or Ferenczi will perhaps perform miracles once or twice in their lives. But practice, experience, luck, the quality of the patient and the fortuitous interplay of so many other unpredictable factors are necessary for the miracle that I think it is only with great difficulty that we can speak of practical analysis today. In my opinion, however, it is not its therapeutic effectiveness that gives analysis its significance. What Freud realised, when at Charcot's side he noticed that the hypnotised hysteric will reproduce the symptoms of hysteria even in a state of subconsciousness – where do these symptoms retreat when we switch off self-consciousness and will in the patient? – Freud asked himself, and came up with the answer: into the subconscious), Ferenczi realised in parallel to him, and he had the courage to accept the consequences of the realisation. This great spiritual act is the result not only of genius and expertise, but also great moral courage. It is impossible to imagine today the spiritual x-ray image of this century without the Freud and the things Ferenczi improved and added to his work. This little word, "repression" is today being used by conservative politicians, who burn analytical literature in the streets, and who don't know that this short word and the way that Freud pronounced it just at the right time, illuminated the new celestial universe of the intellectual world.

In Hungary, it was Sandor Ferenczi who undertook this work of cleansing, which met with the determined opposition of official science all over the world. What does it mean to be an 'analysed' person? We can give a brief answer here: it means being a person with no illusions. Is the analysed person asocial? Not according to Freud and Ferenczi he's not; in fact, he's more social than the collective type of person, who seeks solace and relief in the herd. No wonder that this new science is detested with the same limitless passion: the Bolsheviks think it "counter-revolutionary", Hitler and his friends think it harmful and revolutionary, American bourgeois critics call it the "Jewish science", the Church has placed it on the Index, because it "dissolves" the unity of the soul, "gnaws away" at faith. The loneliness of Freud and Ferenczi was enormous and analysis is still undoubtedly isolated today. But *The Interpretation of Dreams* is thirty years old and it still stands, as solid as a rock – in vain do people push away at it: today it is canonical. Analysis isn't the answer – there is no answer. Analysis simply established a positive, which we had not discovered before, it filled in a piece of the jigsaw in soul-searching, without which it could not have gone on: the concept of the subconscious. This is what Freud brought to the table. The significance of the discovery is on a par with that of gunpowder, printing, or relativity. This is what Ferenczi realised.

Of his sixty years, he spent forty teaching, healing. Of course, he did so without a pulpit, without title, derided at first, despised later. People in Hungary do not even begin to suspect the significance of his work. It was he who stood most energetically against the charlatans of analysis: he created an orthodox circle of a small number of selected doctors, and this circle kept at bay all those who wanted to make a business of analysis, like some sort of fashionable fad. Not one doctor came to his funeral, only his analyst friends. He knew more about human life than any of the soul searchers in Hungary before him. It's my suspicion that he was a poet. Not that he wrote poems, mind you. But he knew what poets know: to feel out that something inexpressible in words, which is the real secret of a soul, a life. When I was with him, I always looked at him expectantly, as though he might let it slip. But he never let it slip, and in fact he died. I feel I've been left without an answer. That's why his death makes me angry.

*   *   *

The literary circle, of which Ferenczi was very much a part, included not only Márai and Ignotus, but Dezső Kosztolányi and Frigyes Karinthy, all of them household names in Hungary at the time, as well as today. Their contacts existed on various levels. They were all habituées of the various Budapest coffee houses, especially the Royal, where Ferenczi held court. They all contributed to Ignotus's literary journal, *Nyugat*. Several of them and/or their spouses had been analysands of Ferenczi's and they all shared a fascination with the insights of psychoanalysis, as well as the gossip surrounding Freud and his circle. Kosztolányi (1885–1936) was especially close to early psychoanalytic thinking, strongly reflected in his various novels. In *Édes Anna*, which can be described as a novel about repression, he gives an excellent portrait of Ferenczi in the guise of his Dr Moviszter character (Kosztolányi, 1991).

Karinthy (1887–1938) and Kosztolányi were close friends, ever since their university days. The former was a very prolific humorist, satirist, poet, and critic, whose work, in the main, does not translate well, though *A Journey Round my Skull* and *Capillaria* (Karinthy, 2008 and 2010, respectively) have appeared in English. His second wife, Aranka Böhm, was a psychiatrist and psychoanalyst, and he was known to regularly transcribe his dreams. A great many of Karinthy's shorter pieces had the human psyche and psychiatry as subjects. Titles such as "My study of the psyche", "Visiting the psychiatrist", and "Melancholy", speak for themselves ("Tanyulmányozom a lelket" (Karinthy, 1913); "Az idegorvosnál" (Karinthy, 1912); and "Melankolia" (Karinthy, 1911), respectively). In his "Kötéltánc" ("Dance on the tightrope", Karinthy (1923), he portrayed a Ferenczi, as well as a possible Freud, character (Szalay, 1961). Although initially Karinthy was a great proponent of psychoanalysis, he seems to have changed his mind somewhat, and in this last work was generally critical of the psychoanalytic school. *Kötéltánc* generated much critical comment and, as a consequence, Ferenczi published an article in *Nyugat*, entitled "The sleeping and waking science; a letter to Frigyes Karinthy" (Ferenczi, 1924), which in turn generated Karinthy's "Response to Sandor Ferenczi" (Karinthy, 1924). In spite of this public airing of their differences of opinion, the two men remained the best of friends and Karinthy published the following bitter-sweet obituary of the analyst (Karinthy, 1933).

Soul Diver – on the occasion of Sandor Ferenczi's passing by Frigyes Karinthy (translated from the Hungarian original by Mark Baczoni)

After lunch, I was oppressed by sleep; I instructed the maid to wake me without fail so that I could attend Sandor Ferenczi's funeral. She failed to wake me, but that was not really important – if I had really wanted to go, I should have woken up by myself. Gathering my wits, still foggy with sleep, the alarmed glance I directed at the clock found,

Novelist, playwright, and satirist, Frigyes Karinthy (1887–1938).

in place of the hour hand, the extended warning finger of the deceased, his gentle, wise refined smile and the gentle caress of his inquisitive look: so, why were you afraid to come to my funeral? Let's see now – where is the knot in the thread? Is it in your throat? Or is it perhaps somewhere deeper?

For he dissected the soul like the very greatest surgeons dissect the body: perfectly anaesthetised, with that fine gift of dexterity with which one is born, and cannot learn. Many have accused the doctors associated with the Freudian method of psychological therapy of introducing the infectious material themselves, during their treatment (like midwives before Semmelweis), but Sandor Ferenczi cannot be tainted with that brush. I am witness to the perfectly aseptic way in which he worked, opening festering wounds or the psyche's lumps that turned away even from themselves (he only accepted patients, never solicited them). The process itself, the cleansing of the soul by natural means, took place in that modern confessional, which thus science is trying to conquer with almost religious awe and – let's be clear – open determination from the toolkit of dominant religion. Even despite his priestly kindness and wisdom, he would not be pleased with my cheap comparison – and he would be right. Sandor Ferenczi was a born doctor, and what's more, a born doctor of the mind. It is my conviction that if the great Teacher, Sigmund Freud, had not yet been born, but had made the world await his coming another century, Sandor Ferenczi would nonetheless have found his own way – without his model, master and friend (at least professionally) – of approaching the root of emotional traumas. The true disciple's, the first disciple's (and Ferenczi was the first) enthusiasm for his master, and the way he discovers his master, is not a coincidence. This is a meeting of soul mates, a meeting of equals, and it is often merely a question of chance as to which comes first. (The Apostle Paul!) Precisely for this reason, he does not merely announce his master, but continues and crowns his work: it is often the case that he can grasp that simple and easily understandable outward form of the Teaching that it needs to conquer the world. What the inventor started, expressed, becomes a communication, a universal message in his mouth.

In Freud's case, this was not necessary. The Master himself is an excellent writer, a virtuoso master of expression and communication too. He made his discovery known in a form as perfectly fine and delicate as its nature demanded. In this, too, he was an example to his disciples; Sandor Ferenczi was handed the method of exploring the mind, in form and content, like some modern mine, with brand new drills and cranes, with comfortable lifts to the already – explored minefaces. He had the opportunity to express his talent in a manner befitting his uprightness, and he took it. Instead of joining the primitive side-show of the sectarians and early reformers, jockeying for position in Utica. He remained true to his master, to be second in Rome. Instead of questionable extension, he chose the harder task of digging deeper in the well-defined area which a genius' magic arrow had demarcated, promising unknown treasures to the adventurer willing to explore it.

Thus were born his works on moral questions and particularly – for me – "Catastrophes in Sexual Life", which significantly underpins the vision of *Capillaria*. This exciting book, over whose daring and surprising deductions Freud, as an old man (Ferenczi would recount proudly) would, with great affection and an old man's cautiousness, shake his head. And I used it often, in those joking battles against exaggeration (as if I didn't, deep down, expect a strict interrogation at the final judgement for exaggeration and paradox . . .). Ferenczi was well aware of this: during our two decades of friendship, our many heartfelt conversations, we often carried on like this and he only accused me of disloyalty once (on the prongs of *Nyugat*, on a moral issue); otherwise, like many true and passionate seekers of the secret of life, he valued constructive criticism more than blind adulation.

A few weeks ago, we met for the last time, on Kelenhegyi Street. He was walking his dog. The sun shone dimly, he smiled, we exchanged a few words about our dogs. Those who have a lot to say are mostly modest. Bunglers compromised the noble art of debate, and only the parrot and the gramophone speak fluently. Before we parted, he made a seemingly unimportant comment, which I later pondered a lot. As a passing impression, he told me that I reminded him of someone he knew, who was, in type and in his understanding of life, all I consider the opposite of me.

The discipline of analysing the emotions was built, solidly and lastingly, on the logic of opposites, like a roof on the crossbeams. They, making known the equality of opposites, term this duality ambivalence and are aware that their enlightening work builds, and at the same time, destroys. It takes away from us the last remaining idol, after the religious idols, the belief in the reliability of self-knowledge, when it proves that we do not want what we think we do. In exchange, it illuminates in a dim ghostly light, a new world: the Hades of our souls, the Mystery.

Their efforts relate to external questions, like every great effort of human intelligence. In the end, they too, proclaim some mystical Law, just as myths do. Predestination, Fate and Destiny – the only difference is that religion sees the complex mesh of wires that guide man from cradle to grave outside and above. The soul divers discovered the directing forces in the depths of the me, and we are left with the point: that it is not up to us what happens to us, at least not up to that individual who concerned us in this World: the Conscious Ego's insights, desires and love.

Sandor Ferenczi was something like the conscience of this generation. Believers and non-, none could miss the fact that he was here among us, he taught us and brought us up. And now, unbelievers and believers, we gaze after him, touched and disappointed: thus the Spirit has become silent, with whom we walked the underworld, you have nothing to say about this Third state, the Third possibility, where Spirit becomes one with the matter it came from?

*   *   *

The relationship between Ferenczi and his famous disciple, Michael Balint (1896–1970) needs no elaboration here. Suffice it to say that, for many years after Ferenczi's death, it was Balint who, virtually single-handedly, kept the Ferenczi flame alight. Naturally, as we have seen in the newspaper report of the funeral, it was Balint who addressed

Portrait of a young Michael Balint, painted by Olga Székely-Kovács, circa 1923.

the gathering on behalf of the school of psychoanalysis, which Ferenczi had founded. There is no record of what was said, but Balint did publish an appreciation of Ferenczi the following year. The version below includes changes made after publication by Balint in his own hand, and, as such, has never before been published.[2]

Dr. Sandor Ferenczi as psycho-analyst by Michael Balint (1934)[3]

If I had to say in one word what our master really was at heart, I would say: a physician, in the finest, richest sense of the word. This does not mean that other things did not attract his interest. His was an active, one could say a restless mind, ever alert, ever inquiring, and so naturally his scientific activity could not be limited by the confines of medicine. He knew that he had attained considerable success beyond its borders, was pleased with this success, even proud of it, but it was never important to him. The only thing which could permanently hold his interest, in which his restless spirit found rest, was: helping, healing.

Ferenczi was not brought to the sick-bed by a combination of circumstances. He did not make the detour through the laboratory as, for instance, his master Freud. As soon as he had finished his studies, he began at once with the treatment of sick people. In the beginning, he was equally interested in organic and functional nervous disorders; later, as he became acquainted more thoroughly with psychoanalysis, he devoted his whole activity to this science. His only aim, and one which he never lost sight of, became to relieve the sufferings of psychically sick people. And it is almost entirely due to Ferenczi that psychoanalysis today is able to help a considerably larger number of people with much greater sureness than 15 to 20 years ago.

In the years before the war what was called, and not by chance, the classical technique of psychoanalysis, had already been worked out. This was almost entirely the result of Freud's work. The technical writings of Freud which appeared from 1912 to 1915 included an excellent résumé of the method of that time. Since then Freud has scarcely touched on technical problems in his writings. His interest turned, on the one hand to clarification of the fundamental analytical ideas and theories, and on the other, to the exposition of the great cultural connections. His last work on technique, the lecture at the Budapest Congress in 1918, was already under the influence of Ferenczi's investigations.

The therapeutic technique of that time was based entirely on the method of free association. One knew at this time that under the pressure of resistances working in them, patients periodically disobeyed the law of free association, or more correctly, were incapable of obeying it. It was Ferenczi who recognised the methodological importance of this phenomenon, and it was Ferenczi who added to the hitherto prevailing definitions of the final aim of the treatment (overcoming of resistances and removal of infantile amnesia) the new task of teaching the patients to be able to associate really freely. From this endeavour derive his changes in technique which not only make the therapeutic technique richer and more effective, but have also essentially deepened our understanding of the criteria of final recovery.

The point of departure was the question as to how one can teach patients to associate freely. According to the analytical conception of that time resistances are at work in the patient; he was thought to be able to say everything that was necessary in the interest of the cure, and yet obviously somehow he was not able, even seemed not to care to do so. The aim was described very characteristically in the unusual analytical slang: these resistances must be overcome, that is to say: greater and more serious efforts are necessary.

The first works of Ferenczi on technique reflect this spirit. First, one has to show up the insincerity of the patient, e.g. his misuse of the freedom of association. Secondly, one must incite the patient to greater efforts. Starting from a technical idea of Freud's, Ferenczi worked out a whole arsenal of such technical devices. Formally, these all represent tasks for the patient. He shall either give up certain pleasant, possibly sensual, actions which have already become a habit; or, for a time, take on himself, unpleasant, possibly painful actions. Through this intervention, the mental tension is increased, and this greater driving force sets the blocked associations in motion. Naturally, the final aim remains the same; to bring hitherto uncontrolled functions under the control of consciousness.

As we see, the essence of this technique – called active technique – is that the patient should do something or renounce something. The result of this intervention, when made at the right time and in the right manner, was always an intense emotional experience. The associations prompted by these experiences always lead to the discovery that these recommended (or forbidden) actions and renunciations were strictly determined by the former experiences of the patient. They are, so to speak, repetitions of significant events of his life. The aim of the activity is the direct provocation of this repetition. From these clinical experiences, Ferenczi drew the conclusion that our patients are incapable adjusting some experiences of their lives merely through free associa-

tion and recollection. It is not enough if we only allow them to reproduce, as it were, these experiences in words in the course of the treatment, in the analytical situation, occasionally the patients must be
helped to repeat them in action.

The results of these experiences were summarized in the book written
jointly by Ferenczi and Rank. Here, it was first emphasized that the
whole analytical treatment really is a shattering experience for the
patient, that it forms one of the most important stages of his libido
development. Freud pointed out some time ago that the peculiarity of
the analytical situation lies just in the fact that the physician does not
react to the repeated by his patients to the emotions transferred on him
from former persons, but endeavours to make the patient conscious of
the transferred and repetitional character of these phenomena. Active
technique lays a new burden on the physician, a further demand on
his elasticity; for as soon as he abandons the attitude of simply listening and interpreting, it becomes of still greater importance that he
should not transfer his own emotions on to the patient in the form of
commands or prohibitions. This is one of the reasons why Ferenczi
became one of the most decided advocates of a thorough didactic
analysis, and it is largely due to him that this extremely important
requirement is to-day internationally recognised.

At this stage of the development of technique, the analyst stood
behind his patient as a powerful protector, his sharp eye seeing
through every attempt at concealment and intervening with his commands and prohibitions at the right point in the conflict between the
resistances and the healing tendencies. Experience showed however,
that this kind of intervention did not bring about the intended results
in all cases. In some cases the ineffective advice had to be revoked,
which naturally considerably lessened the authority of the physician.
Yet, in many cases, a complete collapse of authority, the analysis
started to progress again, and often it went much better than in the
period of the oppressive authority.

From this experience resulted the second period of Ferenczi's technical innovations. Ferenczi never forgot that psychoanalysis was really
discovered by a patient, Miss Anna O., and for him, the merit of the
physician, Dr. Breuer, lay just in the fact that he was always ready to
accept the guidance of his patient and to learn from her this new
method of healing. When in these times of barren results his patients
strongly opposed his authority, Ferenczi was always willing to accept
this as a sign of the necessity for deepening his own analysis. He laid

down the principle, above all for his own use, that if a patient is willing to continue the analysis and the work still does not proceed, then it is physician and his method who are at fault. Obeying this principle to its last consequences, he was always prepared to revise his technique anew. As the first step in this revision; the strict injunction was reduced to that of giving advice. Then he experimented with allowing the greatest possible relaxation instead of heightening the tension. This proved of decisive importance for his later technique. Later he had to extend this revision to the whole behaviour of the physician in the analytic situation. He shrank from no sacrifice if the treatment, in the opinion of the patient failed to progress because of his (Ferenczi's) personal peculiarities. He revised his words, his usual modes of expression, his gestures, even the pitch of his voice, if his patients criticised these. And he was always prepared, at whatever cost to himself, to examine the limits of his sincerity. He did not allow himself a single false or even a vacant tone in the presence of a patient.

Why was this very great effort necessary? He had to learn that in certain cases, his otherwise well-substantiated interpretations or advice had proved useless in so far as they could not succeed in setting the associations going again. Looking for the cause of this failure, he discovered that at such times his patients mistrusted him, feared and suspected him. They obeyed him only out of fear, not from insight, and only the failure, the patient's unaltered condition, showed him that behind the inobedience, mistrust and resistance lay hidden.

This anxiety and fear, which is to be found at the back of all neuroses, is an old problem of psycho-analytic theory. For a long time, it seemed assured that some kind of shattering infantile experience, a trauma, had first aroused this emotion. Rank believed he had found the first cause of the anxiety in the trauma of birth. Ferenczi at first accepted this interpretation, but soon had to recognise that the true cause of the anxiety lay deeper. Another attempt was to trace back the origin of the anxiety in the threat of castration suffered, one could say regularly, during childhood. Doubtless this threat plays an important role in the genesis of the anxiety, but it offers no satisfactory explanation of the general mistrust which may be observed already between child and adult, and which causes the patient hard effort before he can entrust himself to his physician, without suspecting any harm. This mistrust is often concealed behind exaggerated faith, attachment and gratitude. Ferenczi had to sacrifice a good deal of his medical narcissism, before he was able to discover the hidden anxiety behind this affection and gratitude of his patients. Thus it appears that every neurotic really pretends, or lies, but only because he has no other possibility. In the same way as children are made to lie only because the grown-ups, through their hypocritical behaviour prevent them from being sincere. What is felt to be good for the child, such as noisy games, romping about, messing, is naughtiness in the eyes of adults and vice-versa, the adults call good what is really bad for the child, such as sitting still, behaving properly, taking care of his clothes, etc. Education not only forbids many pleasurable activities, but also hypocritically demands him to condemn these pleasures morally. So it becomes impossible for the child to admit his wishes, his pleasures. In many cases – masturbation, Oedipus-wishes – his sincerity appears in the eyes of the grown-up as the worst depravity. The neurotic, but also most so-called healthy people, have remained children many respect; it is therefore understandable that their first reactions to every authority, hence also to the physician's, are those of suspicion, anxiety, and mistrust.

Accordingly, there is no point in combating the obstacles in the way of free association, instead one must endeavour to understand them. The patients test their physician of whether they can talk to him sincerely and frankly, or as Ferenczi has called it, – the tact the physician is of paramount importance. This inner freedom or elasticity is not so easy to achieve; we analysts had to endure the same hypocritical education as our patients. Ferenczi has shown us how we have to watch every tone, every movement, every gesture, so that only true sincerity should lead us and not the "professional 'hypocrisy" which reduces the patients to silence.

These new views fundamentally altered the role of the analyst. He is no longer the powerful protector who, in the time of the active technique, laid bare every hidden, unconscious desire or satisfaction and, as it were, directed the experiences of his patient with his advice; he became, the well-meaning, motherly, tender, understanding companion with whom it is possible for the patient to live through the painful events of his early life, in order to find jointly new and healthier solutions for the mental conflicts which gave rise to the illness. One must sacrifice a large amount of medical narcissism to make this change of role possible. A sacrifice of this kind represents perhaps the most difficult task anyone can be set. Many an analysis has broken down before the unsurmountable narcissistic barrier. Ferenczi often said he was being analysed by his patients; his writings show how serious this analytical work, was. The deserved result was not lacking either. From all parts of the world, Ferenczi was sought out by sick people who had found no help from other treatments, and by physicians who wanted to learn from him. The scientific result is still more significant. Ferenczi with his technique reached such depths of the human mind as no-one before him.

Ferenczi was predestined for this task: the understanding mind of the neurotic soul, and by it, that of the child. He chose subject for his first analytical paper; the title of his address at the First Psychoanalytical Congress, Salzburg in 1908 was "Psychoanalysis and pedagogy." Perhaps his favourite theme, to which he returned time and again, was the fantasy of the "wise baby", who all at once began to speak from his cradle and spoke so wisely that the grown-ups opened their mouths and eyes in astonishment. He himself was in many respects a child, brisk, cheerful, always ready for a joke. Children discovered a comrade in him at once, and became friendly with him amazingly quickly. He always regarded himself as belonging to the younger generation of research workers; justly, for his whole scientific work is one continual impetus without any trace of the flagging of age. His active mind was always ready to forget every conclusion, however respectable, and to regard anew, naively, wonderingly, phenomena seen a thousand times. He could not bear empty formulas and pompous pretentious learnedness; on the contrary, he prized above all concrete clinical observations and a through examination of the condition of the patient. The academicians of our science did not like him, they feared his 'élan', regarded him as "enfant terrible". Ferenczi took note of this nickname with a bitter smile, it hurt him, but also made him feel proud. He felt that he was not understood, that mutual misunderstanding, the "confusion of tongues" also surrounded him, when he had devoted his life and work to the removal of this confusion between the child and the grown-ups, between the patient and his analyst.

Although each of his papers on technique is independent from the others, and it probably never occurred to him to regard them as parts of a series, I believe that taken together these provide the best picture of the man and of his scientific development. This series represents a worthy counterpart to Freud's "Interpretation of Dreams". Here as there the author had to reveal a considerable part of his private life, also the highly personal intimate details usually suppressed, for the sake of presenting a scientific truth. Both works had the same aim: the relentless search for truth, even at the cost of complete disregard of every personal interest and vanity, but with one essential difference. Freud belongs to the classical type of investigator. His "Interpretation of Dreams" is the result of an already crystallized and accomplished achievement, worked out to the smallest detail. Searching and striving after truth is hardly discernable any more. Ferenczi's work leads us through every perplexity of the seeker for truth, through every hope and disappointment. Each subsequent paper is a just but strict and incorruptible criticism of the former.

Ferenczi's work remained unfinished. The situation is not yet ripe for the final verdict. In his last months, – for he worked till a few weeks before his death – he already knew that some of his technical experiments and innovations were not confirmed by experience. The predominant part of his work, however, will ever belong to the eternal and inimitable treasures of psychoanalysis. Today, we cannot yet estimate the possible changes in our technique and point of view which will result from this work. But whatever destiny is to be assigned to the ideas thrown out by Ferenczi, the list of his works will remain an everlasting document of the enquiring human spirit.

* * *

Like Balint, Ernest Jones (1879–1958) needs no introduction. His relationship with Ferenczi was rooted in the early days of psychoanalysis, when Jones received from Ferenczi in Budapest what is generally seen as the first training analysis. The development of the relationship between the two men was documented one-sidedly by Jones himself,

Ernest Jones.

in his Sigmund Freud biography. The imminent publication of the correspondence between Ferenczi and Jones (Erős, Robinson, & Szekacs-Weisz, forthcoming) will, no doubt, shed new light on this relationship. In his Freud biography, Jones famously, and incorrectly, assigned mental problems to Ferenczi in his last years. We shall see later in this volume, that Imre Hermann for one, having visited Ferenczi in person during the latter's last week of life, totally disagreed with the conclusion drawn by Jones. In view of Ernest Jones' ambivalent attitude to Ferenczi, it is of interest to read his obituary alongside the others in this chapter.

Obituary: Sandor Ferenczi, by Ernest Jones[4]

It is my painful duty to announce to you the death of one of our most distinguished and well-beloved colleagues After a long and distressing illness, Sandor Ferenczi died on May 22nd, shortly before the celebration of his sixtieth birthday. With him we lose one of the leading pioneers of psychoanalysis, an inspiring personality and a trusty friend.

Younger colleagues have perhaps seen Ferenczi through a tinted glass, his personality impaired by chronic illness and his later work not readily to be understood or appreciated. It is therefore not easy for me to convey to them the tremendous significance that Ferenczi had in the earlier development of psychoanalysis, both as a branch of science and as an organization of our combined work. Let me relate a few of the actual facts of his life in this connection He had practised for ten years in Budapest as a neurologist and psychiatrist before seriously working at psychoanalysis. In these years he became familiar with both the powers and the limitations of the hypnotic method. On reading the *Traumdeutung* on its appearance he had not been able to assimilate its teachings, and it was only on recurring later to the *Studien über Hysterie*, a book he had casually read years before, that he was impressed by the new perspective there opened out; the *Studien* remained his favourite among Freud's writings, and he could point out in them the most astonishing hints of Freud's later ideas. One may date his real contact with psychoanalytical work to 1907, the year he first met Freud. From then he remained for many years in the closest friendship, scientific and personal, with Freud. They travelled much together, and during the war he underwent a personal analysis with him. At Freud's suggestion he proposed in Weimar, at the Second International Congress, in April 1910, that a permanent International Association be founded, and on that occasion he played a not inconsiderable part in reconciling the rival Viennese and Zurich groups. His own wishes were that a much more intimate "Brüdergemeinschaft" be formed than has proved feasible or than perhaps is humanly possible, but the foundations he built were securely laid. In May 1913, just twenty years before his death, he founded the Hungarian Psycho-Analytical Society, and so has functioned as a group leader longer than any other. At the Budapest Congress, 1918, which was subsequently recognized as an International one in spite of the war exigencies, he was elected President. In this capacity he granted me permission to reorganize the British Psychoanalytical Society in March 1919, and in this connection and in recognition of his distinguished services to psychoanalysis, we elected him an Honorary Member – the first – of our Society. The eccentric position, and virtual isolation, of Budapest led him to resign his Presidentship of the International Association in 1919, and a favourable occasion for re-electing him, which we all wished and intended, was prevented by various turns of fate. He was, I think, the last of our members to be present at all the International Congresses that have so far been held, and it is hard to contemplate our meeting together in the future without his genial presence. He spoke – I say spoke, for only at the last Congress did he actually read a paper – at nearly every Congress, and his turn was always the pinnacle of interest for the audience. The richness and warmth of his personality, together with his gifts of oratory, heightened the never-failing value of his communications.

Ferenczi was a stimulating rather than a systematic organiser. His contribution was the spirit of enthusiasm and devotion which he also expected, and aroused, in others. He was above all an inspiring lecturer and teacher. Before an audience, even of one, his imagination worked at its best, and every theme flowered and developed into far-reaching directions. He was a highly gifted practical analyst, as many present – including myself – know from personal experience; his sympathetic intuition was of a quality that cannot be acquired. Of his more personal attributes I do not find it easy to speak, for he was one of my nearest and dearest friends. His kindliness was unfailing and showed the genuine nature of his charm and loveableness. Two other outstanding qualities – honesty and loyalty – were developed to so high a degree that one might almost apply the word ruthless to them; one could trust him to the last. There was a vein of determinedness in his nature which made him never flinch from any path he decided on, however painful the consequences might be. His life and achievements bespeak of an intense endowment of energy. He complained at times to me of his 'laziness', but that only measures what he demanded of himself. Though sensitive to the opinions of others, he was the sternest critic of himself and his work. Last, but not least, was his extraordinary power of imagination. This showed itself not only in his capacity for understanding and identifying himself with others, but also in more intellectual realms. Observations, discoveries, conclusions he never accepted empirically as finalities. They fertilized his mind and stimulated him to further thought or even distant speculation. I will quote two instances of this out of hundreds or thousands. His observation of the special feeling tone attaching to obscene words – one which with many workers would have remained a banal fact – led him to propound a series of interesting reflections on the psychical significance of the development of speech in general. Again, his discoveries concerning the aetiology of ejacolatio praecox were the starting point of his theory of pregenital amphimixis, ideas which later were extended into the farthest realms of biology.

Several circumstances make it not easy for us at present to make a final judgement on Ferenczi's place in science. Freud always gave him generous credit for ideas they had worked out in common, and it is not possible at times to distinguish their respective shares. Many of Ferenczi's most original and valuable contributions are now so generally accepted as axiomatic that one is apt to forget their source. I might instance here his penetrating essay on 'Stages in the Development of the Sense of Reality' – in my opinion the best he ever wrote; his inestimable contribution to our knowledge of homosexuality and paranoia; his keen observation of the phenomenon of transitory symptom-formation, and endless others. Again, what many consider as his most impressive work, the *Versuch einer Genitaltheorie*, seems to have stunned rather than stimulated the minds of his readers, and opinions differ widely about whether this is because the ideas there expressed are still too far beyond us or whether they were too subjective. It may well be that a future generation will find in them inspiration for a great advance in thought; but perhaps not. Probably many have been deterred from intensively studying and pursuing the line of thought there opened up by the fact that in his still later writings Ferenczi showed unmistakable signs of mental regression in his attitude towards fundamental problems of psychoanalysis. Ferenczi blazed like a comet, but did not shine steadily till the end. In this course he illustrated one of his own most important teachings – the astoundingly close interdependence of mind and body.

Leaving aside, however, all future estimates of his work in detail, we may be sure that as a creative and original thinker, and as the most stimulating pioneer Freud's young science of psychoanalysis has yet seen, Ferenczi's name will remain emblazoned in letters of gold. And what touches us more nearly: we recognise with our hearts that we have lost the most devoted of fellow workers, the most inspiring of teachers, the truest of friends. We shall not look upon his like again.

*   *   *

From Ernest Jones, it is but a short step to John Rickman (1880–1951), both having been eminent Presidents of the British Psychoanalytical Society (Jones 1919–1944, Rickman 1947–1950). They had both been in analysis with Ferenczi in Budapest (Jones in 1913, Rickman between 1928 and 1930), but, unlike Jones, there has never been a question mark over Rickman's genuine friendship with Ferenczi, or his standing as a supportive colleague and follower. Rickman's background

John Rickman and family around the time he was in Budapest.

could hardly have been more different to Ferenczi's. Tall and athletic, he grew up in a Quaker family in the South of England, studied at King's College, Cambridge and was a member of the university's rowing eight (King, 2003). Soon after qualifying, he left for Russia, where he was a country doctor until forced to move by the Bolshevik revolution. He had no option but to return to the UK "the wrong way round", crossing Siberia by train and sailing to the USA from Vladivostok. He was only back in the UK for a short while when, having became interested in psychoanalysis, he wrote to Freud and asked to be analysed by him. On receiving a positive response, Rickman moved to Vienna to be close to Freud and stayed for two years. After returning to London, he became very active in the British Society, but he must have felt that his analysis was incomplete, for six years later he was on the move again. This time he went to Ferenczi for analysis, which involved him staying in Budapest for a further two years. He had been back in London for less than three years when he heard of the death of his friend, colleague, and analyst, Ferenczi. Interestingly, Rickman published his obituary in the *Journal of the Psychical Society*, of which both men were members. (Ferenczi joined in 1911 and wrote to Jones in 1913 asking him to present a paper on Ferenczi's behalf— see letter No 5 in Erős, Robinson, & Szekacs-Weisz (in press).)

Obituary: Sandor Ferenczi, by John Rickman (1934)

By the death of Dr Ferenczi the Society loses one of its most adventurous speculative researchers. For over 30 years he published (first in Hungarian, later in German and English) papers on the phenomena of mental energy expressing itself in physical forms, the expression of instinctual longings in alterations of physiological states. The factors which lead to the employment of unusual physical means of expression were on the whole of less interest to him than the mechanisms of such "conversions from psychical to somatic" spheres, so he stood midway between the group of workers whose main interest is the effect of anxiety and guilt in mental life (the present-day tendency in psycho-analysis) and those whose work lies more especially in the descriptive field of psychical research.

His most important contributions bearing on psychical research lay in his stimulating papers on "The Development of the Sense of Reality", in which he showed how the child's developing perception of the external world is a slow relinquishing of phantasies and again how these phantasies are based on the child's notion of himself. In line with these researches are his penetrating observations on the way in which the mind, to conceal from itself its own defencelessness in the presence of what is felt to be overwhelming and disruptive internal excitement, either attributes to the external world what really belongs within itself or attributes to itself what is really external. His two most distinguished pupils have carried his main contributions into fields which every psychologist has sooner or later to master; Dr Géza Róheim now works on the magical beliefs of aborigines, Mrs Melanie Klein on similar beliefs in civilized children.

After Prof. Freud himself no one has contributed more to the psychoanalytical instruments of thought used in the critical analysis of psychical research; he stood second to none in his enthusiasm for new ideas. To the neurologist the notion of telepathy must be accounted a new idea; he hailed the notion as an important one to study. Although he did not publish observations of a kind usually classed as supranormal, it is well known that he had been collecting data for years, but he had not sufficient evidence to warrant a paper. If anyone scouted the notion of telepathy being other than coincidence, *jamais raconté* or other obvious explanation, he reprimanded the unscientific attitude shown and warned the scoffer of the almost unceasing error that scientific people fall into when they dogmatise, and pointed out that even wish-fulfilments serving a personal neurotic advantage might be objectively true. When asked for the evidence of the supranormal phenomena that he was so ready to welcome, he regretted that even a welcome did not always bring the guest.

Such is the scientist we have all lost; a smaller number mourn the passing of a personal friend. His endowments in science sprang from his gift for friendship, his capacity to accept and thoroughly enjoy whatever was before him without being easily fooled. By his insight he saw what was genial, productive and solid in everyone he met, as he saw what was useful in a scientific theory of an old wives' tale. His life was a rare unity of mind and heart working together. Eager and romantic in temperament he maintained his youthfulness even through the years of suffering, and his kindliness even when bitterly opposed and misunderstood.

*   *   *

No further words are necessary.

Notes

1. The inspiration for this chapter came from the Hungarian publication, *In Memoriam Ferenczi Sándor*, J. Mészáros (Ed.), Budapest: Jószöveg Kiadó.
2. A copy of the annotated version was kindly provided by Nigel Cochrane, Albert Sloman Library, University of Essex.
3. Based on a paper read before the Memorial meeting of the Hungarian Psycho-analytical Association, 3 October 1933.
4. Presented to the British Psychoanalytical Society, 13 June 1933.

References

Balint, M. (1934). Dr. Sandor Ferenczi as psycho-analyst. *Indian Journal of Psychology*, 9: 19–27 [as modified after publication by M. Balint].

Erős, F., Robinson, K., & Szekacs-Weisz, J. (forthcoming). *Sandor Ferenczi & Ernest Jones, Letters 1911–1933*. [see also the same authors in *Thalassa*, 19(2): 3–112, 2008 (in Hungarian)].

Ferenczi, S. (1924). Altató és ébresztő tudomány (Levél Karinthy Frigyeshez) [The science which lulls and the science which awakens; a letter to Frigyes Karinthy]. *Nyugat*, 17: 72–73 [reprinted in F. Erős (Ed.), *Ferenczi Sándor* (pp. 220–221). Budapest: Új Mandátum Kiadó, 2000].

Ignotus (1933). Búcsúztató [Eulogy]. *Magyar Hírlap*, 43(120): 5 (28 May 1933) [reprinted in J. Mészáros (Ed.), *In Memoriam Ferenczi Sándor* (pp. 37–41). Budapest: Jószöveg Kiadó, 2001].

Jones, E. (1933). Sandor Ferenczi, 1873–1933. *International Journal of Psycho-Analysis*, 14: 463–466.

Karinthy, F. (1911). Melankolia, *Nyugat* 1911, I: 1063–1069.

Karinthy, F. (1912). Az idegorvosnál [Visiting the psychiatrist]. In: *Görbe tükör* (pp. 63–64). Budapest: Szépirodalmi Kiadó, 1975.

Karinthy, F. (1913). Tanyulmányozom a lelket [My study of the psyche]. In: *Görbe tükör* (pp. 218–219). Budapest: Szépirodalmi Kiadó, 1975.

Karinthy, F. (1923). Kötéltánc [Dance on the tightrope]. Reprinted in *Karinthy Frigyes összegyűjtött művei. Regények I*. Budapest: Akkord Kiadó, 2000.

Karinthy, F. (1924). *Altató és ébresztő tudomány (Válasz Ferenczi Sándornak)* [The sleeping and waking science; response to Sandor Ferenczi]. *Nyugat*, 17: 155–156.

Karinthy, F. (1933). Lélekbúvár: Ferenczi Sándor halálára. *Pesti Napló*, May 28, 1933 (p. 38) [reprinted in J. Mészáros (Ed.), *In Memoriam Ferenczi Sándor* (pp. 43–46). Budapest: Jószöveg Kiadó, 2001].

Karinthy, F. (2008). *A Journey Round my Skull*, V. Duckworth Barker (Trans.). The New York Review of Books, 2008 [original edition: *Utazás a koponyám körül*, 1937] [reprinted in *Karinthy Frigyes összegyűjtött művei. Regények II*. Budapest: Akkord Kiadó, 2007].

Karinthy, F. (2010). *Capillaria*. Charleston, SC: BiblioBazaar, 2010 [original edition: *Capillária*, 1921] [reprinted in *Karinthy Frigyes összegyűjtött művei. Regények I*. Budapest: Akkord Kiadó, 2000].

King, P. (Ed.) (2003). *No Ordinary Psychoanalyst: The Exceptional Contributions of John Rickman*. London: Karnac.

Kosztolányi, D. (1991). *Anna Édes*, G. Szirtes (Trans.). London: Quartet and New Directions, 1991 [original edition: *Édes Anna*. Budapest: Révai, 1936].

Márai, S. (1933). Élők és holtak. Ferenczi Sándor [The quick and the dead]. *Brassói Lapok*, June 14, (pp. 11–12) [reprinted in J. Mészáros (Ed.), *In Memoriam Ferenczi Sándor* (pp. 47–50). Budapest: Jószöveg Kiadó, 2001].

Márai, S. (2001). *Memoir of Hungary*, A. Tezla (Trans.). Budapest: Corvina and Central University Press [original edition: *Föld, fold . . .!* Toronto: Vörösváry–Weller Publishing, 1972] [reprinted, Budapest: Akadémiai Kiadó, 1991].

Márai, S. (2002). *Embers*. New York: Vintage, 2002. C. Brown Janeway (Trans.), from the German-language work *Die Glut*. Munich: Piper Verlag GmbH, 1999 [original edition: *A gyertyák csonkig égnek* (The Candles Burn Down to the Stump). Budapest: Révai, 1942].

Márai, S. (2004). *Casanova in Bolzano*, G. Szirtes (Trans.). New York: Alfred A. Knopf [original edition: *Vendégjáték Bolzanóban*. Budapest: Révai, 1940].

Márai, S. (2007). *The Rebels*, George Szirtes (Trans.). London: Picador [original edition: *A zendülők*. Budapest: Pantheon, 1930].

Márai, S. (2008). *Esther's Inheritance*, G. Szirtes (Trans.). New York: Alfred A. Knopf, 2008 [original edition: *Eszter hagyatéka*. Budapest: Révai, 1939].

Rickman, J. (1934). Obituary. Sandor Ferenczi. *Journal of Society for Psychical Research*, *28*(1933–1934): 124–125.

Szalay, K. (1961). *Karinthy Frigyes*. Budapest: Gondolat, 1961.

CHAPTER TWO

Sandor Ferenczi the man[1]

Imre Hermann

I first met Sandor Ferenczi in 1911 when he was thirty-eight years old and in the initial phase of his career as a psychoanalyst. I was twenty-two, a fourth-year medical student at the time; I had heard that Ferenczi was recruiting students for an introductory course in psychoanalysis that he was about to start. I presented myself and was given a friendly reception.

After his last lecture, Ferenczi invited remarks and criticism from us students—an invitation that I took up. In a token of friendship, Ferenczi invited me to the evening meetings of his circle of friends, which included the writers Ignotus, Frigyes Karinthy, and Dezső Kosztolány,[2] the pianist Sándor Kovács, the drama critic Sándor Hevesi, and the manufacturer Antal Freund.

The years passed. I had been on voluntary service in the army for a year, followed by four years of wartime service. At the end of this period, in January 1919, Ferenczi not only had me admitted to the Hungarian Psychoanalytical Society (founded in 1913) but had me elected secretary.

He supported me in my practice, gave me professional advice, and it is likely that the early publication of my studies is also due to him. In 1932, he pressed for a German edition of my book on methodology

(Hermann, 1963), despite the fact that I had not pointed out Ferenczi's innovative recommendations in this work. I believe he gave similar support to my contemporaries: Zsigmond Pfeifer, Géza Róheim, and Sándor Radó. In 1919, he received a university professorship under the Revolutionary Council Republic (the first professor of psychoanalysis anywhere in the world), but this in no way altered his friendly attitude. And when he was bedridden with pernicious anaemia, a disease that was barely treatable under the primitive liver therapy then applied, in 1933, a few days before his death, he sent for me, received me with his usual kindness, and asked me to do him a favour as a friend.

How can I describe this friendly attitude of his? He was always ready to help, he never made one feel conscious of his superiority, and he never wished to give the impression of being better than others. Occasionally, other features of his personality did clash with his modesty. His sparkling wit sometimes burst forth under the stimulation of a friendly atmosphere and could give others the impression of his being supercilious. I remember one occasion, probably in 1917, when, on leave from the front, I visited him in his room in the Royal Hotel in Budapest. I related earlier psychological experiments of mine on choice processes. When speaking of edge reactions and centre reactions and saying that, in principle, adults would also opt for the same choice as six- or seven-year-old children, he became excited and exclaimed, ". . . *greift nur hinein ins volle Menschenleben*" (just seize upon the full life people live!) a line from Goethe's Faust. This strange, appropriate, though, at first hearing, not quite fitting comment, confused me; I should have known at the time that what he wanted was to express his sympathy with me.

Later, I myself heard Ferenczi say that when a colleague approached him with a patient's problem he was often overwhelmed by the feeling that it would be best if the patient were transferred to him. This did not come from a sense of superiority, but from sympathy and his strong sense of vocation.

This friendliness can also be seen in his introduction to *Aus der Kindheit eines Proletarmädchens* (On the childhood of a lower-class girl) (Ferenczi, 1929). Ferenczi felt great sympathy for this unfortunate, intelligent girl. He explained to her that someone wanting to kill herself was ill and arranged a date to begin treatment. Even before then he had received her several times. He had her diary translated and published. He regretted deeply that he was unable to save her. In his postscript to the diary, Ferenczi wrote,

> The beauty and fidelity of her description of landscapes and natural phenomena make the girl's diary unforgettable. And above all her misfortunes the inexhaustible love of her mother for her hovers like gentle sunshine; her exquisite sensitivity and intuition in all her misfortune and social exclusion merit admiration.

(The girl's parents looked after the garden of a building in return for a flat: the father, when not drunk, was an odd-job man; the mother struggled to make both ends meet.) The diary says,

> Rich children are lucky, they can learn many things, and (learning) is a form of entertainment for them with which they are spoilt at home and they are given chocolate if they know something. Their memory is not burdened with all the horrible things they cannot get rid of. Furthermore, the teacher treats them with artificial respect. It was like this in our school . . . I believe that many poor children learn poorly or only moderately for similar reasons and not because they are less talented.

Ferenczi took responsibility for the above words, which were considered subversive in those times (1929).

I have mentioned Ferenczi's sense of vocation; his friendliness had a role here, too: the analyst should be kind to his patient even to the point of being humble and be always ready to give help. Ferenczi thought that Freud's treatment was unfriendly. This is stated in the fourth volume of his collected works, *Bausteine zur Psychoanalyse* (Ferenczi, 1964). The analyst should be sincere with his patient and give credence to his criticism. At the beginning of therapy, he dispensed commands and prohibitions, but friendship soon got the upper hand and these were softened to friendly recommendations.

The other ingredient of his kindliness was his modesty. He wanted to be as modest in his treatment of patients as he was in everyday life. He said that an analyst's self-effacement should not be a studied pose, but an admission of the limits of his knowledge. "I for one," he said in 1929, "have become truly modest through the constant oscillation in my concepts. Therefore what I have said here is doomed to the same fate: much of it can be considered true only in part" (1964, Vol. 3, p. 475).

The sense of vocation was accompanied by a search after truth, a sharpness of observation, and a fineness of description. He searched for truth within and without. Hence, he proclaimed that the analyst should discard "professional" hypocrisy. The patient must hear the truth from us. There exists a higher order of truth for the sake of which even the imperative of compulsory secrecy must be discarded (ibid., Vol. 4, p. 268).

And: affection for the patient cannot go so far that when the analyst is asked to make too great a financial sacrifice, then that sacrifice should be made. But in this case he must admit the true state of things and the impossibility of limitless affection (ibid., p. 267). One may suggest an interpretation, but that must be true (ibid., p. 282). The same applies to children, they also must be told the truth. And a neurotic person is a child (ibid., p. 292). The sense of justice requires us to admit our mistakes to the patient.

The ambition of achieving inner truth demands self-analysis. Ferenczi pursued this even during his final illness. He said that self-analysis could be completed only with the help of patients. He agreed with Jung's thesis that the physician's duty towards himself was to rid himself of his fears as far as possible, through therapy. Ferenczi, although so weakened by disease that he was barely able to walk, perceived in his self-analysis the phenomenon discovered by Johannes Muller among his patients: when one is deep in silence, with muscles relaxed, the phenomenon of hypnogogy occurs. Dreamlike images, fantastic visual images, appear before one's eyes. Ferenczi said that they replaced sleep at night—at that time he was already unable to sleep (ibid., p. 268). As to the accuracy and beauty of his description, I have never heard anybody presenting dreams or cases as Ferenczi could present them. When he narrated them, they became living realities. Perhaps the reason for this was that he never embellished and everything he said was imbued with the truth, with his sense of vocation, and the purity of his observation. Unfortunately, there is no record of his lectures and text, and his gestures and accents do not come across in writing.

Let us now see how others judged Ferenczi the man. Lou Andreas-Salomé, that friend of great men, thought that he was the most gifted and most spiritual of the psychoanalysts who emerged in the teens of the new century around Freud. His was not the present, but the future. On several occasions, in public, Freud himself praised Ferenczi's many-sidedness, originality, the depth of his talent, his congeniality, humanity, and openness to everything important. He believed that Ferenczi's greatest achievement was his *Versuch einer Genitaltheorie*, published in 1924, and also known under its shorter title of *Thalassa*. This was probably a turning point in his life because afterwards, as Freud put it, "our friend gradually slid out of our circle as if he was retreating into his solitary work. The will to help and heal gained ascendancy over him ... Our science will certainly not forget him" (Freud, 1933c). In Budapest, this retreat was interpreted by us as resentment and the call of vocation.

Here is another witness, Ernest Jones, once president of the English Society. He had been analysed by Ferenczi in the summer of 1913 (and perhaps later, too, on other occasions, for shorter periods). The treatment had been very useful, he himself wrote, as he had become much more balanced. In his 1959 autobiography, he wrote of Ferenczi that he had a winning personality, one full of childlike imagination which made him entirely suited to the work of an analyst. He was a keen observer and very intuitive, and he loved truth. He saw into people's souls but was fair and tolerant. He had many more ideas than those he had put down on paper, but—and here comes the but—his ideas were uneven in quality because he was not blessed with the faculty of objective and critical judgement.

There is a certain ambivalence in these lines of Jones'. I must, however, briefly now refer to a deplorable statement made by him. In his biography of Freud, Jones wrote that Ferenczi had spent his last years in a state of psychosis. Although it is true that pernicious anaemia can be accompanied by mental illness, muscular weakness—funicular myelosis—was in the case of Ferenczi its major symptom. His notes to the end of 1932 are available; these show at most instability, but not mental illness.

Indeed, he wrote a great deal on the state of his muscles. In the fourth volume of *Bausteine*, there is a short study dated September 1932, on a "casus Gehunfähigkeit" (a case of inability to walk), which is presumably a description of himself (p. 263). When writing on his patients, it was his custom to give the initial letters of their names and not refer to them as "cases". Patient A, patient B, patient K are frequently mentioned in his notes, but not in this particular instance. Here is an excerpt:

Suggestion without the will to act. Tiredness, exhaustion. Somebody grabs our arm (without helping physically) we lean (rely) on the person who directs our steps. We think of many things but we care only for the direction indicated by this person. Suddenly walking becomes troublesome. Every action requires a double investment of energy: decision and execution. The inability to make a decision (weakness) can make the simplest movement very difficult and exhausting. If we leave the decision to somebody else, the same movement ceases to become laborious.

Then a discussion of the regressive psychology of hysteria follows. It is also remarkable that he speaks of this case of locomotive difficulty in the first person plural,which is unusual: he refers to himself in the form of reflection. A year earlier, in March 1931, he had written already on "the absolute paralysis of motility", which included the cessation of perception (Wahrnehmung) and thinking (ibid., p. 244). Jones seems not to have known everything.

Though praising his mentor, Jones also found many faults with him. Abundant, published evidence refers to his allegation that Ferenczi was insane in the last years of his life. Jones has been accused of prejudice, but there is no acceptable evidence for this. Jones defended himself by saying that he had referred only to the last days. I, for one, have found an instance of prejudice, which might be said to derive from psychoanalysis. It is on page 109 of Jones' autobiography (*Free Associations*). The text runs: "Semmelweis had been interned in a lunatic asylum in Budapest for daring to proclaim that tubercular patients improved in an open-air regime, but his suggestion had been revived in Switzerland". The text represses the fact that Semmelweis was, in fact, insane, and there are other tendentious mistakes. Semmelweis was placed in a lunatic asylum in Austria, not in Budapest. He did indeed discover the antiseptic prophylaxis of puerperal fever, but it was not this that had him in a lunatic asylum—he was truly insane. The open-air cure had been suggested by Frigyes Korányi, who also made the reference to Switzerland. However, Semmelweis's rival was an Englishman, Joseph Lister, a more successful pioneer of antisepsis. In this particular case, it was true that the Hungarian rival of the Englishman had been transferred to a lunatic asylum. It is this that Jones has repressed; indeed, Jones even contested Semmelweis's discovery, although after several visits to Budapest he must have known of the Hungarian doctor's life and work.

Einstein wrote in his autobiography that the essence of the life of people like him was what they thought and how they thought it, and not what they did or suffered. Ferenczi was a different type of man. In outlining what he thought, I could not omit what he did: he helped and cured people with his best efforts; even through his own suffering, he tried to understand in order to cure.

Notes

1. Address to the Psychotherapy Working Group of the Society of Hungarian Neurologists and Psychiatrists on the centenary of the birth of Sandor Ferenczi, on 1 June 1974.
2. Obituaries by Ignotus, Karinthy and Kosztolányi can be found elsewhere in this volume.

References

Ferenczi, S. (1929). Vorbericht und Schlußbemerkungen zu *Aus der Kindheit eines Proletariermädchens*. Aufzeichnungen einer 19jährigen Selbstmörderin über ihre ersten zehn Lebensjahre. *Zeitschrift für Psychoanalytische Pädagogik*, 3: 141–172.

Ferenczi, S. (1964). *Bausteine zur Psychoanalyse*, Volumes 1–4. Bern: Hans Huber Verlag, 1964.

Freud, S. (1933c). Sandor Ferenczi. *S.E.*, 22: 225–230. London: Hogarth.

Hermann, I. (1963). *Die Psychoanalyse als Methode*. Zweite, neubearbeitete Auflage. Köln: Westdeutscher Verlag, 1963.

Jones, E. (1959). *Free Associations*. New York: Basic Books, 1959.

CHAPTER THREE

Some social and political issues related to Ferenczi and the Hungarian school

Ferenc Erős

A fter a long history of preparation in Freud's personal and institutional conflicts, as well as in his self-analysis, which already implied some of the major later trends, psycho-analysis appeared on the European scene in the early years of the twentieth century. Psychoanalysis was part and parcel of the conflict-ing intellectual, ideological, and spiritual tendencies of the age: for example, the belief in the omnipotence of science *vs.* the disillusion-ment with a unified natural science capable of understanding all sectors of the human individual; individualism *vs.* collectivism, liber-alism *vs.* anti-liberalism, rationalism *vs.* irrationalism. Psychoanalysis shared with other social and political theories of the age a spirit that was directed against the illusions of the enlightenment. It showed the fundamental and tragic weakness of the individual in the face of greater forces within and without the individual psyche; the irrational and unconscious background of all rational thinking and action; the irresoluble conflict between our desires, our strivings for happiness, and our social roles; the hypocrisy and the double standards of the bourgeois society, which does not tolerate us to talk publicly about all these things we know and practice privately. Thus, psychoanalysis was one of the great "unmaskers" that made an essential contribution to the ideological breakdown of classical bourgeois society. The breakdown of bourgeois society and the coming of the age of the masses gave rise to various mass movements, such as Fascism, Nazism, and Bolshevism, that formed the basis of totalitarian regimes. The fictitious world of totalitarian ideology and propaganda (Hannah Arendt) was based on one main fiction: the abolition of the splitting between the public and the private sphere of the individual through the total identification of the individual members of the mass with the movement and its leader. Psychoanalysis, on the contrary, shed light on the fictitious or illusory character of this identification. This was only possible because psychoanalysis was equipped with an inner safeguard against totalitarian ideologies, not so much with a conceptual safeguard as, rather, with a practical one: the nature of the therapy itself. That is, its roots in the very nature of the relationship between the analyst and the patient, which cannot be controlled by any external agency, let alone by the authority of the psychoanalytic movement itself. Paradoxically, secrecy, this absolute privacy of the analytic relationship, became the last bulwark of the autonomous, free, bourgeois individual. In this respect, it might be said that psychoanalysis was the last truly liberal psychology, internally safeguarded against any attempts to control individuals externally, either in a technological way (utilitarian psychology) or in an ideological way (totalitarian psychology).

Psychoanalysis first developed first in the Austro-Hungarian monarchy. One of the main characteristics of this strange political entity was its inconsistency. As Robert Musil put in his novel *Man without Qualities*,

> By its constitution it was liberal, but its system of government was clerical. The system of government was clerical, but the general attitude to life was liberal. Before the law all citizens were equal, but of course, not everyone was a citizen. There was a Parliament, which made such vigorous use of its liberty that it was usually kept shut: but there was an emergency powers act by means it was possible to manage without parliament . . . (Musil, 1979, p. 33)

The atmosphere in Vienna and Budapest was liberal enough to allow and foster such new enterprises as psychoanalysis, but it was conservative and antiliberal enough to exclude the representatives of this new enterprise from the established circles of state power and its institutions, academic and other. Thus, psychoanalysts were doomed to remain in the "underground" world of the modernist culture, in the informal network of writers, artists, poets with whom they shared their marginality, their contempt of the hypocrisy of the official standards, and the love-hate relationship with the powers that be: they felt themselves absolutely different from the formal world of officialdom, whereas, in a paradoxical way, they expected a kind of recognition from it, even if it was a negative one. This was very well expressed in the motto of Freud's *The Interpretation of Dreams*: "Flectere sinequeo superos, Acheronta movebo". The "antipolitical anthropology" of Sigmund Freud (Carl Schorske) and his close look at all political events of the age are two sides of the same coin.

The "underground" character of psychoanalysis was much clearer in Budapest than in Vienna. The contrast between the formal and the informal, the traditional and the modern was much stronger in Hungary, an economically and socially underdeveloped, feudal or semi-feudal country with—in sharp contrast to the rest of the country—a fast developing bourgeois cosmopolitan capital, Budapest. Here, in the capital and in some other urban centres, there were some informal circles of intellectuals who dreamed of a renewal of culture and society, but, at the same time, there was the fundamental lack of an autonomous, self-organising civil society. This might explain why modernist culture in general, and psychoanalysis in particular, were more radical but perhaps less realistic in Budapest than in Vienna.

Since the beginning of its history, psychoanalysis in Hungary had developed in close connection with the progressive cultural and spiritual currents of the age. Interest in psychoanalysis commenced before the First World War, initially within the most enlightened circles of the liberal bourgeoisie. Its first sponsors and popularisers, as well as its first patients, came from the most enlightened—primarily Jewish—intellectual and business elite of the fast developing Hungarian bourgeoisie, predominantly in Budapest. Literary and cultural acceptance also originates in this milieu. Ignotus, the chief editor of the country's most prestigious progressive liberal literary review, the main forum of modern Hungarian literature, with the programmatic title *Nyugat* (West), was a co-founder of the Hungarian Psychoanalytic Association in 1913. Ignotus, also an important protagonist in the Freud–Ferenczi correspondence, opened wide the columns of his review to the cultivators and followers of the new discipline, including Sigmund Freud himself. The impact of psychoanalysis (on a deeper or, sometimes, on a superficial level) can be well documented in the works of some outstanding writers of the age. Writers such as Gyula Krúdy, Dezső Kosztolányi, Géza Csáth, Mihály Babits, and Frigyes Karinthy were the forerunners of a lay, cultural reception of psychoanalysis, similar to the surrealists in France, James Joyce in Ireland, or D. H. Lawrence in the UK (see the volume containing "psycho-analytic" short stories by Hungarian writers, contemporary with Ferenczi, recently published in France under the title *Cure d'ennui*, or Boredom therapy (Moreau-Ricaud, 1992).

In 1936, more than twenty years after the foundation of the Hungarian Psychoanalytic Association, in a special issue of the literary review *Szép Szó*, celebrating Freud's eightieth birthday, Ignotus writes, "Whereas official science is unable to do anything with psychoanalysis, the intellectual world cleaves to it and the arts stand in its service. The *fin-de-siècle* Hungary was in this, as in so many other things, in the vanguard" (Ignotus, 1936).

It is the cultural and literary context that seems to be the most important, but beyond that the members of the first generation of Hungarian psychoanalysts (with Sandor Ferenczi pre-eminent among them) were in close relation to what we call bourgeois radicalism. By this, we mean those groups, circles, and movements that had elaborated radical political programmes to abolish the age-old feudal system in order to modernise the country in all aspects (to change political, social, and economic life, educational and legal systems, and to democratise the particularly tense national and ethnic relations).

As free thinkers, psychoanalysts were in close contact with the Galileo Circle, Hungary's foremost radical intellectual movement before the First World War. The political and social radicalism of Ferenczi's early writings show a particularly deep impact of the thinking and values of the Galileo Circle. Ferenczi's radicalism manifests itself, first of all, on the level of his writings of direct social and political relevance. From his psychoanalytic insights, he came to far-reaching conclusions very early on. Perhaps the most important concept introduced in this early period by Ferenczi was the notion of "unnecessary constraint" (*unnötige Zwang*) or "surplus repression" (*zusätzliche Repression*). This means that repression in our society requires not simply a minimum of instinctual renunciation, but also the subjugation of members of the society, including deprivation of their human dignity and autonomy. "Surplus repression" sets free, according to Ferenczi, those instinctual forces that lead to religious superstitions, to the cult of authority, and to a rigid adherence to obsolete social forms. In other words, the consequence of surplus repression is the insanity of society, that is to say, collective neurosis. In his early paper, "Psychoanalysis and education" (1908), he argues that

> the liberation from unnecessary inner constraint would be the first revolution that brings genuine relief to humanity, while political revolutions result only in transition of external powers or means of constraint from one hand to the other . . . Only people liberated in this way will be able to bring about radical changes in pedagogy, and thus prevent the reappearance of such conditions. (p. 63)

It is instructive to compare Ferenczi's argument with Herbert Marcuse's much later notion of a "psychological Thermidor" (1957). Marcuse maintains that without an inner, radical transformation of the human soul, all revolutions will be, by necessity, "betrayed revolutions".

It should be emphasised that the revolution announced by Ferenczi was not revolution in the traditional political sense. He was a radical reformer of human relations, a Utopian rationalist in the spirit of *Aufklärung*. In another paper before the First World War, "On psychoanalysis and its judicial and sociological significances" (1913), he speaks about a "sound individual socialistic direction" that is somewhere between anarchism and communism, and which serves not only the interests of society, but also the happiness of individuals. Ferenczi's social–political ideas reappear in the writings of such contemporary Hungarian social thinkers as, for example, Oszkár Jászi, Sándor Varjas, Pál Szende, Aurél Kolnai, and others—all of them close to the Galileo Circle and other organs of the radical intelligentsia, such as *Huszadik Század* (Twentieth Century) and *Szabadgondolat* (Free Thinking). The problem of revolution as something that brings about genuine liberation or introduces new and even more repressive forms of power, appears in the psychoanalytic discussion on "the society without the Father" (*vaterlose Gesellschaft*) at the end of the First World War (Paul Federn, Aurél Kolnai, and others) in the socio-psychological discourse of Austrian and Hungarian thinkers.

The antipolitical and antiauthoritarian utopianism of Ferenczi's early writings anticipated also some of the fundamental concepts and theories of the analytical social psychology as elaborated by Wilhelm Reich, Erich Fromm, and other thinkers of Freudo-Marxism and the Frankfurt School. These concepts (surplus repression, authoritarianism, religion, and totalitarian political movements as manifestations of a kind of a collective neurosis) were first outlined by Ferenczi. They were worked out further, after the First World War, by Freud himself in his cultural criticism and in his theory of culture (in such works as *Group Psychology and the Analysis of the Ego* (1921c), *The Future of an Illusion* (1927c), *Civilization and its Discontents* (1930a), etc.). Subsequently, the concepts were reinterpreted in a leftist, revolutionary–messianic spirit by the Freudo-Marxists, especially in their analysis of Fascism.

Ferenczi's radical views and his long-standing connections with the radical groups explain his participation in the events of 1918 and 1919. Hungary saw two revolutions rapidly following one another; the first, the so called "bourgeois" revolution in October 1918; the second a socialist–communist takeover in March 1919. A few days after the climax of his career in the international psychoanalytic movement, that is, after the Budapest Congress in the autumn of 1918, revolutionary students at the University of Budapest in several petitions to the Rector demanded that Ferenczi be appointed as professor of the new discipline. In spite of being supported by the revolutionary government and by a few progressive professors, the demand was refused by the conservative majority of the medical faculty, but, several months later, in the period of the Commune, Béla Kun's Council's Republic, Ferenczi's appointment to the world's first psychoanalytic chair was finally approved. As a matter of fact, quite a few psychoanalysts, future analysts, and sympathisers (e.g., Jenő Hárnik, Sándor Radó, Géza Róheim, Imre Hermann, Sándor Varjas, Jenő Varga) co-operated—more or less actively—with the Communist government. There is an element of truth in the exaggerated statement of the sociologist Oszkár Jászi, the leading theorist and politician of the bourgeois radicalism, who wrote in his 1920 book *Hungarian Calvary – Hungarian Resurrection*: "During the revolutions . . . Freudianism was the idol of Communist youth".

After the collapse of the revolutions in August 1919, the political and social atmosphere that had previously been favourable toward psychoanalysis changed radically. On the one hand, the government of the victorious counter-revolution led by admiral Horthy tried to consolidate the old semi-feudal conservative order; on the other hand, extreme right groups terrorised and persecuted not only those who actively supported the Communist administration, but also people of leftist and progressivist convictions in general and Jews in particular. (They claimed that the Jews, as a group, had been held responsible for the military catastrophe, the revolutions, and the territorial partition of historical Hungary. The topic of anti-Semitism and anti-Jewish purges is also regularly discussed in the Freud–Ferenczi correspondence.)

Anti-Semitism became part and parcel of institutionalised politics. Post-Trianon Hungary, with its institutionalised anti-Semitism (a *numerus clausus* law limiting the number Jewish students admitted to the university was introduced in 1920) and irredenta (revenge politics), announcing territorial claims against neighbouring countries, became an authoritarian state with more or less direct racist tendencies, while maintaining a reduced form of parliamentarianism and legalism. Therefore, psychoanalysis and other progressive intellectual movements largely lost ground; at the very least, the "golden age" was lost forever. As for psychoanalysts, some left the country permanently, some temporarily; others retreated into the "ivory tower" of medical psychoanalysis, of strictly professional activity. Nevertheless, in the more consolidated atmosphere of the 1920s, the Hungarian psychoanalytic movement was able to restart and extend its activity; moreover, unique and creative contributions to the theoretical and technical development of the discipline were born. The key role in this renewal was again assumed by Sandor Ferenczi.

Excluded from the Budapest Medical Association and exiled to the margins of the existing order, Ferenczi apparently abandoned the area of social critique after the First World War.

It is probably true that his resignation was a reaction to the trauma of the two revolutions and their failure, to the final disappearance of "the world of yesterday", to the dissolution of the Habsburg Empire that brought about the partition of historical Hungary, and, most of all, to the violent anti-Semitic outbursts mentioned above.

In the turbulent autumn of 1918, he wrote to Freud,

The beginning of the breakdown of our old political world, among other things also of the Globus Hungaricus, is deeply injuring our narcissism. It is a good thing that one has a Jewish and a psycho-

analytic ego along with the Hungarian, which remain untouched by
these events. (Ferenczi, 1918, p. 297)

It is probably due to these circumstances that, in the 1920s, the
"psychoanalytic ego" came to the forefront: Ferenczi became more
and more involved in the problems of psychoanalytic technique, and,
as a theorist, he submerged himself in the biological, *Naturphilosophie*
side of psychoanalysis.

Ferenczi's contribution to analytical social psychology is, however,
not limited to his early, explicitly socio-psychological works. On the
contrary, it was the alternative psychoanalytic technique that had a
decisive influence on Erich Fromm's early ideas and his evaluation of
psychoanalysis. In his essay, "The social determinants of psychoanalytic therapy", Fromm contrasts Ferenczi's therapeutic attitude to
Freud's "bourgeois-liberal tolerance". Fromm writes,

Ferenczi's premature death is a tragic conclusion of his life. Torn
between the fear of his break with Freud and the insight that a technique different from Freud's was necessary, he lacked the inner
strength to follow his way to the end. His difference with Freud is
fundamental: the difference between a humane, philanthropic attitude, affirming the analysand's unqualified right to happiness—and a
patricentric–authoritarian, deep down misanthropic, 'tolerance'.
(Fromm, 2000, pp. 160–161).

It can be documented that Ferenczi's ideas on "active technique"
had a major role in the development of Fromm's ideas on a critically
orientated, analytical social psychology. His concept of social character and the significance of "matricentrism" are not alone in owing
much to Ferenczi's alternative technique. In Fromm's lifelong critique
of Freud and of the psychoanalytic movement, Ferenczi is the positive
hero who represents a radical challenge to "the doctor's hidden
sadism", that is to say, to the analyst as father-figure.

We should note here that Ferenczi's alternative approach to psychoanalytic technique and theory, especially his emphasis on loving
relationship and the primary importance of mother–infant interaction,
influenced not only Fromm, but other contemporaries also. It is well
known that Ferenczi's disciple Michael Balint imported his master's
ideas to the UK, and was instrumental in establishing the British
school of object relational psychology.

Returning to the Hungarian cultural and social scene, it is likely
that the enthusiastic uptake of psychoanalysis was one of the most

important channels through which the pre-First World War radicalism was transmitted. It is true even for our present day, when the general rediscovery of the *fin de siècle* art, culture, and science is closely connected to the understanding of the significance of psychoanalysis. As for the value system of Hungarian psychoanalysis, the principles of the Galileo Circle remained central: "individual socialism"—as Ferenczi used the term yet again in his 1922 article in *Nyugat*. The radical tradition of psychoanalysis was transmitted through personal contacts (including on the couch), through reading the works of psychoanalysis, and through literary works.

In the late 1920s and early 1930s, a new, radically leftist intellectual culture appears in Hungary. In this culture, next to Marxism, psychoanalysis was one of the leading ideas. As György Balint, an outstanding leftist journalist, critic, and writer expressed in an article, "I have to admit that meeting Freud contributed largely to my world view—if not to my *Weltanschauung*" (Balint, 1966, p. 172).

In his series of autobiographical novels, *Difficult Love*, (published in the 1970s and 1980s), the well-known poet, István Vas, provides us with a detailed account of how young, leftist orientated intellectuals took up psychoanalysis in this period.

> It was in the air in Vienna and in Budapest too, vaguely, almost threateningly, and I received its snatches with reluctance and aversion . . . My resistance did not stop to protest against this neurotic terror; but I was even more annoyed by the preponderant counterattack of Freudianism: of course, our conscious being protests against this truth, since its main purpose is to repress the psychic contents that have already been revealed or are to be revealed later. And with what sublime sophistication psychoanalysis refutes sensible doubts: ambivalence, inversion, symbolism, repression, transference, sublimation – all these are magic words to silence rational arguments! (Vas, 1983, p. 283)

Somewhat later, Vas continues,

> In the meantime, reading Freud, I had to realize that Freud himself, like Marx and Engels, or those philosophers I liked . . . is a master of writing . . . And when I read *Totem and Taboo*, I recognized the possibility that was always inherent in this style: the reason's tolerant but stubborn effort to understand and to counterbalance the dark and irrational forces of the soul . . . I started to understand that *Totem and Taboo*

was about those more general and more important aspects of human collective life for the understanding of which my Marxist education was not enough. Freud, with some great works of his later period, stirred up my thinking and it merged into my poems. (Ibid., p. 284).

It was as a young poet that István Vas published his first psychoanalytically influenced essay in a journal called *Korunk* (Our Age) in 1929. *Korunk* was, at that time, the most important forum of the socialist intelligentsia in the Hungarian language area. The journal was published in Kolozsvár (Cluj, Romania), and was basically a legal forum of the communist party. (In Hungary, the communist party was banned, but this was not the case in Romania at that time.) The review, however, did not follow strictly the "party line"; it was open to various approaches, non-orthodox and even "deviant" views. During the fourteen years of its existence (1926–1940), several hundred articles dealing with psychoanalysis and related issues were published. *Korunk* was probably the most significant forum for the reception of psychoanalysis in Hungarian intellectual life. These articles are stylistically and thematically very different: scientific papers, essays, reviews, journalistic reflections, ideological statements about psychoanalysis and other schools of deep psychology (e.g., Adler's "individual psychology", quite popular in this period among Marxist intellectuals, and Wilhelm Stekel's "medical analysis"). *Korunk* published original papers by Hungarian and non-Hungarian psychoanalysts (including Sandor Ferenczi, Zsigmond Pfeifer, and Wilhelm Reich), published reviews on books and journal articles by Hermann, Ferenczi, Géza Róheim, Wilhelm Reich, Erich Fromm, Oskar Pfister, etc. There are many articles dealing with the evaluation and critique of psychoanalysis, written by philosophers, writers, and socialist physicians. The review was particularly rich in debates—sometimes bitter polemics between the followers and the opponents of psychoanalysis, between orthodox Marxists who opposed Freudianism "ex officio" and Freudo-Marxists, who attempted to synthesise the two systems of ideas. Most notably, such topics predominated in *Korunk*, as, for example, the application of psychoanalysis to social problems (education, legal system; in the tradition of Sandor Ferenczi's early articles), to mental hygiene (prevention of suicide, alcoholism, etc.), and to mass psychology (fascism, war, anti-Semitism). *Korunk* is an excellent source on the subject of Marxist reception of psychoanalysis in Russia.

Freudo-Marxism, so popular among leftist intelligentsia in Hungary in the 1930s, was a Central and East European invention. We are not attempting an evaluation of "classical" Freudo-Marxism here, but state only that the virtues and sins of Reich, Fromm, and other Freudo-Marxists came from the same source: their sincere effort to take both Marx and Freud seriously. The result of this attempt to synthesise the two spiritual fathers was an enormous broadening of perspective for both Marxism and psychoanalysis. After Freudo-Marxism, psychoanalysis cannot avoid social problems and Marxism cannot escape taking the problem of individuality seriously. On the other hand, most Freudo-Marxists were completely uncritical of some basic dogmatic assumptions and political orientations.

Thus, it is true not only for Ferenczi, but also for many Freudo-Marxists, that they were "naively seduced" (as Ernest once applied this term to Ferenczi). Seduced by whom? Not so much by extraordinary women or telepathic abilities, as Ferenczi was, but by the spirit of a utopian messianism, which made many Freudo-Marxists completely blind about the actual Left and its crimes in the Stalinist Soviet Union. In this connection, Freudo-Marxists shared the ambivalent feelings, or even the schizophrenia, of many leftist intellectuals toward the Soviet Union. For them, there were originally two evils: political fascism on the one hand, and "cultural fascism", the alienated, "one dimensional" consumer society and "mass culture" on the other. Communism, far from being attractive or even "progressive", was "the lesser evil". It seemed to retain some elements of hope for the left. At the very least, it was inadvisable to attack Communism too openly in the period of the Cold War, which seemed to end only recently. This attitude of the left is very clearly described by the Hungarian-British author Arthur Koestler in his essay "The god that failed". According to Koestler, "the addiction to the Soviet myth is as tenacious as any other addiction. After the Lost Weekend in Utopia the temptation is strong to have just one last drop, even if watered down and sold under a different label" (Crossman, 1950, p. 74).

It was not the psychoanalysts who were unfaithful to Communism; it was the Communist party that alienated sympathetic, or even enthusiastic, psychoanalysts (e.g., Reich), as well as patients. The case of the famous Hungarian poet and Freudo-Marxist thinker Attila József is a good example; he was excluded from the communist party, for a number of reasons, including the fact that he was in analysis (with Edith Gyömrői-Ludowyk, a Communist). Soon afterwards, in 1937, he committed suicide. Attila József's poetry represents what might be a second, more profound, stage of the lay reception of psychoanalysis. In the words of Arthur Koestler, Attila József's poems constitute "a new branch of poetry . . . the Freudian folksong".

A recently discovered document dramatically illustrates the Communist treatment of psychoanalysis. In 1948, a special intellectual trade flourished in Hungary: the attacking and denouncing of psychoanalysis. One of the main practitioners was a certain Dr István Tariska. Psychiatrist, Communist functionary, a long-time member of the illegal Communist Party, later—until his death in the 1980s—director of the National Institute of Mental and Nervous Diseases, Tariska published several anti-psychoanalysis articles in the journal *Fórum*. One of his articles, entitled "Psychoanalysis, the domestic psychology of imperialism", provoked protest from two Communist members of the Hungarian Psychoanalytic Association, Imre Hermann and Lilli Hajdu-Gimes. They addressed their protest to György Lukács, the world-famous philosopher who was the most influential member of the editorial board of the journal. They begged for Lukács's protection against Tariska's attack. They emphasised that they agreed with the critique of psychoanalysis on many points and they themselves thought it necessary to continue the Marxist–Leninist critique of psychoanalysis. They did not doubt that in their own countries imperialists tried to use psychoanalysis to serve their aims, but this was only possible through falsifying the theory of psychoanalysis. Hermann and Hajdu stressed that Communists should follow the guidance of the Party in all areas, including psychoanalysis.

> Nevertheless, one sentence of the above article cannot be regarded as principled critique and it deeply hurts us as party members as well as honest individuals. After declaring that psychoanalysis arrives at open reaction, Comrade Tariska writes the following: 'This fact remains unchanged by the circumstance that in Eastern Europe, even in Hungary, persecution, stemming from other sources, forced psychoanalysis, for a longer or shorter period, onto a common road with the genuine representatives of human progress and liberation.' In other words: there is only one explanation for the fact that analysis had gone together with the communists or became communists after the war: namely, they were Jewish. This explanation annihilates another explanation, the reality that they had been always convinced antifascists in

the past, and they are convinced Marxists and faithful party members in the present. (Tariska, 1948)

Hermann and Hajdu asked for Lukács's intervention to ensure the publication of a correction.

Lukács answered the protest in a very nervous and irritated tone. He refused the interpretation that considers Tariska's article to have an anti-Semitic bias. Lukács explained that this interpretation—consciously or unconsciously—diverted attention from the most reactionary side of the *Weltanschauung* of psychoanalysis. According to Lukács, the sentence written by Tariska was only open to one interpretation:

> Before the war there were many people who were dissatisfied with the regimes of Horthy, Szálasi and Hitler. But for many of them, this dissatisfaction came from the fact that, instead of such a form of . . . class dictatorship, they were longing for a class dictatorship of Anglo-American kind. It is only natural that after the liberation such elements (irrespective whether or not they were Jewish) turned against the new democracies. This holds true, of course, of psychoanalysis as *Weltanschauung*. Clearly Hitler's oppressive machine did not need psychoanalysis, while that of Truman's can use it very well. (Szőke, 1992)

This peculiar correspondence shows what the "discontents of the Freudian left" (using the phrase coined by the Zurich psychoanalyst Berthold Rothschild) meant in Hungary in 1948, on the eve of the cold war, in the year of the break with Tito and one year before the Budapest show trials. Needless to say, the letter was never published, and a few months later, in early 1949, the Hungarian Psychoanalytic Association was dissolved. Lilli Hajdu subsequently became the director of the National Institute for Mental and Nervous Diseases, but her son Miklós was executed in 1958 and she committed suicide soon thereafter. Imre Hermann continued his psychoanalytic work "clandestinely" and stayed away from politics for the rest of his life. Tariska was imprisoned in the early 1950s, together with János Kádár, later Party leader, and others. In 1954, Lukács published one of his major works, *The Destruction of Reason*, in which he presents psychoanalysis as one of the ideological forerunners of Nazi ideology.

Thus, for many years, psychoanalysis was exiled from intellectual life and dialogue between psychoanalysis and Marxism was not possible. Since they were persecuted in the name of the state religion, and their very persecution showed them how the future of an illusion can be realised, psychoanalysts also exiled Marxism from their hearts. There was a brief period of ideological *détente* shortly before and after 1956. In 1958, Sándor Szalai (a professor of sociology, himself with psychoanalytic training) was able to arrange a very short run, almost secret re-edition of Freud's *Psychopathology of Everyday Life*. Szalai even wrote a kind of Freudo-Marxist preface to this volume. However, until the late 1970s, it was an American ultra-orthodox party philosopher, Harry K. Wells, and a second-rank student of Lukács, István (not Imre) Hermann, who represented the "proper" Marxist standpoint concerning psychoanalysis.

Not only Freudo-Marxism was lost during these dark years. Almost nothing of the developments of modern psychoanalysis, including for example object relation theory, or Lacan, or Mitscher-lich's analytical social psychology, penetrated the ideological iron curtain. Even such well-known Hungarian emigrants as Michael Balint were virtually unknown (although his book *The Doctor, His Patient and the Illness* (1964) was published in the 1970s). There was an intellectual vacuum, or, more precisely, a deep-freezer, where Imre Hermann's ideas and some nostalgia for the good old days of the Budapest School represented psychoanalytic "modernity".

And so, we arrive at the change of the political system in 1990. We now live now in a so-called transition period between "dictatorship and democracy" (and vice versa). Skipping modernity, we came straight to what we call "postmodernism". Instead of Marx, Engels, and Lenin, it is Derrida, Lyotard, Rorty, and even Jacques Lacan who dominate the ideological field. The "postmodern" interpretation of psychoanalysis wants to eliminate the rationalism in Freud and Ferenczi. For "postmodernism", their different "narratives" illustrate the genesis and the structure of different personal and collective myths. But that is another story.

References

Balint, G. (1966). *A toronyőr visszapillant*. Budapest: Magvető.
Balint, M. (1964). *The Doctor, His Patient and the Illness* (2nd edn), with an introduction by John A. Balint. London: Churchill Livingstone, 2000.

Crossman, R. (Ed.) (1950). *The God That Failed. Six Studies in Communism.* London: Hamilton [reprinted Columbia University Press, 2001].

Ferenczi, S. (1908). Psychoanalysis and education. In: F. Erős (Ed.), *Sandor Ferenczi* (pp. 61–67). Budapest: Új Mandátum Kiadó, 1999 [in Hungarian].

Ferenczi, S. (1913). On psychoanalysis and its judicial and sociological significance. A lecture for judges and barristers. In: J. Rickman (Ed.), *Further Contributions to the Theory and Technique of Psycho-Analysis by Sandor Ferenczi* (pp. 424–434). London: Hogarth Press, 1926 [reprinted, London: Karnac, 1994].

Ferenczi, S. (1918). Letter from Sandor Ferenczi to Sigmund Freud, October 4, 1918. In: E. Falzeder & E. Brabant (Eds.), *The Correspondence of Sigmund Freud and Sandor Ferenczi, Volume 2, 1914–1919* (pp. 296–297). Cambridge, MA: Harvard University Press, 1996.

Freud, S. (1921c). *Group Psychology and the Analysis of the Ego. S.E., 18*: 67–43. London: Hogarth.

Freud, S. (1927c). *The Future of an Illusion. S.E., 21*: 3–56. London: Hogarth.

Freud, S. (1930a). *Civilization and Its Discontents. S.E., 21*: 59–145. London: Hogarth.

Fromm, E. (2000). The social determinants of psychoanalytic therapy, E. Falzeder & C. Schwarzacher (Trans.). *International Forum of Psychoanalysis, 9*: 149–165 [original publication, 1935. *Die gesellschaftliche Bedingtheit der psychoanalytischen Therapie. Zeitschrift für Sozialforschung, 4*: 365–397].

Ignotus (1936). Egy német író: Sigmund Freud [A German writer: Sigmund Freud]. *Szép Szó, 1*(3): 193–196.

Jászi, O. (1920). *Magyar kálvária – magyar föltámadás* [Hungarian Calvary – Hungarian Resurrection]. Wien: Bécsi Magyar Kiadó.

Lukács, G. (1954). *The Destruction of Reason.* London: Merlin Press, 1980 [original edition, *Az ész trónfosztása.* Budapest: Akadémiai Kiadó, 1954].

Marcuse, H. (1957). Theory and therapy in Freud. *The Nation* (28 September 1957): 200–202.

Moreau-Ricaud, M. (Ed.) (1992). *Cure d'ennui, écrivains hongrois autour de Sandor Ferenczi.* Paris: Gallimard.

Musil, R. (1979). *The Man without Qualities, Vol. 1*, E. Wilkins & E. Kaiser (Trans.). London: Pan Books [original edition, *Der Mann ohne Eigenschaften.* Bd. 1, Berlin: Rowohlt, 1930].

Szalai, S. (1958). Bevezetés a második, 1958-as kiadáshoz [Introduction to Freud's *Psychopathology of Everyday Life*]. In: Freud, *A mindennapi élet pszichopatológiája* (pp. 10–16) (2nd edn). Budapest: Cserépfalvi, 1991.

Szőke, G. (1992). Egy jövő illúziója [The illusion of a future]. *Köztársaság*, *1*(32): 42–44.

Tariska, I. (1948). Jelszavak és tények – A freudizmus mint az imperializmus házi pszichológiája [Slogans and facts – Freudianism as the domestic psychology of imperialism]. *Fórum, 10*: 799–805.

Vas, I. (1983). *Nehéz szerelem* [Difficult Love] I–II. Budapest: Szépirodalmi Könyvkiadó.

CHAPTER FOUR

Ferenczi in context

Edith Kurzweil

Much has been written about Ferenczi's and Freud's relationship, their close personal friendship and theoretical disagreements, but not much attention has been paid to the influence on them of their surrounding milieu, the contradictions within the *Kaiserreich*, its rampant anti-Semitism and hypocrisy hidden beneath a veneer of politeness and *Gemütlichkeit*, which they took for granted. Of course, both Freud and Ferenczi were delving into individuals' psyches to reach their unconscious, but I am wondering to what extent Ferenczi's subsequent influence, or neglect, by psychoanalysts—on the European continent, in the UK, and the USA—has been due to cultural factors. Therefore, I am using my sociologist's viewpoint, that is, a so-called "scientific bird's eye perspective", that requires a knowledge of psychoanalysis but focuses on the differing cultural circumstances.

So, when asking, for instance, "Why were Ferenczi's innovative techniques forgotten or even maligned?", I cannot zero in on the validity or the details of the disagreements between him and Freud, on the rivalry between the disciples for succession, or on unconscious motives for these. Instead, I have to examine the social context within which these questions arose. This is not to say that sociologists know more than psychoanalysts: they are just as tempted to go beyond their professional expertise, as are psychoanalysts.

In fact, it behoves us to recall that in the early twentieth century both psychoanalysis and sociology were in their infancy; that since then, both disciplines have become established and have split up into ever more professional organisations; and that their ideas have become ubiquitous enough for laymen to think they can psychoanalyse and sociologise by simply asserting that that is what they are doing. However, psychoanalysts as well tend to sociologise and sociologists to psychoanalyse without the necessary qualifications. This habit seems justified by referring to Freud's *Totem and Taboo* (1912– 1913), *Civilization and its Discontents* (1930a), and *The Psychopathology of Everyday Life* (1901b), etc., which, however, are not the works practising psychoanalysts tend to rely on in their clinical work with patients.

Over the years, serious efforts have been made to come to grips with the elusive ramifications of the combined social and psychologi- cal influences on the formation of individual character, the psyche, the ego, or the self, etc. Among these are the collaborative endeavours of sociologists and psychoanalysts in the Frankfurt school (that is, Fromm, Horkheimer, and Adorno already before the Second World War, Mitscherlich and Habermas soon afterwards), the co-operation of Talcott Parsons and Heinz Hartmann in America in the 1940s and 1950s, and a variety of interdisciplinary endeavours between mem- bers of psychoanalytic institutes and sociological societies. In such collaborations, ultimately, one of the two disciplines has ended up overpowering the other. This means that the methods by either disci- pline predominate, and that either psychic or social influences even- tually are thought to determine the events and attitudes of individuals and societies.

Sociologists are divided, roughly, into a variety of so-called humanists, Marxists, and "scientific" quantifiers and poll-takers. Each of these, in turn, has its own networks, and specialities, some of them mainstream and others esoteric. Although they might have as little contact with one another as the followers of Wilhelm Reich with those of Charles Brenner, or of Siegfried Bernfeld with those of Melanie Klein, it is possible for sociologists to jump into another network when fed up with their own, and to have overlapping memberships.

Superficially, the proliferation of sociological organisations parallels that of psychoanalytic ones. But sociologists rarely identify with their mentors in the way psychoanalytic candidates tend to do with their analysts and / or supervisors. And after would-be psychoanalysts have chosen the institute they want to belong to before entering their field, that is where they will obtain their credentials and where they tend to remain for the rest of their professional lives. Thus, they do not have much contact with those who have been trained in a different way. Even when strong differences result in institutional splits, because these are based on convictions by leading individuals, in a discipline whose methods in part depend on intrapersonal and relational factors, might mean that hurt feelings could become part of institutional history. In so far as these must also be incorporated into theory and technique, it makes perfect sense to focus on the quarrels among prominent individuals. Freud himself set the precedent, beginning with Adler, Jung, and Stekel. The rest of the disciples, Ferenczi among them, agreed that the "gold of psychoanalysis"—that is, the discovery of the unconscious—was to be their fundamental concern. But, as its innermost source kept eluding them, they were forced to focus increasingly on the techniques that would be best suited to uncovering it. And, because Freud's unconscious (and his cases) had provided the original material for psychoanalysis, it was bound to be the meat of psychoanalytic theory and technique. In that sense, it became the disciples' property.

As we know, already at the meetings of the Wednesday Society Freud offered the overarching theories that were based on the information the disciples had brought away from their casework. And much later, he even wrote to Ferenczi that he did not care all that much for work with patients. Consequently, the elaboration of technique later on fell to the disciples, who, themselves, brought different backgrounds, talents, levels of imagination and ambitions to this task. As long as Freud was alive, he managed to keep them together for the sake of psychoanalysis. Undoubtedly, his own natural bent was to elaborate on the rational elements that could be distilled from the irrational unconscious. Ferenczi, however, had more courage in so far as he allowed himself to enter more fully into this irrational sphere. In practice, and from the letters, it could be argued that the technique of ego psychology not only follows from The Ego and the Id (1923b), but from Freud's inclination to extensive theorising, and from his rejection of Ferenczi's experiments.

Ferenczi died just after Hitler began to rule Germany. At the time, many psychoanalysts began to emigrate. I have gone into the detailed reasons for the ascendance of ego psychology in my book, *The Freud-ians. A Comparative Perspective* (Kurtzweil, 1989). Here, I just want to state that a combination of the American penchant toward science, the threat of charlatans getting away with practising various types of pseudo-psychoanalyses, along with existing institutional structures, not only was favourable to the success of what since then has been called "American ego psychology" but was "what the doctor ordered". That psychoanalysis was dead on the continent during the war and very much curtailed by it in the UK, and that the Contro-versial Discussions between Anna Freud and Melanie Klein did not exactly further it, was yet another factor that helped establish the Americans (most of whom were European *émigrés*) during the first meeting of the International Psychoanalytic Association (IPA) in 1949.

François Roustang, a Frenchman, likens Freud's disciples to the brothers in *Totem and Taboo*, who were fighting for succession after having killed their tribal father, namely Freud. If we carry this anal-ogy a step further, then Ferenczi was one of those who lost, who was killed by his brothers, under the leadership of Ernest Jones. Although less dramatically than Jesus at Easter, and after fifty to sixty years rather than a few months, the ideas for which he was crucified are being resurrected. Obviously, they had been prematurely buried.

André Haynal has provided a most perceptive overview of the origins of Ferenczi's psychoanalytic technique (Haynal, 1993), and of the milieu in which his psychoanalysis was embedded: among the *émigrés* from the far-flung territories within the Austro-Hungarian empire, the Judeo-Hungarian intelligentsia, and Freud and his disci-ples. Individuals aware of that milieu, of the flavour of that era, histo-rians and other scholars of *fin-de-siècle* Vienna recognise that emotional and scientific issues were intertwined not only among psychoanalysts but in the culture at large. Practising analysts and commentators today cannot be expected to truly tune into an atmosphere that no longer exists anywhere. Thus, they cannot help generalising from our times to Ferenczi's.

Haynal also emphasises that, in spite of their differences, there was instant and mutual enthusiasm and friendship between Freud and Ferenczi, which extended to their personal lives and lasted until Ferenczi died. I might add that any two people who meet as fre-quently as they did, and who have exchanged "more than 1000 letters", are close. The letters Ferenczi wrote to Freud from America, and which are almost the only remaining record of this eight-month visit, are those of an intimate who bares his soul, with no holds barred.

Inevitably, psychoanalysts examine Freud's and Ferenczi's relation in terms of issues touching on psychoanalytic theory, which was Freud's forte, and technique, which was Ferenczi's forte. They look to Ferenczi's *Clinical Diary* and to his *Final Contributions* as well as to the letters. And they point, as Ferenczi also did, to his need for love and acceptance. In addition to that theme, commentators examine his notions of mutual analysis; identification with the aggressor; abstinence *vs.* gratification within the psychoanalytic dyad; definitions of sexual abuse; and the tendency to elevate "emotional" over "scientific" analysis. At the time, psychoanalysis did not yet take much note of the inevitable distortions that might occur in the reporting of cases. Sixty to ninety years later, as we delve into Ferenczi's self-critical observations, these reinterpretations run an even greater danger of being re-evaluated piecemeal, due to a combination of his re-interpreters' biases and the cultural changes that have taken place. However, Ferenczi's penetrating honesty and his ability to take calculated risks by now are inspiring a large number of practising psychoanalysts.

The current revival of Ferenczi's contributions by some so-called mainstream Freudians is based to a large extent on the realisation that components of his "active" method might work better with today's patients than the detached, scientific stance. The opposition to this method, of course, can be traced to Freud's original rejection of it. However, the American basis for neglecting Ferenczi's contributions, though never explicitly, is based not only on his disagreements with Freud, and on the assumption by Jones of his lack of competence at the end of his life, but on an exceedingly acrimonious quarrel within the New York Psychoanalytic Society in 1941. At that time, Karen Horney, with the strong support by Clara Thompson, among others, argued against "scientificity" and held that clinical diagnoses also had to take account of cultural factors, and that, therefore, the analyst's technique ought to focus on the present lives of their analysands and work backwards, rather than the other way around.

In my years of examining the records, I did not come upon Thompson's name except in asides about her support of Horney, and an occasional mention of her own unorthodox analysis. However, after their separation from the New York Psychoanalytic Institute, the

William Alanson White Institute offered a haven for Ferenczi's (dis-parate) sympathisers, among them Erich Fromm and Harry Stack Sullivan, in addition to Horney and Thompson. But they were not members of the American Psychoanalytic Association, or of the International Psychoanalytic Association, after the Second World War. Therefore, none of them then were in a position to reintroduce Ferenczi's ideas on the continent. In addition, the method of *Tot-schweigen* (deathly silence) about dissidents, which had already been practised by Freud, had by then been perfected.

By now, most of the participants in the quarrels of the 1940s are dead or retired from institutional politics. Active members tend not to know about this history, although their training has led them to prac-tise what has been passed down from them. And as we know, with-out conviction in their own clinical methods, psychoanalysts cannot practise successfully. So, I am not faulting psychoanalysts of any denomination for their indispensable professional stance. However, it seems to me that the revival of interest in Ferenczi's psychoanalytic techniques is due to the fact that the strictly scientific method of curing neuroses—despite enormous expenditures in time and money—has not always brought the expected results, and that the search for the unconscious has not been as successful as expected.

The focus on intrapsychic factors alone, I believe, tends to pay too little attention to the changing social situation in which psycho-analysis is embedded. Sociologists speak of a move from the modern to the postmodern age and the accompanying change in conscious-ness. I am not maintaining that sociologists are any less "provincial" than psychoanalysts. However, the changes in presenting symptoms by potential patients are responses also to other than psychic phenom-ena. That many people look for quick-fix therapies that do not touch on the unconscious, and for the most part cannot differentiate psycho-analysts from con-men (and women) and from charlatans, is yet another extra-psychoanalytic factor. Altogether, it seems that even many otherwise knowledgeable individuals living in our speeded-up culture resist spending their time waiting patiently for the uncon-scious to emerge—in the presence of a more or less silent psycho-analyst. Some of these analysts have come upon Ferenczi's "active" technique and expect to explore it, even if, as they learn about it, they find out that it is not as active as they had expected. One should note that many "experimenters" are among the younger analysts, that in

America a good number of them are not medically trained, that they are rather eclectic, and are among those who only recently have been accepted by the International Psychoanalytic Association.

What part of Ferenczi's technique, then, appeals to today's practitioners and motivates them to try out some of his experiments in their sessions with patients? Why the sudden revival? Yes, he was among the first to advocate an extensive training analysis for analysts, and to argue that mastering the countertransference was imperative for every psychoanalyst—practices that by now have become routine for (psychoanalytic) therapists. Moreover, some of Ferenczi's then far-out methods now seem to be better suited to current culture than the purely "scientific" methods. And, finally, his writings have been made available to more than a handful of persons. The following six concepts not only vindicate Ferenczi, but also are attuned to the current ethos:

Love and acceptance

It has been argued, frequently and convincingly, that Ferenczi's own need for love and acceptance helped him identify these needs in his patients, that it was a cornerstone to his technique, and that it was especially strong in his relation to Freud, his "father". For example, while in America, in 1926, and at a time when Otto Rank was more and more pushing the importance of the birth trauma, Ferenczi was proving his allegiance to Freud (Ferenczi, 1955, p. 36):

> In a lecture which I recently gave . . . I attempted to demonstrate . . .
> that the mother, womb-, and birth-fantasies and dreams of neurotics
> are only symbolic representatives of the penis . . . that it is certainly
> unjustified to base a new technique of psychoanalysis on such a highly
> disputed theory as the birth trauma . . . [and that] Freud as well as
> myself rejects this newest theory of Rank's.

Although Ferenczi goes on to explain the context of his own dispute with Freud over psychoanalytic technique, he argues that to rid the patient of his repetition compulsion it is useful for the analyst to encourage the patient's repetition tendency in order to eliminate the neurosis. And he goes on to say that

> Freud accepted my method in so far as he admitted that analyses are
> best carried out in a state of abstinence. I have always emphasized that

this measure can be used only in exceptional cases and then only occasionally. But certain colleagues appear to have misunderstood my
method . . . Active therapy is only a means to an end . . . Exaggeration
of active measures leads to a great heightening of resistance in the
patient and would endanger the analysis. (Ibid., p. 37)

This is just one example that demonstrates Ferenczi's need to remain
in tune with Freud, and which, soon after his return from America, he
appeared to want less strongly.

Both sociological and psychological studies of mass culture and of
peer behaviour have found that children who have their parents'
approval perform better, have higher self-esteem, and generally do
better all around. I am not saying that this is or is not so, but that
Ferenczi's techniques, which assume this primary need, appeal to
therapists dealing with patients who have similar needs.

Mutual analysis

Freud was shocked when Ferenczi informed him that he had given in
to his patient RN's (Elizabeth Severn) wish to analyse him. In the
Diary, Ferenczi states,

> The patient's demands to be loved corresponded to analogous
> demands on me by my mother . . . therefore I did hate the patient, in
> spite of all the friendliness I displayed; this she was aware of, to which
> she reacted with the same inaccessibility . . . Mutual analysis appears
> to provide the solution. It gave me an opportunity to vent my antipa-
> thy. (1932, p. 99)

Ferenczi goes on to list additional advantages to venting his antipathy
toward this patient: finding her less disagreeable and thus able to
show more friendliness, liberating himself of anxieties in relation to
other patients, experiencing less sleepiness and being capable of more
empathy during his sessions with patients, and, thus, becoming more
sensitive in his interventions. As Dupont summarises in her introduction to the *Diary*, mutual analysis was a difficult path; Ferenczi felt as
if he were balancing on a tightrope, and yet he decided to push the
experiment to its limit, but did not continue it when he became aware
of the limitations—RN's grandiose ideas about their "collaboration"
and the subsequent termination of the experiment. Although Ferenczi

gave up this technique, it added immensely to our knowledge about countertransference. At present, this is a central topic in clinical debates, and, in line with our current egalitarian ethos, it makes Ferenczi more popular than the ego psychologists who, even more than they deserve, are being accused of so-called elitism.

Abstinence vs. gratification

If, metaphorically, Sigmund Freud was the father of psychoanalysis, Sandor Ferenczi was the mother, states Hoffer (1993, pp 75–80). (Paradoxically, this so-called mother introduced the active technique, which, in the age of women's liberation, tends to point out that this used to be the father's domain.) When Freud died, Hoffer goes on, psychoanalysis became a one-parent child (ibid., p. 751). Freud had argued that "the treatment must be carried out in total abstinence" (Freud, 1914g). Ferenczi, after having agreed with him for years, gradually gave in to more of his patients' demands for corrective emotional intervention. In this context, he was increasingly made to focus on the analyst's impact on the patient, and on the transference itself as a piece of repetition in the analytic process. Thereby, he gave yet another meaning to the term "countertransference". Recent research on projective identification, among other things, focuses on these issues, which Ferenczi addressed, as it were, *in utero*.

In staying with my sociological focus, I want to add that in the Vienna and the Budapest of the 1920s and 1930s, notions of gratification went against the grain of received opinion: self-control and duty were considered paramount, and to abstain from pleasures, in principle if not always in deed, were the approved mores. Now, gratification of wishes, which frequently is equated to happiness—one of the somewhat elusive rights allegedly guaranteed by the American constitution—is perceived as the due of every citizen. Consequently, Ferenczi's concern with this issue has become an increasingly pervasive "postmodern" theme.

Scientific vs. emotional analysis

It is generally agreed that some of the Freudian ego psychologists applied the notion of abstinence too literally and thereby left out the extra-transferential aspects of the relation between analyst and analysand. Even without reference to Ferenczi, this was a recurring theme in psychoanalytic congresses. I recall, for instance, Ralph Greenson's caricature at the International Meetings in Vienna, in 1971, where he reported on one of his supervisees: his patient had come to the session with half of his body in a plaster cast, and the analyst had abstained from asking him what had happened to him. When the patient did not say much while on the couch, this supervisee had reported on his hostility—without recognising that he might have had reason to be hostile to an analyst who did not even care to know why he was injured, or whether he was in pain.

The British independent school, of course, has stressed the need for the analyst's loving relationship with the patient all along. Aside from Balint, who followed Ferenczi's stress on the importance of the analyst's personal emotional investment in his analysands, Fairbairn, among others, advocated "genuine emotional contact" (Fairburn, 1952), Winnicott talked of "basic ego-relatedness" (Winnicott, 1958), and Bowlby focused on attachment and parental care (Bowlby, 1979). As I indicated above, in the USA the interpersonal school, among them Fromm, Horney, Sullivan, and Thompson, did carry on the spirit of Ferenczi's emotional analysis, though less explicitly. In any event, they were outside the official Freudians' dialogue.

Sexual abuse

In a *Diary* entry in August 1932, Ferenczi notes that "the newborn child uses all its libido for personal growth, and must be loved . . . and in addition to being loved and loving [it]self . . . can also introject persons and things as love objects" (Ferenczi, 1932, pp. 189–190). He adds that satisfaction must be timely, in step with the appropriate ego development, and then goes on:

> It is undoubtedly injurious to the infant if lazy and unscrupulous wet nurses use masturbatory stimulation of the genitals to make children go to sleep. Just as untimely and disturbing to the ego are the frequent, brutally masturbatory assaults of adults on growing children, whose genitality has not yet progressed beyond the period of harmless, non-passionate touching. An undeveloped ego will have to make an even more colossal effort, of course, when it has to endure the violence and shock, as well as the emotions, of real sexual intercourse. But such incidents are much more frequent than one would imagine. (Ibid)

In postmodern society, where traditional norms, when not pur-
posefully attacked, are ignored, and where sexual freedom (including
license) is accepted, incidents of sexual abuse have become much
more pervasive. (This does not mean that Ferenczi's foresight itself
was postmodernist. Yes, he was years ahead of his time. But his "confusion of tongues" referred to emotional, unconscious confusions
rather than to those of postmodern discourse that is based on structures of language.) However, during the last sixty years the abuses by
wet nurses, which then were rather common in Vienna and Budapest,
are no longer being perpetuated. And then, as now, children did not
report incestuous relationships, because they "are deeply shaken by
the shock of the premature intrusion and by [their] own efforts of
adaptation [to it]" (ibid.). Contemporary psychoanalysts, for good
reasons, rely on Ferenczi's perspicacity on the subject. They, too, note
that children, in spite of the more open acceptance of sexuality, still do
not criticise the behaviour of the intrusive adult, and still respond to
accusations of brutality or of lying by withdrawing into daydreams,
into automatic behaviour, compliance, and so on. And all along it has
been exceedingly difficult to know clearly when an abused child is
recounting an incident, is reliving a fantasy, or (in the USA) is
responding to suggestions by a zealous sex therapist to "harmless,
non-passionate touching" (ibid.). In any event, Ferenczi's clinical dis-
tinctions did not speak to societal changes, but to unconscious psychological ones. His insights were path-breaking and brilliant.

Identification with the aggressor

Ferenczi extends these observations by stating that "the early seduced
child adapts itself to its difficult task with the aid of complete identification with the aggressor" (ibid.). He goes on to say that, in analysis,
such a patient must be taken back to the time before the trauma and
the corresponding sexual development have occurred. Ferenczi then
asks "whether a sense of guilt after having suffered an untimely attack
is not bound up with guilt feelings because of having guessed and
shared the aggressor's feelings of guilt" (ibid.). (He also discusses this
issue in "Confusion of tongues" (1933).) These are astute and invaluable insights into the analysis of abused patients. But I tend to question their extension to generalisations about, for instance, victims of
the Holocaust. And I do not believe that Anne Frank's family, the

inhabitants of the Warsaw ghetto, or of Auschwitz, could have been saved by making plans for escape, that they could have stopped the machinery set in motion in the death camps, and elsewhere. (This is not to deny the possibility of less direct unconscious identification.) An analysis of the mediating institutions linked to power, politics, military strength, and international conflict, etc., and which historians and sociologists of the Holocaust have done, I believe, are more appropriate means of judging than the psychological states of helpless inmates whose psychic resolve, at best, could influence only personal decisions: whether or not to commit suicide, to tempt their fate by trying an escape, or an assassination. It is one thing to identify with a personal aggressor and another to do so with an inhuman machinery. I am touching on this topic not to explore it, but to exemplify that psychoanalytic findings can be misleading when applied to sociological realms.

It pays for us to recall that Sandor Ferenczi's strength was in the clinical contributions that put him way ahead of his contemporaries. His work was with patients; his interests were clinical. He lived for psychoanalysis. The only macro-political forecast he made was when he counselled Freud, in 1933, just before he died, to leave Vienna, preferably for England, where one could get good medical treatment. I believe that this was the warning of a friend, the sort of perception intelligent outsiders often possess about a place they know well but to which they do not totally belong. Freud was too much of a Viennese, too identified with his compatriots to foresee the danger. In this instance, I believe, neither Freud nor Ferenczi were making psychoanalytic judgements. Ferenczi's marginality allowed him to be the proverbial participant observer who is both outsider and insider, while Freud was too much of an insider to step outside his milieu. The rest is history.

References

Bowlby, J. (1979). *The Making and Breaking of Affectional Bonds*. London: Tavistock.

Fairbairn, W. R. D. (1952). Schizoid factors in the personality. In: *Psychoanalytic Studies of the Personality* (pp. 1–27). London: Tavistock/ Routledge.

Ferenczi, S. (1932). *The Clinical Diary of Sandor Ferenczi*, J. Dupont (Ed.), M. Balint & N. Z. Jackson (Trans.). Cambridge, MA: Harvard University Press, 1988.

Ferenczi, S. (1933). Confusion of tongues between adults and the child. In: *Final Contributions to the Problems and Methods of Psycho-Analysis* (pp. 280–290), M. Balint (Ed.), E. Mosbacher & others (Trans.). London: Hogarth Press, 1955 [reprinted, London: Karnac, 1994].

Ferenczi, S. (1955). *Final Contributions to the Problems and Methods of Psycho-Analysis*, M. Balint (Ed.), E. Mosbacher & others (Trans.). London: Hogarth Press, 1955 [reprinted, London: Karnac, 1994].

Freud, S. (1901b). *The Psychopathology of Everyday Life. S.E., 6*: vii–296. London: Hogarth.

Freud, S. (1912–1913). *Totem and Taboo. S.E., 13*: vii–162. London: Hogarth.

Freud, S. (1914g). Remembering, repeating and working-through. *S.E., 12*: pp. 145–156. London: Hogarth.

Freud, S. (1923b). *The Ego and the Id. S.E., 19*: 1–66. London: Hogarth.

Freud, S. (1930a). *Civilization and Its Discontents. S.E., 21*: 57–146. London: Hogarth.

Haynal, A. (1993). Ferenczi and the origins of psychoanalytic technique. In: L. Aron & A.Harris (Eds.), *The Legacy of Sandor Ferenczi* (pp. 53–74). Hillsdale, NJ: Analytic Press.

Hoffer, A. (1993). Ferenczi's relevance to contemporary psychoanalytic technique. In: L. Aron & A. Harris (Eds.), *The Legacy of Sandor Ferenczi* (pp. 75–80). Hillsdale, NJ: Analytic Press.

Kurtzweil, E. (1989). *The Freudians: A Comparative Perspective*. New Haven, CT: Yale University Press [reprinted with new Introduction, New Brunswick, NJ: Transaction, 1998].

Winnicott, D. W. (1958). The capacity to be alone. In: *The Maturational Process and the Facilitating Environment* (pp. 29–36). London: Hogarth Press, 1965.

CHAPTER FIVE

Ferenczi now and then: an introduction to his world

André Haynal

I t is instructive to embark on a "now and then" trip, a journey back and forth between problems of contemporary psychoanalysis and some stimulating ideas from the work of Ferenczi.

In the first place, Sandor Ferenczi was a clinician. Examining his world and its possible extensions can provide a better understanding of the psychoanalytical *process*.

As a matter of fact, from the beginning of the psychoanalytical process there is an "entanglement" of the ongoing relationships. The understanding of this *imbroglio*—"you take me for somebody else"— is what the psychoanalytic process consists of. Who would have shown this if not Ferenczi, especially in the case of RN, as presented in his *Clinical Diary* (Ferenczi, 1932). By living in these interactions, based on very archaic scripts, the analyst's efforts are directed toward disentangling them by interpretation, thus achieving a resolution of this adventure that is psychoanalysis. Therefore, for him, there is little difference between psychoanalysis and real life or, in other words, between the inside and outside of the treatment. Psychoanalysis was the world in which Ferenczi lived; for him there were no clear boundaries between life and psychoanalysis, but a continuity between both. Freud's attempt, on the other hand, to draw a clear line between the two areas is somewhat artificial: when Ferenczi came to Vienna to have analysis with him, Freud told him that he "should at least have one meal with us daily", but that "technique will require that nothing personal will be discussed outside the sessions" (Freud, 1916, p 130).

For Ferenczi, the "entanglement" is based primarily on the difference between "two languages", that of the adult and that of the child, which are not equivalent because they do not convey the same meaning. This paves the way for an understanding of the problem of traumatisation, but also for that of its counterpart, the creation of a libidinal bond.

Seduction

Before Ferenczi, seduction was usually viewed as a negative phenomenon; however, it has always occurred at the beginning of human life. Seduction creates the first attachment in the early stages of the highly tense and dramatic relationship emerging between a mother and her baby. To offer the breast to a newborn baby—what else could this be but a great, fundamental seduction? A few hours after our first child was born, the big, black, authoritarian and extremely nice nurse told my wife in an unforgettable imperative tone, "Feed her now or she'll starve." Wasn't that an invitation to seduce? Many women experience sexual pleasure in feeding their baby, and the baby learns the pleasure of taste, of warmth, of repletion. Here, we have both worlds, that of an adult woman and that of a newborn baby. One might say that, in this field, Ferenczi is a forerunner of Winnicott and others, but, unlike Winnicott, Ferenczi does not idealise the mother in a relationship allegedly devoid of any aggression. He does not focus on either a deceptive or a traumatic mother, whereas other authors in the second half of the twentieth century did—that is, the concepts of the "schizophrenogenic mother", or otherwise "traumatising" and abusing mothers. Ferenczi focuses on a complex and ambivalent mother such as usually exists in real life, and, in all likelihood, existed in Ferenczi's own relationship with his mother.

In recent years we have discussed amply Ferenczi's theory of traumatism, but less, or not at all, his ideas about seduction. For him, both topics were equally important and intertwined, so that it is no coincidence that in his Wiesbaden paper Ferenczi (1933) talked about trauma and seduction.

In psychoanalytic theory, discoveries have always started with the observation of something excessive. This was the case with the manifestation of transference in general, or, as one of the best recent examples in this respect, with the concept of projective identification, first viewed as pathological by Klein, and then as "normal" by Bion. Usually, a discovery is provoked by the excessive or exaggerated form of a phenomenon. Only later did clinicians, attentive to nuances, become aware of the existence of incomplete *"formes frustes"*—of less developed or mixed forms, of hints, that actually appear more frequently in the human psyche.

Seduction can be defined as an active movement of soliciting, of establishing contact and a growing *intimacy*. This is the definition of an affective phenomenon that is usually communicated by mostly emotional, non-verbal channels (looks, gestures, voice, posture, etc.). The setting-up of an analytic bond, and thus of the *process* of analysis, takes place by setting in motion a movement of mutual seduction. As many channels of affective communication by visual signs are blocked in analysis, it is the analyst's offer of a presence, his intense listening, his honesty, his expectations, and his demands, which carry the seductive message. In this *perspective*—Bion's "vertex"—we are able to grasp the affective emotional set-up of the process (Bion, 1965, pp. 106–107). Remember that, in his earlier works, Freud's preoccupations revolved around problems of seduction and sexuality raised by the encounters with his analysands. These were the starting point of the adventure he came to call "psychoanalytic treatment". As we know, for different historical reasons, he abandoned these interests and turned to the realm of fantasy life. It was Ferenczi who, on the basis of his clinical observations, came back to this dimension hidden in the therapeutic relationship.

In Freud's later works, it is the "therapeutic alliance" between the ego, weakened by internal conflicts and needing help, and the analyst that leads to what he called the *pact*. And this pact constitutes the analytic situation (Freud, 1940a[1938], pp. 173–174). For him, it is the resulting "positive transference with which" the analysand "meets us" (ibid., p. 181). Is that not the description of a process of seduction without designating it as such? (Did he avoid using this word?) What greater seduction is there than that of the analyst, who offers to listen attentively four times a week and, thus, becomes, on a regular basis, the centre of interest for the Other, who knows about failed seductions, and how these failures can become traumatic?

All this permits us to understand the "honeymoon", as Grunberger (1971) calls it, which follows the seduction, along with the growing awareness of one's wishes and hopes and also of the fears, anxieties, and profound concerns that are aroused in both protagonists.

The child, in its *helplessness* (Freud, 1954, Vol. 1, p. 138), resorts to seduction and tries to activate the people in its environment to fulfil its needs and desires. More recent research on babies has fully demonstrated the extent to which they are active in soliciting the help they need (Stern, 1985); this is done affectively in the form of "seduction". We tend to use the same strategy (often unconsciously) in situations when we feel deprived.

In such an interaction initiated by the psychoanalyst, the analysand will contribute to the creation of that intimacy. This is the first step, leading to further consequences: the setting-up of the ego ideal (the appearance of extraordinarily high, even inordinately megalomaniac hopes), and other so-called "regressive" manifestations, in particular, a certain degree of emotional dependence (which has always been the target of criticism of psychoanalysis by outside people. (One of the more recent versions of this is Masson writing about "emotional tyranny" (Masson, 1988).) It is this fear of dependence or of sexual implications that often mobilises the first major resistances to moving closer to each other as the consequence of the mutual seduction.

It is quite clear that a focus on the *emotional encounter* and on what it mobilises will lead to a conception of psychoanalysis in which the *experiencing* of that emotionality and its eventual, if imperfect, analysis will play an important role. From a historical perspective, the clarification of, and emphasis on, this aspect of psychoanalysis is an important part of Sandor Ferenczi's work. As has often been noted, Freud's emphasis was more on "insight", on "analysis" in the strict sense of the term, on what, in other words, we might call today the "cognitive" aspect. In his wish to link emotionality with that same "insight", Ferenczi thought that the latter must be preceded by an *experience* as deep as possible. Today, it might appear simplistic to oppose "insight" (*"Einsicht"*) and experience (*"Erlebnis"*) in this way; it can only be a matter of *degrees* of experience. One aspect of this question in particular was discussed by Freud and Ferenczi in their correspondence (see the letters from Ferenczi to Freud, December 5, 1931 and December 27, 1931 (Ferenczi, 1931a, p. 421, 1931b, p. 424)), and this was: what degree of sexual manifestation is tolerable? And how much of their inevitable *discharge*, such as the "little kiss" of Ferenczi's patient that initiated an important controversy, can be considered legitimate? (Today, we know that without the analysand "denouncing" Ferenczi to Freud, an important aspect of the case could perhaps not have been analysed. Denunciation of the father was an infantile theme in that patient's history of which she had previously not been aware (Ferenczi, 1932, p. 11).) Should emotions be re-experienced only to a *minimal* degree and for the greater part be discouraged by the clinical frame and by the strict non-responsive attitude of the analyst, as might have been Freud's position? (See the adage according to which the analysand can "say anything and do nothing" in the analytic situation (Freud, 1931).) Again, in today's historical perspective, it is clear that this is a question of *degrees*. The analytic community projected an antagonism on to the dialogue between Freud and Ferenczi that, one might suppose, brought about an attitude of fervent support for Freud's position, while ostracising Ferenczi as a "dissident". Calling him a dissident facilitated the elimination of the problem by creating a "memory gap" in history (Haynal, 1995).

This question touches, evidently, on the analyst's emotions and, therefore, affects a vital personal dimension. The aforementioned two positions were linked to this problem, but obviously did little to solve it. Historically, ego psychology has retained the idea of the *"minima"* of emotions admissible in the analytic cure as it appears in the formulae of the ageing Freud: when Freud had more students than patients, when he claimed to be unenthusiastic as a therapist, etc., he wrote to Ferenczi, "I am saturated with analysis as therapy, 'fed up'" (Freud, 1930, p. 380, and see also Haynal, 1988, pp. 3, 10, 32–33, 140). Ferenczi's heritage in this respect—the expression of *emotionality*, the importance of experience, and the idea of an analytic framework that allows the maintenance of such experience and regressions—surfaces again among all those who have worked with an *object-relation* perspective (for example, in the UK the "middle group", Winnicott, Balint, Rycroft, and others, the Kleinian group, in the USA, Searles and others, in France Bouvet, and others elsewhere). There can be no doubt at all that the majority of psychoanalysts are heirs, in varying degrees, to this conceptualisation.

As a starting point, "seduction" enables us to confront all aspects of *emotionality from the beginning* of the treatment, an emotionality that will subsequently flare up in the course of the analytic process.

Let us come back to the differences between adult and childhood languages. Those differences arise from the fact that the adult's final goal is to completely satisfy the sexual desire, in conformity with the adult stage of sexuality, while the infant's goal is to exchange mostly pregenital tenderness: these different goals do differentiate the one from the other. This is linked to the developmental stage of the infant, different from that of the adult. As Ferenczi underlines, this is all about the confrontation between the infant's and the adult's world, be it a dual or a triangular situation. As already noted, seduction is present from the very beginning. It is worth repeating that seduction was discovered in its caricatured and extreme manifestations, as is always the case in psychoanalysis. Seduction drives the contact between the infant and the adult; between infant and mother, and, later, between the child and the representatives of the Oedipal triangulation.

One could say that if seduction does not appear, then traumatism will. The neglected and abandoned child is the prime example of the child who has not received the normal amount of seduction from his environment, necessary to set in motion the making of contact. Thus, the problem of seduction is very closely linked to the problem of traumatism: a lack of early seduction results in early traumatism. The traumatism of original seduction leads, in the evolution of the history of psychoanalytic theory, to Laplanche's notion of generalised seduction (Laplanche, 1987).

It is clear that seduction is a motor, a motive in libidinal life, an *aspect* of the libido, but it is also clear that it can be used in the service of *resistance*.

Seduction has something to do with *adventure*. Psychoanalysis is an adventure and so, even more, is life. Starting with the "original" seduction, the seductions experienced throughout life make for a great many adventures. Perhaps it is this associative link between seduction and adventure/adventurer that reminds Freud of Ferenczi's affairs as an adolescent and as a young man. Was it perhaps this talent as a seducer that helped Ferenczi feel the importance of emotional communication?

In 1905, after the image of the perverse, seducing father, even *guilty* of having perhaps infected his child, the seducing but innocent mother makes her appearance in a published text, the *Three Essays*. (In fact, the introduction of the mother in the process of seduction precedes this text: Freud alludes to this for the first time in a letter of 6 December 1896, although only in a discreet allusion—in a veiled form—to the mother as an unforgettable seducer (Freud, 1896, p. 213).) The hypothesis developed by Freud in the later famous passage in the *Three Essays* (Freud, 1905d) says that the child's sexuality is precociously awakened by the *care* his mother gives him, due to his helplessness and his original distress. The idea that seduction comes about through maternal care was taken up by Klein, Ferenczi's former analysand, in 1928, when she stated that through the mother's tenderness her child's sexual drives are awakened.

In 1928, Klein went further than Freud did in 1905. As a matter of fact, in 1905 Freud did not yet talk about the seduction by the mother, even if he wrote that due to the care she gives the child, the latter's sexual drives are awakened by her caresses (Klein, 1968, p. 236; Lanouzière, 1991, p. 54). But talking about drives awakened in situations of care and tenderness perhaps does not sufficiently take into account other situations of physical nearness and of verbal and non-verbal libidinal exchanges within the intimacy of a family. In this sense, in *The Psychoanalysis of Children*, Klein (1932)—being the good observer that she was, whatever has been said—speaks of fraternal seduction; this in addition to the seduction by fathers that had already aroused the interest of Freud and of herself earlier. It was Freud's idea that extreme seduction—also an Oedipal one—could simultaneously become intrusion and aggression in the context of a primitive passivity, as in the case of his Russian patient.

In conceptualising the seduction only as a fantasy of the child, developed afterwards because of the little girl's vindictiveness towards her mother and her father, Klein does not elaborate on what this care and these caresses transmit, somewhat despite themselves, of the parents' fantasies, even if she reveals that this fantasy is based upon elements of the reality of their inner world, the mother's care and the father's tenderness.

In not taking into account the activity of the fantasies of both parents, Klein proposes a chrono-historical theory of seduction, in that the seduction is not born in the Oedipal triangle in relation to each of the parents, but in a premature triangulation of the child's proper relations with his two parents. Seduction, according to Klein, is a fantasy correlational to the structuring of the Oedipal situation; its content depends on the succession of libidinal movements that constitute its history: attachment–detachment, love–hate. Freud, in his genetic–historical theory, took into account, besides maternal care as an opportunity for excitement, the unconscious components of sexual life that deposit into the child the first elements of his unconscious together with the germs of his future sexuality. For Klein, on the contrary, the passive attitude of the Russian was determined, as she became convinced in her analyses of little boys, by the excessive range of destructive drives directed against his father, and by the resulting overwhelming anxiety. The passivity of the Russian patient is, still for Klein, the consequence of a "long period of impotence and being in need of the little child" (Klein, 1921, 1923).

In "Fragment of an analysis", Winnicott writes, "Also you have said that in your first analysis you had no aim. At the beginning, like other infants, you had no aim and this problem has remained with you" (Winnicott, 1972, p. 672). Winnicott also reminds us of the fact that it was more or less he who went to look for him. To explain: "When a baby has tasted milk, he knows that his aim is to get at milk, but if no milk is presented, his aim remains undirect" (ibid.). Winnicott added: "There is no solution for you except that something comes from me" (ibid.). Is this not a clear case of gross seduction? The seduction of the analyst!

If this has become a tabooed subject, this taboo concerns first of all the analyst, and perhaps particularly the analyst's wish to make analyses, to have analysands and, thus, be involved in his own self-analysis through hetero-analysis.

Remember the following: Freud put his patients, most of them being women, on a couch: in a way, on his bed: is *this* not seduction? The argument that these are relics of hypnosis might just as well be a denial of deeper motivations, even if it is historically correct. In other words, it might be true, but why did he keep just this particular feature?

Ferenczi's world

Ferenczi's understanding that the work of the analyst can be seen in different perspectives, which Freud already acknowledged in saying that "this technique is the only one suited to my individuality; I do not venture to deny that a physician quite differently constituted might find himself driven to adopt a different attitude to his patients and to task before him" (Freud, 1912e, p. 111), opened the door to the possibility of adopting a working style that would also *suit Ferenczi*. Thus, he paved the way for pluralistic and *non-dogmatic views about psychoanalytical work*. He saw himself in the light of how he imagined Freud wanted him to be, but was unable, in spite of his efforts, to conform to this image. His curiosity, his desire to help and to adapt to different patients and their different personal styles, prevented him from adopting a uniform attitude.

By the way, we know today that Freud also was better adapted to the individuality of his patients than it appears from his early technical writings and also from his being idealised as a hero by his Viennese and Berliner followers and the ensuing ego-psychological tradition. This becomes clearly apparent in Roazen's book, *How Freud Worked* (1995), and the numerous accounts of Freud's analysands: for example, Smiley Blanton, John Dorsey, Joseph Wortis, Marie Bonaparte, etc.

Ferenczi first, and Balint later, showed that the *personality* of the analyst does play an important role in the creation of the analytic situation, so that the analyst is never really "neutral" in this sense. Thus, they paved the way to new considerations on psychoanalytic interaction. In their view, psychoanalytic practice encompasses a certain attitude, creating what Ferenczi and Rank called the *psychoanalytical situation*, the setting (fifty-minute hour, couch, etc.) and also the analyst's personality and convictions expressed, among other things, by the pictures on the wall of the consulting room and other details. As an example, Balint described in a rather amusing caricature what we called the problem of the cushion:

> There are several solutions to this problem: (a) the cushion remains the same for every patient, but a piece of tissue paper is spread over it which is thrown away at the end of the hour; (b) the cushion remains, but every patient is given a special cover, distinguishable from the others by its shade or design, and for each hour the cushion is put into the appropriate cover; (c) each patient has his own cushion and must use only this; (d) there is only one cushion or only two or three of them for all the patients and it is left to them to use them as they like, etc. Moreover these possibilities have to be multiplied by at least three, because the situation differs according to whether the analyst, the patient or a servant manipulates the cushion.

A bagatelle, it may be thought, which it is almost ridiculous to treat at such length. And yet such trifles seem to have certain importance in the formation of the transference situation. For instance, one patient, who for external reasons had to change his analyst, dreamt of his first analyst as working in a highly modern, white-tiled W.C., well fitted with every hygienic refinement, and of the second as working in an old-fashioned, dirty, stinking place. . . . The dream analysis showed clearly that the patient drew certain conclusions as regards his two analysts' different attitudes towards cleanliness from the way in which they treated the cushion problem. No one is likely to dispute that an analysis conducted in an atmosphere corresponding to the first part of the dream will take a different course from what it would in an atmosphere corresponding to the second part. . . . We only wish to assert that differences do exist in the analytical atmosphere which are brought about by the analyst himself . . .

The same is true of a whole number of such details. Another impor-tant point, for instance, is the way in which the end of the session is brought about. Some analysts get up from their chairs, thus giving the signal. Other simply announce it in stereotyped words; others again try to invent new formulas for each hour; some begin to move to and fro in their chairs and the patient has to infer from the sound that the time is over; others again use alarm clocks, or keep a clock in front of the patient so that he may himself see the time passing. Then there is the couch itself, which may be low, broad, comfortable, or quite the contrary; the chair of the analyst; the arrangement of the consulting room – shall it be furnished as a study or as a drawing-room? or shall it be left totally unfurnished apart from the couch and the chair? – the method of . . . (Balint & Balint, 1939, pp. 224–225)

As we have seen, the personality of the analyst determines some aspects of the psychoanalytic process, and Ferenczi came progres-sively to a pluralistic view of psychoanalysis, close to artistic creativ-ity. Let us remember that the history of art is, as Strenger, among others, clearly points out, the history of *competing* styles that coexist within a common cultural space. "The art world is the paradigm of a cultural institution which *thrives* on plurality" (Strenger, 2002, p. 51). Its consequence is the necessity of various ways to judge art, which compete with each other.

This model of the art world has interesting consequences: "The plurality of coexisting approaches becomes a virtue rather than a problem. Psychoanalysis should also thrive on the tension generated by plurality, as Ferenczi recognised it . . ." (ibid., p. 52). In this sense, Ferenczi was already postmodern: he did not think that his alternative theory could be evaluated on the basis of the quality of his style, but, rather, by showing the difference of his narratives, created by himself on the shoulders of Freud. We can say that psychoanalysis has been good at doing two things: describing complexities of human experience and providing narratives that make sense of such experience. The other professional class of people that has been good at this is writers of fiction and poetry. Freud marvelled that his narratives read like novellas (Freud, 1895d, p. 161) and it is little wonder that Ferenczi sought and enjoyed the company of literary people. Their narratives, he thought, are superior to those of psychoanalysts who worked hard, if not slaved, trying to write up their experiences. The artist is offering narratives of life. He also shows a certain relative *validity* of the adult and the childhood discourses, and points to the conflict between these discourses in later life (especially in his Wiesbaden conference). For him, the point is not to neutralise one's personality, but to make constructive use of it (as in his *Clinical Diary*).

Already, for Freud, analysis is an exercise in truthfulness. "[A]nalysis . . . is in the first place an honest establishment of the facts" [*die Analyse . . . ist . . . zuerst eine ehrliche Feststellung*] (Freud, 1922, p. 87) and "becoming deceitful and [to] hide the essentials . . . is in direct conflict with the spirit of PA" (Freud, 1909, p. 32). In this sense, Ferenczi tried to realise Freud's ideal *in extremis*, by striving for *absolute truthfulness and sincerity* (Ferenczi, 1910, pp. 130–132). Freud saw the baby's encounter with his environment, in a situation of helplessness, as a frustrating experience. Ferenczi's *frustration with Freud* in his analysis with him made him think that the psychoanalytical encounter and attitude can provoke even more than frustration, sometimes possibly also traumatisation. In this context, the history of failed seductions, Ferenczi's attempts to seduce Freud, without receiving the expected or desired response, comes to mind. It is true that not only in life but, as we saw it, also in psychoanalysis, there is a first moment of mutual *seduction* (that can be tied subsequently to fears of dependence or of sexuality), followed by a moment when the *trauma* reappears or, in more general terms, when the individual is re-exposed to the fundamental *difficulties* of his life (i.e., to everything with a painful, anxious, or depressive connotation linked to failure, to what has fallen short of the idealised image, and what might, therefore, been likely to have been pushed away, not grasped, expelled from communication). The process of "working through", of transformation, of change (these difficulties culminate, as it is, in trauma and its consequences) refers to loss and to mourning to be done, and, ultimately, to the symbolism of limitation, that is, death.

Psychoanalysis presents us with a fundamental alternative: either wish fulfilment or the work of mourning. During therapy, the work of mourning, made possible by the presence of the analyst, predominates. Once this work is accomplished, hope slowly arises, and the analysand is able to experience in greater harmony the newly reconciled inner imagoes that have replaced his former conflicts and inner struggles. To reach that stage, loss had to be accepted and certain neurotic aspects of the self to be renounced that were at the root of those conflicts. The analyst adapts to the analysand and to his rate of working through. Leaving behind his own world and the relative harmony he has managed to achieve, he enters into the world of the Other to participate in the Other's inner journey, which requires constant self-questioning and brings with it all the risks that this entails. The analyst's ability to forget, to give up his own wish and even knowledge (as Bion (1967) has it), is called into play.

The analysand's mourning causes the analyst to relive his own. He should give up, to a great extent, his theoretical models and framework as well as personal ideas, in order to meet the Other on his own ground, sometimes even coming up against the very limits of psychoanalytic theory. He must also overcome his temptation to function *on behalf* of the Other and, the journey ended, must accept *his own death* in an intense relationship. Our resistances to change, to mourning, our defences against depression, are put harshly to the test. Unearthing memories, the memories of dead parents, of losses, can be compared with the process of repression followed by the lifting of repression: bad experiences that were buried, encapsulated, encysted, are dug up so that suppression can give way to true mourning.

Conclusion

In his last works, Ferenczi seeks unconventional ways of expression in order to break through the wall of words that had become all too familiar and automatic, with the assumption that "if we only stick to a strictly defined setting, we will automatically further the positive outcome of the therapy". That is to say that we would be rewarded for the merits of our discipline, by strictly adhering to the rules, tying the analysand to a procrustean bed and stretching or cutting him to fit the bed size. As a matter of fact, the therapeutic encounter is a mess, so to speak, of sheer humanity, where no reliable laws apply, as Ferenczi experienced it for the worst and the best in the cases described in the *Clinical Diary*, without the paternalism implicit in purism. He is aware of our epistemic fallibility and he does not forget our propensity to err, "the map should never be confused with the territory", as he writes (Ferenczi, 1932, p. 75). The personality of the analyst, as we have seen in Balint's humorous sketches, cannot be ignored; the little trifles, the spices, are often more important than strictly following the instructions of the recipe. Ferenczi anticipated this difference, as is mirrored in his texts. For a long time, Ferenczi feared that, if he did not follow Freud's lines and "recipes", this would make him a poor analyst. In the early 1930s, however, he underwent a positive change towards more independence. He developed and increasingly trusted his own way of thinking, as is reflected in the *Clinical Diary*.

"She reminds me very much of my mother", says Ferenczi about Severn. He forcefully introduces this subjective element into his thinking about his patient. In Freud's narratives on fathers and sons, you will scarcely find anything involving himself. In his clinical cases, there is never a mention of him, Freud, not even when the Rat Man calls him "My Captain". Freud explains,

> He repeatedly addressed me as 'Captain', probably because at the beginning of the hour I had told him that I myself was not fond of cruelty like Captain N., and that I had no intention of tormenting him unnecessarily. (Freud, 1909d, p. 169).

He is not the captain; on the contrary he is *not* fond of cruelty . . . Even in Freud's correspondence with Ferenczi, where he always plays the role of the father, never of the son, and thinks that he really *is* this father, about whom there is *no room* for fantasies. Together with Rank, Ferenczi opened a new path, a new tradition, the intersubjective discourse, but, in contrast to the interpersonal schools, he did not deny the existence of an *underlying motivational* system (like the *drives*) or the communication through *affects* (i.e., he conceived emotions as a communication system). Nowhere in Freud's works can we find the same clarity about these topics, which later formed an important part in object relations theories and are also present, to some extent, in Kohut's self psychology. Generally speaking, what was not accepted or integrated from Ferenczi's heritage later re-emerged in other forms in related traditions, especially in the British Middle-Group and in self psychology. Likewise, another heritage of the Budapest School (here, I think in the first place of Imre Hermann, Ferenczi's disciple) can be seen as a forerunner of the later *attachment* theories, a specific kind of relationships.

The same holds true for the problem of *seduction*. I think it is an example of how emotional theoretical disputes can create a taboo on topics that, however, are fundamental for a better understanding of the elements constituting the *psychoanalytic process*. Seduction should not be eliminated by a denial, but recognised as an important factor in the transference of ancient, primeval events and interactions. The repetition of traumas may have been the subject of many useful discussions over the past years—in fact, in Ferenczi's footsteps. However, the problem about the mobilisation of libidinal forces is worth considering as an important part of his heritage for a better understanding of ourselves.

To conclude, let me express my hope that I have been able, at least to a certain degree, to seduce you to think over these subjects and particularly that of seduction . . .

References

Balint, A., & Balint, M. (1939). On transference and counter-transference. *International Journal of Psycho-Analysis, 20*: 223–230. Also in: *Primary Love and Psychoanalytic Technique* (pp. 201–208). London: Karnac, 1985.

Bion, W. R. (1965). *Transformations; Changes from Learning to Growth.* London: W. Heinemann Medical Books [reprinted, London: Karnac, 1984].

Bion, W. R. (1967). Notes on memory and desire. *Psychoanalytic Forum, 2*: 271–286.

Ferenczi, S. (1910). Letter from Sandor Ferenczi to Sigmund Freud, February 5, 1910. In: E. Brabant, E. Falzeder, & P. Giampieri-Deutsch

(Eds.), *The Correspondence of Sigmund Freud and Sandor Ferenczi, Volume 1, 1908–1914* (pp. 130–132). Cambridge, MA: Harvard University Press, 1993.

Ferenczi, S. (1931a). Letter from Sandor Ferenczi to Sigmund Freud, December 5, 1931. In: E. Falzeder & E. Brabant (Eds.), *The Correspondence of Sigmund Freud and Sandor Ferenczi, Volume 3, 1920–1933* (p. 421). Cambridge, MA: Harvard University Press, 2000.

Ferenczi, S. (1931b). Letter from Sandor Ferenczi to Sigmund Freud, December 27, 1931. In: E. Falzeder & E. Brabant (Eds.), *The Correspondence of Sigmund Freud and Sandor Ferenczi, Volume 3, 1920–1933* (pp. 424–425). Cambridge, MA: Harvard University Press, 2000.

Ferenczi, S. (1932). *The Clinical Diary of Sandor Ferenczi*, J. Dupont (Ed.), M. Balint & N. Z. Jackson (Trans.). Cambridge, MA: Harvard University Press, 1988.

Ferenczi, S. (1933). Confusion of tongues between adults and the child. In: M. Balint (Ed.), *Final Contributions to the Problems and Methods of Psycho-Analysis* (pp. 280–290). London: Hogarth Press, 1955 [reprinted, London: Karnac, 1994].

Freud, S. (1895d). *Studies on Hysteria. S.E., 2.* London: Hogarth.

Freud, S. (1896). Letter from Freud to Fliess, December 6, 1896. In: J M. Masson (Ed.), *The Complete Letters of Sigmund Freud to Wilhelm Fliess 1887–1904* (pp. 207–214). Cambridge, MA: Harvard University Press, 1985.

Freud, S. (1905d). *Three Essays on The Theory of Sexuality. S.E., 7*: 123–243. London: Hogarth.

Freud, S. (1909). Letter from Sigmund Freud to Ernest Jones, October 31, 1909. In: R. A. Paskauskas (Ed.), *The Complete Correspondence of Sigmund Freud and Ernest Jones 1908–1939* (pp. 32–33). Cambridge, MA: Harvard University Press, 1993.

Freud, S. (1909d). *Notes Upon a Case of Obsessional Neurosis. S.E., 10*: 151–249. London: Hogarth.

Freud, S. (1912e). Recommendations to physicians practising psychoanalysis. *S.E., 12*: 109–119. London: Hogarth.

Freud, S. (1916). Letter from Sigmund Freud to Sandor Ferenczi, June 1, 1916. In: E. Falzeder & E. Brabant (Eds.), *The Correspondence of Sigmund Freud and Sandor Ferenczi, Volume 2, 1914–1919* (pp. 130–131). Cambridge, MA: Harvard University Press, 1996.

Freud, S. (1922). Letter from Sigmund Freud to Oskar Pfister, 25 July 1922. In: H. Meng & E. L. Freud (Eds.), *Psychoanalysis and Faith. The Letters of Sigmund Freud and Oskar Pfister, 1909–1939* (pp. 87–88). London: Hogarth Press, 1963.

Freud, S. (1930). Letter from Sigmund Freud to Sandor Ferenczi, January 11, 1930. In: E. Falzeder & E. Brabant (Eds.), *The Correspondence of Sigmund Freud and Sandor Ferenczi Volume 3, 1920–1933* (pp. 380–381). Cambridge, MA: Harvard University Press, 2000.

Freud, S. (1931). Letter from Sigmund Freud to Sandor Ferenczi, December 13, 1931. In: E. Falzeder & E. Brabant (Eds.), *The Correspondence of Sigmund Freud and Sandor Ferenczi, Volume 3, 1920–1933* (pp. 421–424). Cambridge, MA: Harvard University Press, 2000.

Freud, S. (1940a[1938]). *An Outline of Psycho-Analysis. S.E., 23*: 139–208. London: Hogarth.

Freud, S. (1954). *The Origins of Psycho-Analysis; Letters to Wilhelm Fliess, Drafts and Notes 1887–1902.* London: Imago. Partially in: *S.E., 1*: 318.

Grunberger, B. (1971). *Le narcissisme.* Paris: Payot.

Haynal, A. (1988). *The Technique at Issue. Controversies in Psychoanalysis from Freud and Ferenczi to Michael Balint.* London: Karnac.

Haynal, A. (1995). Ferenczi – dissident. In: *Disappearing and Reviving. Sandor Ferenczi in the History of Psychoanalysis* (pp. 101–107). London: Karnac, 2002.

Klein, M. (1921). Eine Kinderemtwicklung. *Imago, 7*: 251–309.

Klein, M. (1923). The development of a child. *International Journal of Psychoanalysis, 4*: 419–474.

Klein, M. (1928). Early stages of the Oedipus conflict. *International Journal of Psycho-Analysis, 9*: 167–180 [Les stades précoces du conflit Œdipien. In: M. Klein (1968), *Essais de psychanalyse* (pp. 229–241)].

Klein, M. (1932). *The Psycho-Analysis of Children. International Psycho-Analysis Library, 22*: 1–379. London: Hogarth Press.

Klein, M. (1968). *Essais de psychanalyse.* Paris: Payot.

Lanouzière, J. (1991). *Histoire secrete de la seduction sous le regne de Freud.* Paris: Presses Universitaires de France.

Laplanche, J. (1987). *Nouveaux fondements pour la psychanalyse.* Paris: Presses Universitaires de France.

Masson, J. M. M. (1988). *Against Therapy. Emotional Tyranny and the Myth of Psychological Healing.* New York: Atheneum.

Roazen, P. (1995). *How Freud Worked. First Accounts of Patients.* Northvale, NJ: Jason Aronson.

Stern, D. N. (1985). *The Interpersonal World of the Infant. A View from Psychoanalysis and Developmental Psychology.* New York: Basic Books.

Strenger, C. (2002). *The Quest of Voice in Contemporary Psychoanalysis.* Madison, CT: International Universities Press.

Winnicott, D. W. (1972). Fragment of an analysis. In: P. L. Giovacchini (Ed.), *Tactics and Techniques in Psychoanalytic Therapy* (pp. 455–693). New York: Science House, 1972 [reprinted, Northvale, NJ: Jason Aronson, 1990].

Healing boredom: Ferenczi and his circle of literary friends

Michelle Moreau-Ricaud

"Ferenczi's turn must come"

(Andreas-Salomé, 1913)

I would like to suggest, first, that I experienced a theoretical and aesthetic shock with Hungarian psychoanalysis and literature during my analytic training and later.

As I was in difficulty in my first analysis under supervision (called *analyse quatrième* in my organisation), I was looking for enlightenment in historical articles on the subject. I discovered Kovács, and my very first paper her innovation to that of Eitingon's (Moreau, 1977). As I was interested by Ferenczi, the Balints (Michael and Alice), Róheim, Loránd, Pető, etc., I chose to write on the Budapest School for my second doctorate.

On top of this, I fell in love with Kosztolányi (and early twentieth century literature). His *Kleptomaniac Translator* is so funny and so well observed. Was he a pre-Lacanian? He shows us that the symptom might change but the structure does not. An aesthetic shock during a public reading drove me to learn Hungarian. But, alas, it was so difficult and, to investigate the influence of analysis on Hungarian writers,

I asked Peter Adam to help in my research. The results were beyond my expectations. Unlike in Vienna, the cultural circles were open to the new, the modern. The reception of psychoanalysis in Hungary, so long and so difficult in the medical field, was, on the contrary, immediate and passionate in *Les Belles Lettres*. It was Ferenczi (1876–1933) who had brought about this cross-fertilisation.

It is "pure gold", said Freud, speaking of Ferenczi's writings. We could say the same for the work of Ferenczi's writer friends. And my desire to share with others these little wonders unknown in France received the friendly help of Gribinski and Pontalis (1990) in the *Nouvelle Revue de Psychanalyse*. Pontalis also published works in his collection *Curiosités freudiennes* (Gallimard) under the title (half-stolen from Kosztolányi) *Cure d'ennui. Ecrivains hongrois autour de Sandor Ferenczi* (Moreau-Ricaud, 1992).

Ferenczi, a young doctor "attracted by the arts and artists"

In the beginning of the nineteenth century, Hungary experienced a cultural revolution, leaving behind the medieval way of thinking for modernity. But we know that changing mentality is a long process; it might be helped by intellectuals, artists, and others. Budapest (nicknamed "Judapest", as Lukács reminds us) opened herself to the West in many different ways: politics, science, art, music, literature, and the new science, psychoanalysis.

Writers, engrossed by this young science, were in the *avant-garde*, conscious of their commitment. Psychoanalysis fertilised the public mind through novels, plays, short stories, poems, etc. Ferenczi was the bridge between these two worlds. He was the driving force behind the integration of the young science and *Les Belles Lettres*, a turning point for literature, because he was passionate about it. Kosztolányi recalled how Ferenczi "was attracted by the arts and artists" (Moreau-Ricaud, 1992).

It is true that he was very young when he fell in the cauldron . . .

Sandor: a literary upbringing

Many books have been written on Ferenczi (Barande, Haynal, Jimenez, Lorin, Sabourin, etc.) but not on his infancy. He seemed to have been a "wise baby", a wise pupil, a joyful student, and a scholarly young man.

He was born in the last forty-five years of the Austrian–Magyar Empire. He was educated in an atmosphere of revolutionary ideas. In fact, his father, Baruch Fränkel, from Cracow, settled in Miskolc after his participation in the Insurrection of 1848; he changed his Jewish name, "magyarising" it into Bernát Ferenczi, and became a bookstore owner, a printer, and a publisher. Not forgetful of his first commitment, he published the revolutionary poems of Mihály Tompa, a Calvinist pastor famous for his poetry against the House of Habsburg.

In the family, the atmosphere was "too severe", "not loving enough" (Ferenczi, 1921, p. 8), but intellectual and artistic. At nine years old, Sándor went to the Calvinist gymnasium and received a very good education there—a classical one with German, French, Latin, and Greek literature (*"Thalassa"*, instead of *"tenger"*, is a reminiscence of his translation of Xenophon and Herodotus)—and a modern education as well, since his school had just introduced new teaching methods. He learned a lot of poetry, in the cultural *Society Kazinczy*, and also wrote his own poems, some dedicated to his mother (Moreau-Ricaud & Mádai, 1991).

There is a significant anecdote related to the recitation of his poetry (Freud, 1901b). One day he made a slip of the tongue, reported by Freud in the third edition of *The Psychopathology of Everyday Life*:

> When I was in the first form at the Gymnasium [Secondary School] I had, for the first time in my life, to recite a poem in public (i.e. in front of the whole class). I was well prepared and was dismayed at being interrupted at the very start by a burst of laughter. . . . I gave the title of the poem '*Aus der Ferne* [From Afar]' quite correctly, but instead of attributing it to its real author I gave my own name. The poet's was no less than Sándor Petőfi! (p. 85)

Ferenczi explained,

> The exchange of names was helped by our having the same first name; but the real cause was undoubtedly the fact that at that time I identified myself in my secret wishes with the celebrated hero-poet. Even consciously my love and admiration for him bordered on idolatry. (Freud, 1901b, p. 85)

The lapsus shows his heroic identification and his ambition to be *"un homme de letters"*: every boy in Budapest had the desire to become a poet.

While he was an adolescent (fifteen years old), he wrote an essay for a competition, "The founding of the Magyar Kingdom: causes and consequences", along with a fellow student, D. Reisz, the son of a Miskolc doctor. They won the prize and deserved it, though there were no rivals because the other pupils were discouraged by the difficulty of the task! The jury judged the work "fine and complete", and its style "good and stimulating the interest" (Moreau-Ricaud & Mádai, 1991).

Sándor idealised the old independent nation, particularly after the death of his patriotic father. We know from the *Correspondence* how his everlasting love for Hungary suffered under the Horthy regime: he said, ironically, that he was helped by his "Jewish Ego" and his "Analytic Ego" (Ferenczi, 1918a, p. 297). He studied medicine in Vienna, and returned to Budapest in 1896. We know he had a difficult time as a young doctor in Rókus hospital, but he took advantage of it and wrote a great deal (Lorin, 1993). But his very first writing, prior to that discovered by Lorin, is a psychologically orientated paper that we know he wrote before he read Freud (since he confessed to Balint that he had lived a joyous life and had never heard of Freud at the time of his medical studies (Balint, 1968). Thanks to Peter Adam, I had the chance to discover this paper, entitled "Psychology of tourism" (1897), in the National Library of Budapest: I published it in the French Freudian review *Topique* (Moreau-Ricaud, 1994). It is a reflection on that new modern "symptom", tourism. It could have influenced Balint—who was an accomplished sportsman—in his research into the quest for intense feelings in dangerous sports, and in his concepts of philobatic and ocnophilic object relations and attitudes. Ferenczi was himself a keen climber, as were Freud, Abraham, and others.

He had some intuition of the necessity of psychology (Ferenczi, 1909). He read Georges Dumas and Pierre Janet. Under the influence of the French School, he experimented with "automatic writing" in "Spiritism": the article was published by Miksa Schächter, the Editor of *Gyógyászat* (Therapeutics), a progressive medical journal opposed to the academic *Orvosi Hetilap* (Medical Weekly). Ferenczi then became Schächter's collaborator, and was so influenced by this fatherly figure that he was nicknamed "Schächter-miniature" (Ferenczi, 1917).

Ferenczi and his conversion to Freudianism

He was already a medical researcher, having published some fifty medical articles (see Lorin, 1993; Lorin & Wiener, 1985) when, in the year 1907, the "plague" of analysis spread its bacillus to him and to his friends—writers and poets.

The disease

After neglecting to review *The Interpretation of Dreams* in 1900, while he was working with Schächter and *Gyógyászat*, Ferenczi read it again in 1907, influenced by Dr Stein and maybe by his writer friends, and this time felt convinced. Then he devoured all the analytic literature, met Freud in 1908, and fell under his charm. In the same year, the poet Hugo Ignotus launched the *Nyugat Movement* (Haynal, 1987, pp. 67–68). We may suppose both men had the same intention—to open the mind, to awaken Hungary, and to build a synergy for a revolution of ideas. The mutual interest in new and progressive ideas, and a mutual friendship and admiration, had bridged the two fields of psychoanalysis and literature. After 1908, Ferenczi propagated analytic ideas in the *Gyógyászat* and in other reviews (*Nyugat*, etc.).

Ferenczi had contaminated the writers

In the following years (1908–1913), the medical field remained resistant to the young science, in spite of Ferenczi's valorous efforts. We will not be surprised to find in the first embryo of the Psychoanalytic Hungarian Association and its office a President (Ferenczi), a vice-president (Hollós), a secretary (Radó), a treasurer (Lévy), and only one member (Ignotus) (Moreau-Ricaud, 1990, 1997)! Another writer, Szilágyi, became an analyst later.

Ferenczi was at home with the writers

Ferenczi was part of the *intelligentsia*. Loránd spoke of him as a wonderful professor; he was not a traditional sad and severe scholar; on the contrary, he was a very sociable and playful person, and he remained so all his life. Let us remember Freud teasing him about his "third puberty"! Imagine him, armed with a chronometer, performing

Jung's Association Test on the clients of the coffee houses—the first step towards psychoanalysis for the clients (a psychoanalytical café?).

Kosztolányi recalled that Sándor "played" at society games. "He was interested in linguistics, in theatre, in puns, in gossip, in all that is human". It is not surprising, then, that he was so welcomed in social circles and in coffee houses, where his "greedy infantile curiosity" could be a stimulation for all. Balint described him as a generous and warm personality. He used to meet with his friends (Ignotus, Kosztolányi, Karinthy, etc.) in the *kávéház* (a Turkish-style coffee house), or at the table in the Hotel Royal (where he lived as a bachelor, in spite of himself), or in the wonderful Café New York. These "popular universities" were full of writers, journalists, and students, according to Lukács. One could hear Kosztolányi's unusual order, "Waiter, a bottle of . . . ink, please!". In 1914, he wrote a nostalgic poem about the deserted Café New York. Even Sándor Petőfi was an *habitué* in the 1840s:

> Coffee house was a true Hungarian institution, a place where one could live. One of my friends left his house-coat in the coffee house, with his books and his medicine. Everyday, without a word, the waiter brought him his valerian and his book, open at the page he had left it the day before! (Kosztolányi, 1914, p. 33)

Allow me to share a personal anecdote: In the New York restaurant, in 1987, I was astonished to experience what Braudel called "*la longue durée en histoire*" (the long duration of history), thanks to a witty waiter who "refused to take the order in French because Clemenceau behaved very badly in 1920 (at Trianon!)". Happily, André Haynal and Mark Paterson were my helpful witnesses . . .

Clinicians "ès-lettres": literary clinicians

In the coffee houses, Ferenczi was used to being bombarded "with questions about the new science, and he, a brilliant and witty man, full of humour and a very good storyteller, talked to them until dawn, so amused by the game".[1] And they were all plague-stricken! A sort of poets' circle was taking form. Poets and analyst were under a reciprocal influence: Ferenczi taught and the writers created. For Ferenczi, the poets' influence was as a forum where he tried out his ideas. And as he was mocked for his "blistered style", he changed it for the simple and clear one that pleased us so much (Ferenczi, 1924). He said he was "the analyst with the shortest breath".

For the book, Peter Adam and I chose to publish six writers: Babits, Csáth, Füst, Karinthy, Kosztolányi, and Krúdy. They belonged to the same period and were of the same generation; thus, we did not include the great Márai. We chose a pot-pourri of their representative styles. The book is composed of short stories, portraits of important figures (Ferenczi by Kosztolányi, Groddeck by Füst, who was cured by him in Baden-Baden), and also some authentic contributions to analytic research.

"My mother", by Karinthy, shows six years of mourning by a young boy: the short story is autobiographic, and is now of interest to a film-maker. In Csáth's "Rehearsal of suicide" (1906), the "death drive" is doing its self-destructive work, anticipating Freud's theory. We find it also in Babits' romantic and tragic "The lake in the mountain", and also in Krúdy's "At the White Horse Tavern". Füst's "Hypertrophia of the 'I'" (1935) reveals his knowledge of narcissism, and Karinthy's '"Big I" and 'little I'" plays with the psyche's agents.

Some short stories are funny, mocking both analysis and the analyst. In Karinthy's "At the psychiatrist's", someone has to rush—before going mad—to the famous "Berenczy"(!), who behaved in a sadistic way, shouting after the patient and taking out his money. "The mysterious healing of F.F." mocks professors, cocooned in their knowledge, whose diagnosis of an "olfactive hysteria" or a "Macbethian case of olfactive hallucination" is wrong. Only a modest general practitioner (like Dr Moviszter in the trial of *Édes Anna*) could understand the real problem and "extract" the pseudo-malignant tumour.

"*Healing Boredom*" or "*Boredom Therapy*"—only a writer could invent that—is a parody of the medical treatments existing at the time, such as rest therapy, fresh air,[2] balneology (not yet Thalassotherapy!), and certainly the new one, analytic therapy! This short novel was written in 1922, some four years after Ferenczi's article "Effet vivifiant et curatif de 'l'air frais' et du 'bon air'" (the reviving and curative effects of 'fresh air' and 'good air') (Ferenczi, 1918b). In his article, Ferenczi denounced false ideas in medicine and preached a new idea: the organism is not only a *working machine* but also needs *joie de vivre*. For this 'patient', *Taedium vitae* is impossible! Life is so interesting: a mere fly on the wall launches him into analysing a metaphysical problem, and it is a "new beginning". This typically Middle European humour or irony is a pure joy!

In conclusion, if anyone still doubts the reciprocal influence of Ferenczi and his circle, I propose a game, linked to *Kleptomaniac Translator*. Read Kosztolányi's short novel *About a Patient* (1931); then take the third volume of the *Freud–Ferenczi Correspondence* (2000) and read Ferenczi's letter to Freud from America (8 April 1927), sixth paragraph: we have twenty lines in Ferenczi, thirty-four in Kosztolányi: plagiarism? No: there are the inverted commas. Kleptomaniac translation? No: there are additions this time! I think it was a gift from Ferenczi to a very intimate friend.

This osmosis reminds me of the sudden emotional insight of an audience member in Strasbourg, in 1994. She said that she suddenly realised that when she read this literature under Stalinism, it was as if she were reading (forbidden) psychoanalysis *"par ricochet"* (by rebound). I think her feelings reflect the following statement by Ferenczi: "Doctors and scientists have completely given up the rich source of psychological science, and without hesitation, have left this impassioned material to writers" (Ferenczi, 1901).

Psychoanalyst and novelist: two ways of being a *Seelensucher*.

Notes

1. Zsófia Dénes, quoted by Peter Adam in Preface to *Cure d'ennui. Ecrivains hongrois autour de Sandor Ferenczi* (Moreau-Ricaud, 1992).
2. H. Brehmer (1826–1889) and P. Dettweiler (1837–1904) were the "inventors" of air and rest cures at sanatoria in the mid-nineteenth century in Germany. Thanks are due to Luc Canet for this information (2004).

References

Andreas-Salomé, L. (1913). *In der Schule bei Freud. Tagebuch eines Jahres, 1912/1913*. München: Kindler Taschenbücher, 1965.

Balint, M. (1968). Preface to *Sandor Ferenczi, Psychanalyse 1, Œuvres complètes 1908–1912* (pp. 7–10). Paris: Payot, 1968.

Ferenczi, S. (1901). L'amour de la science [Love in science]. In: C. Lorin (1981), A propos de "L'amour de la science". *L'Évolution psychiatrique*, 46(3): 755–771.

Ferenczi, S. (1909). Des psychonévroses. In: *Psychanalyse 1, Œuvres complètes 1908–1912* (pp. 57–72). Paris: Payot, 1968 [English edition: Ferenczi, S. (1909). The analytic conception of the psycho-neuroses. In: *Further Contributions to the Theory and Technique of Psycho-Analysis* (pp. 15–30)].

Ferenczi, S. (1917). Mon amitié avec Miksa Schachter. In: *Psychanalyse 2, Œuvres complètes 1913–1919* (pp. 288–292). Paris: Payot, 1970.

Ferenczi, S. (1918a). Letter from Sandor Ferenczi to Sigmund Freud, October 4, 1918. In: E. Falzeder & E. Brabant (Eds.), *The Correspondence of Sigmund Freud and Sandor Ferenczi Volume 2, 1914–1919* (pp. 296–297). Cambridge, MA: Harvard University Press, 1996.

Ferenczi, S. (1918b). Effet vivifiant et effet curatif de l'"air frais" et du "bon air". In: *Psychanalyse 2, Œuvres complètes 1913–1919* (pp. 304–307). Paris: Payot, 1970.

Ferenczi, S. (1921). Letter from Sandor Ferenczi to Georg Groddeck, December 24, 1921. In: C. Fortune (Ed.), *The Sandor Ferenczi–Georg Groddeck Correspondence, 1921–1933* (pp. 7–15). London: Open Gate Press, 2002.

Ferenczi, S. (1924). Ignotus le compréhensif. In: *Psychanalyse 3, Œuvres complètes 1919–1926* (pp. 248–249). Paris: Payot, 1974.

Freud, S. (1901b). *The Psychopathology of Everyday Life. S.E., 6.* London: Hogarth.

Gribinski, M., & Pontalis, J. B. (1990). *Nouvelle Revue de Psychanalyse.* Paris: Gallimard, 1990, no. 41 & 42.

Haynal, A. (1987). *La technique en question.* Paris: Payot.

Kosztolányi, D. (1914). Budapest, ville des cafés. In: *Les cafés littéraires de Budapest* (p. 33). Nantes, France: Le Passeur, 1998.

Lorin, C. (1993). *Sandor Ferenczi de la médecine á la psychanalyse.* Paris: PUF.

Lorin, C., & Wiener, P. (1985). A propos de "Le jeune Ferenczi. Premiers écrits 1899–1906". *L'Evolution Psychiatrique, 50*(4): 957–962.

Moreau, M. (1977). "Analyse quatrième, contrôle, formation", et traductions de documents sur le contrôle psychanalytique. *Topique, 18*: 63–67. Paris: Epi.

Moreau-Ricaud, M. (1990). La création de l'Ecole de Budapest. In: *Revue Internationale d'Histoire de la Psychanalyse, 3*: 419–437. Paris: P.U.F.

Moreau-Ricaud, M. (Ed.) (1992). *Cure d'ennui. Ecrivains hongrois autour de Sandor Ferenczi. Coll. Curiosités littéraires.* Paris: Gallimard.

Moreau-Ricaud, M. (1994). Bénéfique montagne pour Ferenczi et Freud. A propos de "La psychologie du tourisme" de S. Ferenczi. *Topique, 54*: 391–393.

Moreau-Ricaud, M. (1997). La filiation analytique: une filiation hongroise? *Topique*, *61*: 421–432. Bouscat: L'Esprit du Temps.

Moreau-Ricaud, M., & Mádai, G. (1991). Sandor Ferenczi les années de lycée (1882–1890). *Revue Internationale d'Histoire de la Psychanalyse*, 4: 659–669.

CHAPTER SEVEN

Ferenczi and Ortvay: two boys from Miskolc

Tom Keve

Ortvay

Rudolf Ortvay was a distinguished Hungarian scientist, Professor of Physics first in Szeged and later in Budapest. He was a member of the Hungarian Academy of Sciences and is still commemorated today: there is an annual Rudolf Ortvay International Physics Competition for high-school students world wide and Ortvay Colloquia are held regularly at ELTE Eötvös Loránd University in Budapest.

After the great scientists, the likes of Eugene Wigner, John von Neumann, Theodore von Kármán, George Hevesy, Dennis Gábor, and others left Hungary in the 1920s and 1930s, Ortvay became the

Physicist, Rudolf Ortvay (1885–1945).

number one physicist in this country, by default. He never attained the international fame of the others, but he was in close contact with the leading physicists of his day, the émigré Hungarians, especially von Neumann, Wigner, and Hevesy, but also with others like Wolfgang Pauli and Werner Heisenberg. Ortvay's correspondence with these men is full of deep, insightful ideas on many subjects on Ortvay's side, while the replies from these younger men are respectful, friendly, with some personal information, but short on technical content. Quite possibly, Ortvay was a disappointed man, for although he was in the number one spot in Hungary, his younger émigré colleagues undoubtedly excelled him both in original published work and in international fame and recognition.

But let us return to Ortvay's roots. Rudolf was born in Miskolc in 1885, twelve years after Ferenczi. His family were of German Catholic origin and were originally called Orthmayr.[1] His father, Miksa, was a judge in Miskolc, one of the pre-eminent figures in the city. *His* mother, that is to say Ortvay's grandmother, was a Jendrassik girl. The Jendrassiks were a dynasty of eminent medical men and engineers. The name of Ernő Jendrassik appears in the Freud–Ferenczi correspondence; he was a well known and influential opponent of psychoanalysis, who tried to prevent Ferenczi from being appointed to the Chair of Psychoanalysis.[2] According to one source (Tóth, 1999), this same Ernő Jendrassik was Ortvay's cousin, according to another (Tóth & Zsigmond, 2003), Ernő Jendrassik was Ortvay's uncle. (Given that Füstöss states that it was Ortvay's grandmother who was a Jendrassik, the most likely relationship was that Ortvay's mother and Ernő Jendrassik were cousins.)

Rudolf Ortvay attended primary school in Miskolc, then the Jesuit Gymnasium in Budapest. In 1906, he entered the University of Budapest, not as a physicist, but as a medical student; however, after two years he transferred to physics and mathematics. Between 1909 and 1912, he was a physics lecturer in Kolozsvár. Later, he worked under the world famous physicists, Debye in Zurich and Sommerfeld in Munich.

Ferenczi–Ortvay links

Undoubtedly, the Ferenczi and Ortvay families would have known of one another in Miskolc. On the one hand, we have a well-known judge from an upper-middle-class intellectual milieu and, on the other hand, we have one of the largest and the best-known bookstores in the centre of the city. Whether Sándor and Rudolf knew one another in their Miskolc days is not known, but is unlikely. A twelve-year age difference in childhood is, of course, enormous.

By the time Ortvay was a young man in his mid-twenties, however, they clearly did know each other, as some of their correspondence survives. Two letters from Ferenczi to Ortvay can be found in the archives of the Hungarian Academy of Sciences.[3] The first letter is undated, although the context makes it clear[4] it was written in the second half of July 1910. The second letter is dated July 22.

The letters, with translation, are reproduced below:

Dr FERENCZI SANDOR Budapest, VII, Erzsébet Körút 54

Kedves Ortvay Ur!

Örültem hogy levelével felkeresett. Magam is úgy hiszem, hogy a nyári szünidő nem alkalmas a psychoanalitikus kúra megkezdésére, mert minden valoszinüséggel nagy megszakitásokkal járna.

Örömmel vettem tudomást arról is hogy kisérletei annyi nehézség lekúzdése után kedvezőbb stádiumba jutottak. – Kolozsvár talán nem is rossz nyári tartozkodási hely.

A repülőversenyen én is jelen voltam egyszer – a Frey bukását követő vasárnapon.

A munka most már csak félgőzzel megy. Freud elutazott Hollandiába. Nincs kizárva hogy aug. végén ott találkozunk és Antwerpenben hajóra szállva, a csatornán, Liszabonon és a Gibraltáron át Afrika érintésével Siciliába utazunk néhány hétre. De ez még csak terv és kivitele attol függ, milyen lesz a Freud egészségi állapota.

A Freud nevéhez fúzödő irányzat ellen az ellenállás egyre erősödik és sokszor kellemetlen alakban nyilvánul meg. Egyes orvosok megvetéstöl és dühtől tajtékzó cikkeket írnak és előadásokat tartanak róla íly értelemben. Olvassa el a Berliner Klinik (Klinische Rundschau) ujság egyik utolsó számában Hoche prof cikkét "Eine psychische Epidemie unter Angsten" cím alatt. Freudnak szerinte csak kor-történelmi jelentősége van, t.i. annyiban hogy ilyen absurdumokat hogy lehetett manapság elhinni.

Szivélyessen üdvözli igaz hive,

Ferenczi Sándor

Dr FERENCZI SANDOR Budapest, VII, Erzsébet Körút 54

Dear Mr Ortvay,

I was very pleased to receive your letter. I tend to agree with you that summer vacation is not the best time to commence psychoanalytic treatment, most likely there would be too many interruptions.

I was very pleased to read that after overcoming many difficulties, your experiments have reached a favourable stadium.[5] Perhaps Kolozsvár is not a bad place to spend the summer.

I too attended the air race, on the Sunday following the fall of Frey.[6]

My work is progressing only at half speed. Freud has left for Holland. It is possible that we shall meet there at the end of August and take a boat together from Antwerp, through the Channel, via Lisbon and Gibraltar, touching North Africa to Sicily, where we may stay for a few weeks. But this is just a plan, its execution depends on the state of Freud's health.

Resistance to the direction associated with the name of Freud is becoming stronger all the time, and often manifests itself in a most unpleasant manner. There are doctors who write articles brimming with contempt and rage, and give lectures about the subject in the same vein. You should read the article by Professor Hoche in one of the most recent numbers of the Berliner Klinik (Klinische Rundschau), entitled "Eine psychische Epidemie unter Angsten". According to Hoche, Freud only has socio-historical interest, in the sense that there are men, even today, who can believe in such absurdities.

With heartfelt greetings, yours truly,

Sandor Ferenczi

We can make a few observations.

1. It would seem that prior to this date (July 1910) there had already been a pre-existing, close relationship. Evidence for this is found in the tone of the letter, which is friendly, much less formal than was the custom in those days. It also contains personal as well as professional information about Freud, which would only be shared with a friend or close mutual acquaintance.
2. It would also seem that in a prior letter Ortvay had suggested going into analysis with Ferenczi. Perhaps he suggested doing so

in the autumn, as Ferenczi agrees with him that summer is not a good time to begin analysis.

3. It is also of interest that the opposition to Freud is such a strong element in their exchange, given that it is Ortvay's cousin, Ernő Jendrassik, who would turn out to be the main professional opponent of psychoanalysis in Hungary.

The second letter is as follows:

Dr FERENCZI SANDOR, Budapest, VII, Erzsébet Körút 54

Jul 22

Kedves Ortvay Ur,

Megörvendeztetett levelével, melynek tartalma elárulja milyen mélyen behatott a psychoanalytikus eszmekörbe – valószinüleg beható auto-analysis segitségével.

A Freud elleni támadások egyelőre a summaris gorombaságok jegyében mozognak; – füszerezve néhány hizelgő, (de általános és így semmitmondó) megjegyzéssel. Az objektív kritika kora még nem jött el.

Kétségtelen (rég tudjuk!) hogy a beati poszidentesek közül kerül ki az ellenzők, az elégületlenek közül a támogatók túlnyomó többsége. De ez mindig, minden revoluciónál így volt -, az elégületlenség éleslátová teszi az embereket. – Maga Freud ellenben beatus poszidentes volt, míg teoriáival ki nem lépett – azután 10 évig anyagilag és erkölcsileg izolálva maradt.

Jung-nak iagaza van. Gyakorlatban az analysis csak annál jár eredménnyel, aki maga már túl van a kétkedés és ellentállás időszakán. Aki magamagával nem kész, vak és süket lesz a patiensek komoly complexumainak felismerésénél. A "meggyőződés" tulajdonképen szintén gyógyúlás. *Gyógyításra* csak az alkalmas, ki maga már gyógyult. – Ez nem egészen azonos a spiritisták és a katholikus vallás hívési kényszerével. –

Az antisemitizmus *egyik* gyökere kétségkívül a Freudtól feltételezett castratió (circumcisio) complex. Egy másik a következő (: N.B. ezért már nem Freud felelős :)

A zsidó vallás ritus bizonyos törvények betartására (imák, tízparancsolat, böjtölés) reducálja, vagyis "kényszercselekedetek" formájába önti a vallásosságot – de azonfelül teljes gondolati és cselekvési szabadságot enged. Ezt a zsidók alapossan ki is használják és főleg anyagi, de erkölcsi téren is merészebbek, szemérmetlenebbek, önzőbbek. Ellenben a buddhizmus és keresztény vallás óriási "verdrangung"-al jár (: nem *belátás* hanem infantil *elfojtás* és *önletagadás* útján uralkodik az ösztönökön. :). A zsidók reprezentálják a keresztény elött az ő saját öntudatlan "bűnös" és merész velleitásait. Már pedig az ember "gyűlöli a bűneit" [gyűlölöm mint a bűnömet – mondja a magyar közmondás]. Tehát gyűlöli a zsidót.

A megoldás szerintem 1.) a zsidó szabadosság korlátozása belátással, 2.) a keresztény "verdrangung" analitikus átváltoztatása célszerüségi *belátássá*, a tiltások kiküszöbölése. Ez a jövő pedagógia feladata lesz.

Antisemitizmus = antiniggerizmus amerikában ugyanezen alapon. A "finom", "tiszta", "becsületes" absztinens amerikai gyűlöli a durva, piszkos, tolvaj és libidinosus négert.

Minden *Angst* neurotikus, vagyis kielégítetlen unbewust libidinozus tendentiák reaktiója. Az *ideálisan* önmagán uralkodó ember minden – még a legfélelmessebb situatióba is – mint változtathatatlanba – filozófikussan belenyugodnék. Az analysis (bár asymptotikusan) ezen ideál felé vezet.

Ha a *sex* szó ebben a kapcsolatban még shockirozza – maradjon egyelőre a "lust–unlust" szó mellett. Idővel meg fog győződni a sexualitás alapvető fontosságáról.

Rég tudjuk a suicidiumok erotikus gyökerét. Még a suicidium *formái* is sex[uálissan] determináltak. *Mérgezés álomban* úgy mint *neurotikus nyelven* = conceptio = (nők suicidium módja).

Lövés álomban, neurozisban = sex[uális] aggreszió folklore-ban). Igen szépek az Öntől idézett példák!

Szivélyessen üdvözli hive,

Ferenczi

u.i. Analyzisnél sokszor *téved* az ember, illetve kiegészíteni, korrigálni kénytelen egy előbbi felvételt. *Freud* sohasem volt "consequens"; változtatott, kiegészített, elejtett dolgokat. *Ez a fejlődés útja.*

Dr FERENCZI SANDOR, Budapest, VII, Erzsébet Körút 54

Jul 22

Dear Mr Ortvay,

You made me very happy with your letter, the contents of which demonstrate how profoundly you have been able to penetrate the psychoanalytical intellectual milieu, no doubt assisted by effective auto-analysis.

For the moment, the attacks against Freud amount to no more than boorishness, spiced with a few flattering (but general and therefore insignificant) comments. The era of objective criticism has not yet commenced.

It is beyond doubt (and we have known for long), that the opposition are primarily from *beati possidentes*,[7] while the vast majority of supporters come from the ranks of the discontent. But this has been the case with all revolutions – it is discontent that allows men to see clearly. *Freud* himself was a *beatus posidentus* until he formulated his theories, after which he remained in financial and moral isolation for the next ten years.

Jung was right. In practice analysis only brings results in the hands of those who have themselves gone through and beyond the period of doubt and resistance. He who has not yet come to terms with himself will be blind and deaf to the serious complexes manifested by his patients. It is true to say that conviction is also healing. Only one who has been healed can be a *healer* himself. – This is not quite the same as the conditions imposed by spiritism or by catholic religious dogma.

One of the roots of anti-Semitism is, without a doubt, the castration (circumcision) complex discovered by Freud. Another is the following (this time Freud is not responsible):

The Jewish religion[8] ritual reduces religiosity to keeping certain rules (prayers, ten commandments, fasting), that is to say it moulds religion into "compelled actions" – but beyond these, it permits total intellectual freedom and freedom of action. The Jews use this freedom to the full, and are more audacious, more unabashed and more egotistic, primarily in the material, but also in the moral sphere. On the other hand, Buddhism and Christianity bring with them an enormous *verdrangung*,[9] (dominating instinct not through *understanding*, but via infantile *repression* and *self-denial*). It is the Jews who, for Christians, represent their own unconscious "guilty" and audacious inclinations. It is the case that man "loathes his sins", [I detest him like I detest my sins – says the Hungarian proverb]. So he detests the Jew.

In my view, the solution is (1) limiting Jewish licentiousness through increased understanding, (2) transforming Christian "verdangung" into objective *understanding* through analysis and the elimination of taboos. This will be the task of the pedagogues of the future.

Anti-Semitism = anti-Negroism in America on exactly the same basis. The "genteel", "clean", "honest", abstinent American detests the rough, dirty, thieving, libidinous Negroes.

All *Angst* is neurotic, or in other words it is a reaction caused by unsatisfied, unconscious libidinous tendencies. The man capable of controlling his own emotions to an *ideal* degree, will be able accept stoically even the most frightening circumstances if they are deemed inevitable. It is towards this ideal that analysis strives (*asymptotically*).

If you still find the word *sex* too shocking in this context, remain, for the moment with the expression "lust–unlust". In time you will be convinced of the fundamental importance of sexuality.

We have realised long ago the sexual roots of suicidal behaviour. Even the *forms* of suicide are determined by sexual parameters. *Poisoning* in *a dream*, in the *language of neurosis* = conception = (form of suicide favoured by women). *Shooting* in dream, in neurosis = sexual aggression in folklore. The examples you quote are very pertinent.

With friendly greetings, yours

Ferenczi

P.S. One often makes mistakes in analysis, i.e. one is forced to extrapolate, or correct the prior record. *Freud* was never "consequent", he altered, extrapolated and dropped items. *This* is the way of progress.

The tone of this highly interesting letter indicates close contact and a deep level of trust between the two men. Ferenczi holds Ortvay in high enough esteem, both as an intellect and as a student of psychoanalysis, to treat him—a much younger man—as an equal.

1.   In the intervening letter, Ortvay must have made remarks about psychoanalysis which elicited positive reaction from Ferenczi. Clearly, Ortvay has made a study of psychoanalytic ideas and has apparently indulged in self-analysis. Again, they are discussing the wave of opposition to Freud's ideas.

2.   Ferenczi not only quotes Jung as the source, but also agrees with Jung's idea that before an analyst can heal others, he must first have progressed beyond doubts and resistance himself. After the split, Freudians in general were not so generous in giving credit to Jung.

3. Ferenczi not only discusses anti-Semitism with Ortvay, a Roman Catholic, but advances his own theory as to some of its causes and compares it with anti-negro sentiments. He even proposes a solution.

4. Then Ferenczi discusses the psychoanalytical symbolism of various methods of suicide. He also mentions two examples of sexual symbolism in suicidal dreams. Interestingly, the sexual motif in dreams also forms the bulk of Ferenczi's letter No 155 to Freud, written just two weeks later on August 10 1910.

5. Ferenczi refers to Ortvay's excellent examples (apparently on the subject of sexuality in dreams), demonstrating that this exchange must be part of an ongoing discussion between the two men. Perhaps Ortvay has sent Ferenczi a manuscript for his comments. Or he simply explained his ideas in an earlier letter. Again, the tone is a discourse between colleagues rather than an expert talking to a layman.

6. Finally, the postscript. One possible interpretation is that when Ferenczi accuses Freud of being inconsequent, he is accusing him of being unscientific. Can it be that Freud changes case histories to suit his theories? "This is the way of progress", Ferenczi writes. Is he in agreement and making a supportive statement? Or is he critical of Freud, or even being sarcastic? The reader must make up his own mind. It seems that Ferenczi is indeed criticising his master, which is all the more remarkable if one recalls that this letter was written in 1910, at the time when the relationship between Ferenczi and Freud was at its most positive.

We know that Ferenczi's contact with Ortvay continued, for he is mentioned by name in the Freud–Ferenczi correspondence. Letter No 423 is, in fact, a picture postcard with the caption *"Intérieur d'un temple"*. It reads:

Budapest, October 11, 1913

Dear Professor,

This card was given to me by a certain Dr. v. Ortvay, who spent the month of September (very bearable!) in Egypt. He thinks one could use this month very well for an Egyptian journey. Maybe we'll do it next year!!

Ferenczi

Ortvay's interest in psychoanalysis continued. At about this time he published a learned paper in the *Internationale Zeitshcrift für Artzliche Psychoanalyse* with the title "Eine biologische Paralelle zum Verdrängnisvorgang" (Ortvay, 1914). In this work, he proposes a link between the emergence or suppression of homosexuality and/or bisexuality, on the one hand, with the Mendelian ideas of recessives and dominants in heredity, on the other. These ideas were certainly familiar to Ferenczi, for we can read the following footnote in Ferenczi's *Thalassa* (Ferenczi, 1924): "Ortvay refers to the fact that the psychoanalytic doctrine of repression is capable of explaining the Mendelian phenomenoa of the 'dominance' and 'recessiveness' of unit characters" (p. 87).

There seems to be no further trace of Ortvay and psychoanalysis after this time, although the social contacts with Ferenczi probably continued. Indeed, there is interesting evidence for this social link. Von Neumann's younger brother, Nicholas, wrote a memorandum entitled "John von Neumann as seen by his brother", in which he describes the goings-on in the parental home. He writes (Vonneuman, 1988):

> Frequent guests for dinner or otherwise, including family friends such as . . . Rudolf Ortvay . . ." and elsewhere, "Rudolf Ortvay . . . was . . . a frequent visitor and family friend. And so was Sandor Ferenczi, one of the big 5 associates of Freud . . . (p. 12)

In fact, Ferenczi was more than just a family friend. Ferenczi's brother-in-law, Gizella's brother, Ágoston Alcsuti (originally called Altschul), was also the brother-in-law of Miksa Neumann, father of John and Nicholas von Neumann. Miksa Neumann and Ágoston Alcsuti were old friends who had married sisters. The Neumanns and the Alcsutis lived in the same Budapest block, 62 Vilmos császár körút (Bajcsi-Zsilinsky út today), which was owned by the family patriarch, the father-in-law of both men. Ferenczi was part of the extended family, so it was natural that he should be invited there. What Ortvay's exact connection to the household was is not clear. One must presume he was a friend of the father, Miksa Neumann.

Ortvay kept up a very extensive correspondence with John von Neumann when the latter resided in the USA. These letters are also very friendly and cover a wide range of topics. On 26 September 1939,

Ortvay wrote a long letter to von Neumann (see Nagy, 1987). After a short paragraph bemoaning the outbreak of the Second World War, he says, "I want to note another current event – Freud's death". In this letter, Ortvay states that he had been a keen student of Freud's works and that he had been in contact with several of Freud's disciples. He then continues with a critique of Freud: Ortvay is very positive about Freud as the prime explorer of the unconscious, he appreciates the importance of sexuality with some reservations, but Ortvay has mixed feelings about psychoanalysis as therapy, which he considers suggestive. Unfortunately, we do not know whether he was ever in analysis with Ferenczi, or, indeed, anyone else.

During the 1930s, Ortvay concentrated on physics, more as a teacher and as a missionary for the gospel of quantum physics than as a researcher. He kept up a correspondence with the *émigré* Hungarians and also other physicists, such as Pauli and Heisenberg. He instituted regular colloquia at the university and used his international contacts to get first class speakers to Budapest, including Heisenberg, Dirac, Sommerfeld, Wigner, von Neumann, Hevesy. and Lánczos.

According to his biographer, Ortvay was a stiff man, a closed personality who preferred letter-writing to personal contact. From his letters, it is clear that Ortvay was longing for the company of his colleagues and intellectual equals, who were all abroad. In all likelihood, he was a disappointed and a lonely man. He lived a bachelor's life in Budapest, sharing his home only with an elderly aunt. The war years took a major toll on him. There is a record that he personally tried to intervene with the Germans—possibly with Eichmann—to save a Jewish colleague who had been sent to Auschwitz. Needless to say, the intervention was without success.

Ortvay's story ends rather sadly. On 1 January 1945, in the middle of the siege of Budapest, Ortvay committed suicide. It was his sixtieth birthday.

Notes

1.   Biographical information from Füstöss (1984); Rudolf Ortvay's curriculum vitae is reproduced in Nagy (1987).

2. Ferenczi to Freud, letters No 295, April 23 1912 and No 802, April 4 1919, in Brabant, Falzeder, & Giampieri-Deutsch (1993), and Falzeder, Brabant, & Giampieri-Deutsch (1996) respectively.
3. Magyar Tudományos Akadémia Kézirattár, Ortvay K785/331 and K875/332.
4. There is mention of the Budapest air-race, which took place in 1910. Ferenczi also writes that Freud had recently left for Holland—we know that Freud arrived at The Hague on 17 July 1910, for this is the date of his picture postcard (letter No 148) to Ferenczi. The trip Ferenczi describes is the same as his proposal on July 14 1910 in his letter No 147 to Freud.
5. It is unclear what experiments are being referred to.
6. There was an International Air Race in the summer of 1910 in Budapest. André Frey was a well known French aviator.
7. Blessed are the possessors.
8. Crossed out in the original.
9. Repression.

References

Brabant, E., Falzeder, E., & Giampieri-Deutsch, P. (1993). *The Correspondence of Sigmund Freud and Sandor Ferenczi, Volume 1, 1908–1914*. Cambridge, MA: Harvard University Press.
Falzeder, E., Brabant, E., and Giampieri-Deutsch, P. (Eds.) (1996). *The Correspondence of Sigmund Freud and Sandor Ferenczi, Volume 2, 1914–1919*. Cambridge, MA: Harvard University Press.
Ferenczi, S. (1924). *Thalassa, a Theory of Genitality*. London: Karnac, 1989.
Füstöss, L. (1984). *Ortvay Rudolf*. Akadémiai Kiadó, Budapest, 1984.
Nagy, F. (Ed.) (1987). *Neumann János és a "magyar titok" a dokumentumok Tükrében* [John (von) Neumann and the "Hungarian secret" as mirrored by documents]. Budapest: Országos Műszaki Információs Központ és Könyvtár.
Ortvay, R. (1914). Eine biologische Parallele zu dem Verdrängungsvorgang. [A biological parallel to the displacement process] *Internationale Zeitschrift für ärztliche Psychoanalyse*, 2: 25–26.
Tóth, V. (1999). A Kerepesi úti temető II. Jobboldali falsírboltok, No. J. 2680. [Kerepesi road cemetery, right hand wall memorial wall, No J 2680] *Budapesti Negyed*, 9(3). In: http://epa.oszk.hu/00000/00003/00020/adat002.htm (30.03.2011).

Tóth, V., & Zsigmond, J. (2003). A Farkasréti temető 2003-ban (adattár) No. 1–57. [Frakasrét Cemetary, 2003, No. 1–57] *Budapesti Negyed, 11*: No. 2, 3, 4. In: http://epa.oszk.hu/00000/00003/00030/adattar.html (30.03.2011).

Vonneuman, N. (1988). *John von Neumann as Seen by His Brother*. Meadowbrook PA: Private Printing, 1988. Library of Congress Cat 87–91777.

CHAPTER EIGHT

Ferenczi and trauma: a perilous journey to the labyrinth

György Hidas

T
he interpersonal context of trauma, its effects on the psyche, and resolution of its consequences were fundamental problems for Sandor Ferenczi in his psychoanalytical career. The topic of trauma was central in his therapeutic activity, especially in his healing experiments in the last decade of his life. The innovations of his healing work, the method of child analysis with adults, relaxation analysis, and mutual analysis were grouped around the concept of trauma. Considering Ferenczi's analytical life's work, a hypothesis offers itself, which is that the trauma concept and the associated neocatharsis were a return of the repressed in his personal world. Taking a look at the personal, the subjective aspect, a touch of "psychologising", seems to be permissible in this case; making the reservation, however, that the role of this problem in Ferenczi's world might have been over-determined in several aspects.

Ferenczi was a medical student in Vienna, and graduated there in 1894. In the spring of 1908, soon after he met Freud personally, he delivered a lecture in Budapest with the title "Actual and psychoneuroses in the light of Freud's investigations and psychoanalysis". In this paper, Ferenczi wrote,

I delivered several years ago a lecture on *Neurasthenia* – I made a mistake difficult to remedy when I left out of account Professor Freud's investigations of neuroses. This omission was all the greater as I was acquainted with Freud's work. In 1893 I had read the paper he wrote together with Breuer, concerning the psychic mechanism of hysterical symptoms, and later, another independent paper, in which he discusses infantile sexual traumata[1] as the causes or starting points for the psychoneuroses. Today, when I have convinced myself in so many cases of the correctness of Freud's theories, I may well ask myself why did I reject them so rashly at that time, why did they, from the first, seem to me improbable and artificial, and particularly, why did the assumption of a purely sexual pathogenesis of the neuroses rouse such a strong aversion in me that I did not even honour it with a closer scrutiny? (Ferenczi, [1908]1926, p. 31)

When, soon after the publication of *The Interpretation of Dreams*, the book was handed to Ferenczi by Miksa Schächter, the editor-in-chief of the medical journal *Gyógyászat*, Ferenczi started to read it, and put it down as being not interesting enough to review. He did so in spite of being interested in the topic, for, in 1902, he reviewed a book by Sante de Sanctis, an Italian writer, on dreams (*I Sogni*), and even translated a part of this book for the journal *Gyógyászat*. As many as fourteen years had to pass from 1893 until, taking *The Interpretation of Dreams* in hand for a second time, Ferenczi became an enthusiastic follower of Freud's science. This time, he wrote in the book, "*Aere perennius*" (more lasting than bronze). Ferenczi published numerous articles in the *Gyógyászat* even before 1908, several of which were on the subject of psychiatry and psychology. He wrote about love in the sciences, transvestism, homosexuality, and so on. His writings show that he might have had a special aversion, probably connected to the childhood sexual aetiology of neuroses. Presumably, this resulted from his own, non-conceptualised unconscious childhood conflicts.

Ferenczi was in analysis with Freud twice. We know that he was dissatisfied with his analysis and always wished to continue it. Freud speaks of him in the *Endliche und unendliche Analyse* as his colleague who reproached him for his negative transference not being analysed. Freud's counter-argument was that only what appears, what gives signs about itself, can be analysed.

Reading Ferenczi's *Clinical Diary* (1932a) and his correspondence with Georg Groddeck, outlines of a self-image evolve, which, together with the above quotation, well support the hypothesis that, for Ferenczi, the revival of the trauma concept had very personal, subjective elements.

The following, mosaic-like self-portrait of Ferenczi has been left to us. He writes to Groddeck at Christmas 1921,

> My mother had eleven living children – I was the eighth of them. Either I was all too demanding, or my mother was all too rigorous, but my memories suggest that I surely received too little love and too much strictness from her. Sentimentality and fondling were unknown in our family. All the more they preferred emotions like fearful respect. What else could be the result of such a rearing than hypocrisy?

The fight against hypocrisy runs like a thread through Ferenczi's professional career:

> . . . to keep up appearances, to hide any 'immorality', this was all absolutely important. That's how I became an eminent pupil and a secret onanist; prudishly, I never used obscene words—and secretly I visited prostitutes on stolen money. Now and again I made cautious attempts to be discovered. Once, 'by chance' I got into my mother's hands the list of all the obscene words I had known. What I was given was a moral lesson instead of enlightenment or help. (Ferenczi & Groddeck, 1986, p. 38)

Elsewhere, he wrote, "my mother . . . was hard and energetic and of whom I am afraid" (Ferenczi, 1932a, p. 45). When one of his analysands held that Ferenczi could never fully feel her experiences, he answered, "Except if I sink down with her into her unconscious, namely with the help of my own traumatic complexes" (ibid., p. 38).

In his childhood, a housemaid had probably allowed him to play with her breasts, and then she clasped his head between her legs, so that the child was flooded with anxiety and was choking. This is the source of his hatred toward women. That is why he wants to kill them. "This is why my mother's accusation, 'you are a murderer', cut to the heart" (ibid., p. 61).

> The continuous protests (from the deepest unconscious) that I do not in fact have any real empathy or the compassion for the patient, that I

am emotionally dead, was in many respects analytically proven (in 'counteranalysis') and could be traced back to deep infantile traumata ... possibly to a traumatic event in earliest infancy. (ibid., p. 85)

It is obvious that traumatic experiences of childhood have become conscious, or Ferenczi was convinced of their reality, only in the period of mutual analyses. Unconsciously, these memories formed his aversion to Freud's ideas conceptualised at the time of the seduction theory, and made him sensitive later to the trauma problem. Trauma and catastrophe, as events that form both the individual and the species, are of the utmost importance for Ferenczi. Note that the Hungarian title of *Thalassa: A Theory of Genitality*, translates as "Catastrophes in the development of sexual life".

Ferenczi's insight, based on his own experience, was that

if the present process is to have a different outcome from the original trauma, then the victim of traumatic shock must be offered something in reality, at least as much caring attention, or genuine intention to provide as a severely traumatized child must have. It appears, however, that even the child thus affected demands, as compensation for and counterweight to this suffering, inordinate amounts of love, in both a qualitative and a quantitative sense. (ibid., p. 28)

Ferenczi's ability to relax was substantially limited by "terrifyingly rough treatment" by a nurse because of "an incident of anal soiling" (ibid., p. 36). Relaxation had to be mutual, as well.

In his analysis with RN, Ferenczi revealed that he felt guilty because of the death of a sister of his (Vilma), who was two years younger than him (ibid., p. 121). It turned out in the same "counteranalysis" that, "since the more profound investigation of the causes of my sympathies and antipathies, a large share of the latter have been traced back to infantile father and grandfather fixation with corresponding misogyny" (ibid., p. 155).

In October 1933, the Hungarian Psychoanalytic Society held a session in memory of Sandor Ferenczi. At this meeting, István Hollós spoke of Ferenczi's life and work, while Michael Balint recalled Sandor Ferenczi as a doctor. The three papers by Ferenczi on the topic of trauma were introduced by Imre Hermann; in his paper, he made a meaningful attempt to compare Freud and Ferenczi from an epistemological viewpoint.

In Hermann's opinion, in the progress of psychoanalysis Freud revealed a biologically founded developmental psychology: when general, coherent, laws and principles evolved, distinct steps of development were distinguished, while the traumatic shock as experience and as focus of therapy was pushed into the background. Experiences were only given a motive role in the necessity of development. While, in psychoanalysis, emphasis is laid on the individual, the concept of trauma stands at the centre, and it loses its importance only when general laws and principles become the focus of interest. Hermann cites Ferenczi in "Disease or pathoneuroses" (1918):

> The original psycho-analytical traumatic theory of the neuroses has maintained itself till the present day. It was not set aside, but supplemented by Freud's theory of sexual constitution and of its predisposing significance for the development of neuroses . . . (Ferenczi, 1926, pp. 80–81)

This quotation demonstrates that there was no polar opposition at that time for Ferenczi between the trauma concept and psychoanalytic developmental pathogenesis. Hermann underlines that

> Ferenczi has come to the real core of the issue when in the last years of his life he was engaged in hidden traumas which emerged only after overcoming the resistances, and which seemed to be unbelievable and fantastic from the point of view of the learned moral of the time. (Hermann, 1934)

This latter wording indicates the shock that Ferenczi caused the psychoanalytical world by reviving the theoretical and methodological importance of trauma and by placing himself in opposition to Freud.

A "pathognomic" sign of this situation was, among others, that "Confusion of tongues between adults and the child" (1933), originally published in German, was not published either in English or in Hungarian until 1949 and 1971, respectively. Haynal argues that the Freud–Ferenczi controversy was caused not so much by the revival of the trauma concept, but, rather, by psychoanalytic technique, consequential regression, and the deviation of Ferenczi's attitude from the Freudian recommendation. Nevertheless, even in our day, the psychoanalytic community is convinced that, since the summer of 1897, Freud had given up the seduction theory and replaced it with the determinative role of genetically programmed developmental stages and structures, and by psychic reality, claiming that "up to our days we could not find a difference in the consequences according to whether fantasy or external reality has a larger part in these childhood issues" (Freud, 1966, p. 259). Masson goes so far as to accuse Freud of making "an assault on truth" for this reason.

In Ferenczi's trauma concept, the following elements can be distinguished: the reality of sexual and destructive acts against the child, the conditions that make the event pathogenic, and conditions that are able to neutralise the consequences of this trauma. In the psychoanalytic process, conditions imposed by the framework, which enable the re-enactment of trauma, appear as factors that can convince the patient of the reality of the trauma, and that might resolve the consequences of the trauma.

Khan (1978) distinguished the following stages in the development of the trauma concept in psychoanalysis and states that these stages do not annihilate one another, but, rather, one strengthens and corrects the other. The first stage lasts from 1885 to 1905, the trauma reaches the individual from the environment, and he is unable to cope with it, either by abreaction or associational elaboration. The paradigm of this traumatic situation is sexual seduction. The neurotic anxiety comes from transformed libido. The main defensive mechanism is repression.

The second stage lasts from 1905 to 1917. The trauma is composed of the force of sexual drives and the fight of the ego against them. The paradigmatical traumatic situations are: (a) castration anxiety, (b) separation anxiety, (c) the primal scene, and (d) the Oedipal complex. All these exert their effect through unconscious fantasies, through internal reality.

The third stage lasts from 1917 to 1926, and is characterised by intersystem (drive) traumatism, in which the determinants are the life and death instinct, the psychic structures (ego, id, superego) and the repetition compulsion.

The fourth stage lasts from 1926 to 1939. Here, the essence of the traumatic situation is the experience of helplessness, which is caused by accumulation of excitation, and this automatically elicits anxiety as a signal. In this stage, the role of the environment (the mother) and the necessity of external help in the problematic situation come to the fore. The roots of ego psychology can be found in this stage.

The last stage begins in 1939. In this, the infant–mother relationship is decisive (Kahn, 1978, pp. 89–91).

Ferenczi's trauma theory goes back to the first stage, that is, the trauma is caused by the environment, but he underlines the protective, trauma-resolving role of the mother, and so anticipates the present-day fifth stage.

Khan speaks of the protective barrier role of the mother; Ferenczi also built on the hypotheses of the third stage, which consist of the death instinct and repetition compulsion. His paper, "The unwelcome child and his death instinct" (1929a) fits into this stage; his hypothesis was verified by the later observations of Spitz.

Ferenczi's trauma concept is multi-factorial. In "The unwelcome child", he claims that the mother–child relationship can become destructive, and he speaks of the imbalance between the equilibrium of life and death instincts. This is the essence of the trauma.

> Those [unwelcome children] who develop so precocious an aversion to life give the impression of a defective capacity for adaptation similar to those who, in Freud's grouping, suffer from an inherited weakness in their capacity for life, but with the difference that in all cases the innateness of the sickly tendency is deceptive and not genuine, owing to the early incidence of the trauma. The trauma is a conscious or unconscious sign of the aversion or impatience of the mother. (Ferenczi, 1929a, p. 106)

"Severe or prolonged suffering, but above all something unexpected and thus traumatic, exhausts the instinct of self-assertion and allows the forces, wishes, and even characteristics of the aggressor to invade us" (Ferenczi, 1932a, p. 42).

> The effect of a shock – whether it be a sudden fright or fright plus physical injury – is particularly dangerous when trauma occurs in exceptional states (of consciousness). ... S.J.('s) mother ... launched an insane, terrifying attack on the sleeping child, because of some sort of masturbatory activity during sleep. (ibid., p. 45)

Ferenczi describes shock as follows:

> Shock = annihilation of self-regard – of the ability to put up a resistance, and to act and think in defence of one's own self: perhaps even

the organs which secure self-preservation give up their function or reduce it to a minimum . . . shock always comes upon one unprepared. It must be preceded by a feeling of security, in which, because of the subsequent events, one feels deceived, one trusted in the external world too much before; after, too little or not at all. One had to have overestimated one's own powers and have lived under the delusion that such things could not happen, not to me. Shock can be purely physical, purely moral, or both physical and moral. Physical shock is always moral also; moral shock may create a trauma without any physical accompaniment. (Ferenczi, 1932b, pp. 253–254)

In Ferenczi's words, the essence of psychotrauma is as follows: "great unpleasure, which, because of its sudden appearance, cannot be dealt with. But what is the meaning of 'dealing with'?" Laplanche and Pontalis (1973) define it as follows: "An event in the subject's life defined by its intensity, by the subject's incapacity to respond adequately to it and by the upheaval and long lasting effects that it brings about in the psychical organization" (p. 465).

By the end of the 1920s, Ferenczi had arrived at a standpoint that the role of the trauma, mainly childhood sexual trauma, cannot be overestimated in the aetiopathogenesis of neuroses. With this argument, he went back to the early concepts of Breuer and Freud, and, emphasising the importance of the theme, he brought about the renewed use of catharsis as a therapeutical instrument.

In the course of the trauma, Ferenczi saw phases with several actors in interpersonal relationships. Prior to the trauma, the child has an emotional, confident, and/or dependent relationship with the attacking, sexually traumatising person. The traumatic event finds the child unprepared: the child speaks and communicates in the language of tenderness, while the adult, from his own level, speaks and communicates in the language of passion and genitality. This is confusion of tongues. The traumatic event, which, according to Ferenczi's examples in the *Clinical Diary*, might even be vaginal or anal penetration, can also be associated with behaviour jeopardising vegetative functions. The traumatic event generally undergoes repression. In Ferenczi's opinion, the model of this repression is a pre-primal trauma in connection with the mother. In his cases, it is the mother or the father who commits the sexual or vital aggression. As a consequence of the event, the victim identifies with the aggressor:

the weak and undeveloped personality reacts to a sudden unpleasure not by defence, but by anxiety-ridden identification, and by introjection of the menacing person or aggressor. Only with the help of this hypothesis can I understand why my patients refused so obstinately to follow my advice to react to unjust or unkind treatment with pain or with hatred and defence. (Ferenczi [1933]1955, p. 163)

The introjection might also involve guilt feelings of the adult; the child might incorporate these guilt feelings. "Traumatic confusion arises mainly because the attack and the response to it are denied, by the guilt ridden adults, indeed are treated as deserving punishment." If the child, after the shock, turns to his mother or to some other confidential person to seek alleviation for his emotional stress, and he is not taken seriously, and the story is qualified as mere fantasy or a lie, the pathogenic effect of the trauma grows ever stronger by this—in present-day wording—double-bind situation. Repression of the trauma, based on primal repression, denial instead of consolation and care, introjection of possible guilt-feelings—these are the components of the dyadic or triadic script of the trauma.

Ferenczi argued that if, after the traumatic experience, the child is able to relate the story to someone, if he can complain, if he gets realistic information, if he can express his emotions, then the pathogenic effect of the trauma will diminish or not develop at all. Referring to Ferenczi ten years later, Hermann wrote in his book *Primaeval Instincts of Man* (Hermann, 1943), that if the child who witnessed the primal scene receives sincere, sympathetic information from his mother at some later time, then the traumatogenic effect can be alleviated. At this time, Hermann conceptualised the primal scene as the only external trauma.

In his letter to Freud dated December 25 1929, Ferenczi explains,

1) In all cases, where I penetrated deeply enough, I found uncovered the traumatic–hysterical bases of the illness, 2) where the patient and I succeeded in this, the therapeutic effect was far more significant, 3) . . . psychoanalysis deals far too one-sidedly with obsessive neurosis and character-analysis – that is, ego-psychology – while neglecting the organic–hysterical basis of the analysis. This results from overestimating the role of fantasy and underestimating that of traumatic reality in pathogenesis . . . 4) the newly acquired experiences (though in essence they refer back to the distant past) naturally also affect some particular features of technique. (Ferenczi, 1929b, p. 376)

Ferenczi's trauma concept is well illustrated by the following thoughts, which also apply to the therapeutic treatment of the traumatic experience:

> Theoretically important in these ... observations is the relation between the depth of unconsciousness and the trauma, and this justifies the experiments of searching for the experiences of shock in an intentionally induced absorption in trance. An unexpectedly unprepared for, overwhelming shock acts like, as it were, an anaesthetic. How can this be? Apparently by inhibiting every kind of mental activity and thereby provoking a state of complete passivity devoid of any resistance. The absolute paralysis of mobility also includes the inhibition of perception and (with it) of thinking. The shutting off of perception results in the complete defencelessness of the ego. An impression which is not perceived cannot be warded off. The results of this complete paralysis are: 1) the course of sensory paralysis becomes and remains permanently interrupted; 2) while the sensory paralysis lasts, every mechanical and mental impression is taken up without any resistance; 3) no memory traces of such impressions remain, even in the unconscious, and thus the causes of the trauma cannot be recalled from memory traces. If, in spite of it, one wants to reach them, which logically appears to be almost impossible, then one must repeat the trauma itself and under more favourable conditions one must bring it for the first time to perception and to motor discharge. (Ferenczi, 1931, pp. 239–240)

The problems are: the memory of the traumatic event, its effect, as well as the possibility and way of recalling this event. Apparently, Ferenczi's therapeutic work and mental efforts try to solve this problem in the period of the "Confusion of tongues". He writes in his *Clinical Diary*,

> By no means ... can I claim to have ever succeeded, even in a single case, in making it possible for the patient to remember the traumatic processes themselves, with the help of symptom-fantasy ... submergence into dreams, and catharsis. It is as though the trauma were surrounded by a retroactively amnesic sphere as in the case of trauma after cerebral contusion ... For the present it is not quite clear in what way the centre of the explosion can be incorporated, if it can be, in the analysand's mind as a conscious event, and therefore as a psychic event, which is capable of being remembered. (Ferenczi, 1932a, p. 67)

Since a specific feature of the trauma is that it undergoes repression, probably primal repression right at the moment of its actual occurrence, this is well supported by Ferenczi's therapeutical experience about the lack of memory, the lack of remembrance.

If we think of the trauma in the concept of primal repression, then we have to have a look at the arguments of Cohen and Kinston: ". . . in what sense is the memory unconscious and how is it kept that way? The answer sounds simple – there is no memory" (1984, p. 411). They quote, at this point, Freud, from *An Outline of Psychoanalysis*, to support their opinion:

> And if for instance, we say: 'at this point an unconscious memory intervened', what that means is: 'at this point something occurred of which we are totally unable to form a conception, but which, if it had entered our consciousness, could only have been described in such and such way. (Freud, 1940a[1938], p. 197)

Cohen and Kinston continue,

> The patient is in a mental state which is not structured as a memory: and primal repression is seen as an absence of structure due to the trauma of environmental failure. The state observed in analysis has been perpetuated precisely because it reflects unmet needs . . . personal urges which demanded but have not obtained adequate mediation." (Cohen & Kinston, 1984, p. 415)

Ferenczi's experience, cited earlier, that he could not succeed in helping the patient to remember the traumatic processes even in a single case, agrees with one of the four arguments of an 1897 letter of Freud, in which he rejected the seduction theory of trauma. "Fourthly, there was the consideration that even in the most deep-reaching psychoses the unconscious memory does not break through, so that the secret of infantile experiences is not revealed even in the most confused states of delirium" (Freud, 1897, p. 265).

Unlike Freud, Ferenczi did not question the reality of childhood trauma just because of a lack of memory.

> The fact that the trauma had really occurred or it was mere fantasy is a very important issue for the psychic reality, as the symptomatological and characterological consequences of the childhood abuse and the

real incest give eloquent evidence of it. The problem of abused children and patients stands not in the fact that they make fantasies of a
non-occurred trauma, but rather in that they deny one that had really
occurred. The cessation of this disavowal and the recognition of the
reality of traumatisation are in many cases a decisive turning point in
treatment. (Domes, 1993, p. 235)

We know that Ferenczi considered it decisive for the resolution of
the consequences of the trauma that the patient might develop a conviction that the trauma had really occurred, and was not only a
fantasy or a dream. In Ferenczi's concept, a condition of the real traumatising situation is when children do not receive immediate remedy,
and where the adaptation, that is, "a change in their own behaviour,
is forced on them". "If a trauma strikes the soul, or the body, unprepared, that is, without countercathexis, then its effect is destructive for
the body and mind, i.e. it disrupts through fragmentation" (Ferenczi,
1932a, p. 69).

Ferenczi's thoughts on the trauma go back to the earliest
mother–child relationship. He rejects Rank's hypothesis on the trauma
of birth, and asks

whether the primal trauma is not always to be sought in the primal
relationship with the mother, and whether traumata of a somewhat
later epoch, already complicated by the appearance of the father,
could have had such an effect without the existence of such a pre-
primal trauma (*ururtraumatischen*) mother–child scar? (ibid., p. 83)

Re-enactment of the trauma, healing

Ferenczi thinks the following about trauma analysis:

1) Deep (traumatogenic) analysis is not possible if no more favourable
conditions (in contrast to the situation at the original trauma) can be
offered: a) by life and by the external world, or b) – mainly – by the
analyst. a) is partly contained in the contra-indications of analysis by
Freud (misfortune, age, helplessness); b) may partly replace a), but
here emerges the danger of a lifelong fixation to the analyst (adop-
tion—yes, yet how to 'disadopt'?),

– Trauma

Amnesia – Childhood

– Childhood dreams

cannot be remembered because it has never been conscious. It can be re-experienced and recognized as the past. . . . The unpleasurable memories remain reverberating somewhere in the body (and emotions). (Ferenczi, 1932b, pp. 278–279)

These thoughts, dating from 1932, are of prime importance. Sterba, writing on Ferenczi's last papers in 1936 argues, "Both the analysand and the analyst have to regress to the infantile level. And, as a result of the interrelationship between theory and technique, the reuse of the cathartic method had to bring about the revival of the trauma concept" (Sterba, 1936, p. 41).

According to Ferenczi, the conditions for recall of the pathogenic trauma are the following: confidential atmosphere which is created by the analyst's sincerity, freedom of professional hypocrisy, accepting, loving attitude, abundant time investment and mutuality. This emotional atmosphere is different from the asymmetric, double-bind, hypocratic atmosphere of the patient's childhood. The re-enactment of childhood trauma can occur under these conditions. However, the recalling itself, which happens in a regressive trance, lacks the indication of reality for the patient. We know that Ferenczi did not succeed in recalling the direct memory of the original experience; he reconstructed it from derivates. He observed a therapeutic effect from the re-enactment, which is the derivative of the original experience, only if the atmosphere, contrastive to the original situation, and the verbal connection with the analyst during the re-enactment, had formed a conviction in the patient that the recalled experience had really happened, it was neither a fantasy nor a dream. According to Ferenczi's thesis, re-enactment is the emotional basis of therapy. "Without sympathy: there's no healing" (Ferenczi, 1932a, p. 288).

Two further technical terms of Ferenczi's are worth attention: (a) dream interpretation during relaxation: an attempt to take back the patient into the dream itself during the analytical session, and (b) symptom-fantasy (fantasies around a symptom). To quote from the *Clinical Diary*,

Observation of a case in which in relaxation ('trance') opisthotonic positions did appear: when contact could be established with the patient, she reported that the position was a reaction to a feeling of a painful excitation in the genital passage, which the patient described as painful hunger: in this position, psychic unpleasure and defence against ardent desire are simultaneously represented. With the help of exchange of questions and answers it could be established that this state of excitation has been implanted by the father, with the help of gentle shaking and seductive words and promises . . . a scene is reproduced in which the father takes the child in his lap and actually makes use of her ('. . .und regelrecht gebraucht'). (Ferenczi, 1932a, p. 64)

A question arises, what meant Ferenczi, for example, by the term "reproduction": remembering, re-enactment, alone or together with Ferenczi?

The further fate of his ideas and conceptions was, for a long time, sealed by the survivors' loyalty to Freud, and a series of other factors, not to be detailed here due to lack of space.

The Freud–Ferenczi disagreement acted as a trauma on the psychoanalytical world. Hollós described it thus (1934, p. 309),

> In the last years Ferenczi was dealing with the problem of the unfortunate child who suffered traumata. I wonder if the binding that connected the happy child in Ferenczi with his adulthood in a harmonic way up to then, became loose in his own self. His big struggle with the 'hundred-headed enemy' of healing – the resistance of the patient – could not consume all his strength. But I guess it used up his energy and it is Ferenczi's tragedy that during his struggle . . . he experienced conflict with the master, his spiritual father. The title of his last paper [Ferenczi, 1933], 'Disturbances in the mutual understanding between the child and the adults' [Hollós's translation] probably speaks about the wound that caused the death of the eternal child inside Ferenczi, the wound caused by Freud turning away from Ferenczi.

Michael and Alice Balint brought Ferenczi's concepts to the UK, while Imre Hermann remained in Hungary and became the chief psychoanalytical theorist in the country. From Ferenczi's trauma concept, Hermann retains only the primal scene as a trauma in his major work, *Primaeval instincts of Man* (1943), while in his important book, *Psychoanalysis as a Method* (1933), he does not refer to the "Confusion of tongues" at all. Being the leader of the group of psychoanalysts in Hungary, his influence was decisive in letting Ferenczi's trauma theory sink into oblivion.

Lilly Hajdu, and Alice and Michael Balint understood and took on the progressive thoughts of Ferenczi, but, for example, in her 1936 paper, "Treating transference according to Ferenczi's experiments", in Vienna, Alice Balint stated, "I couldn't talk about the cathartic abreaction of pathogenic traumata since I haven't tried it myself . . . I didn't want to talk about the traumatogenesis of neurosis either, for my experience isn't sufficient to declare something definitive" (A. Balint, 1936, p. 55).

Michael Balint revives Ferenczi's trauma theory in 1970, in his three-phase concept based on Ferenczi's ideas: (1) the first phase is the confidential dependence of the child on the adult; (2) in the second phase the adult drastically misuses the child's expectations (overstimulates him through tenderness or cruelty, and a passionate interaction takes place); and (3) the adult disrupts this by rejection in the third, the traumatising phase (M. Balint, 1970).

Very early on, based on Ferenczi's concepts, Balint described a "new beginning" as the continuation of development from the point where the trauma had diverted it from its original direction.

From the end of the 1920s, Lilly Hajdu-Gimes practised analytical therapy on the basis of Ferenczi's theories with schizophrenic patients. In her opinion, infant and adulthood traumata (especially starvation, cruelty of the mother, and her lack of devoted behaviour) play a significant role in the aetiopathogenesis of schizophrenia. Psychotics should be treated the same way as children; as the psychotic does not relax, the therapist has to relax him. She was convinced, in the spirit of Ferenczi, that psychotics should be adopted, meaning that we can only succeed in achieving a good result by living among and with them.

During the decades following Ferenczi's death, therapeutic regression, catharsis accompanied by emotional and somatic symptoms and the aim to enact and abreact the trauma, shifted towards intellectual processing, in Hungary also.

And now it is time for us to bring Ferenczi home.

Note

1.   When I now looked up the English translation of Ferenczi's paper published in German in *Populäre Vorträge* in 1922, I found a lapse of the

translator who rendered the word "Traumen" ("traumata") in English as "dreams". The lapse occurs in the dimensions of external reality and psychic reality—the relationship and the distinguishability of the two was a conceptual subjective problem for Freud and Ferenczi as well, and formed a part of their controversy. The fact that the translator makes a misreading at this point demonstrates the high emotional tension of the problem.

References

Balint, A. (1936). Handhabung der Übertragung auf Grund der Ferenczi-schen Versuche [Treating transference according to Ferenczi's experiments]. *Internationale Zeitschrift für Psychoanalyse, 22*: 47–58.

Balint, M. (1970). Trauma und Objektbeziehung. *Psyche, 24*(5): 346–358.

Cohen, J., & Kinston, W. (1984). Repression theory: a new look at the cornerstone. *International Journal of Psychoanalysis, 65*: 411–422.

Domes, M. (1993). *Der Kompetente Sangling*. Frankfurt: Fischer.

Ferenczi, S. (1908). Actual and psycho-neuroses in the light of Freud's investigations and psychoanalysis. In: Ferenczi (1926) *Further Contributions to the Theory and Technique of Psycho-Analysis* (pp. 30–55), J. Rickman (Ed.), J. I. Suttie & others (Trans.). London: Hogarth Press, 1926 [reprinted, London: Karnac, 1994].

Ferenczi, S. (1918). Disease or pathoneuroses. In: Ferenczi (1926) *Further Contributions to the Theory and Technique of Psycho-Analysis* (pp. 80–81), J. Rickman (Ed.), J. I. Suttie & others (Trans.). London: Hogarth Press, 1926 [reprinted, London: Karnac, 1994].

Ferenczi, S. (1922). *Populäre Vorträge über Psychoanalyse*. Leipzig: Internationaler Psychoanalytischer Verlag.

Ferenczi, S. (1926). *Further Contributions to the Theory and Technique of Psycho-Analysis*, J. Rickman (Ed.), J. I. Suttie & others (Trans.). London: Hogarth Press, 1926 [reprinted, London: Karnac, 1994].

Ferenczi, S. (1929a). The unwelcome child and his death instinct. In: Ferenczi (1955) *Final Contributions to the Problems and Methods of Psycho-Analysis* (pp. 102–107), M. Balint (Ed.), E. Mosbacher & others (Trans.). London: Hogarth Press, 1955 [reprinted, London: Karnac, 1994].

Ferenczi, S. (1929b). Letter from Sandor Ferenczi to Sigmund Freud, December 25, 1929. In: E. Falzeder & E. Brabant (Eds.), *The Correspondence of Sigmund Freud and Sandor Ferenczi, Volume 3, 1920–1933* (pp. 374–376). Cambridge, MA: Harvard University Press, 2000.

Ferenczi, S. (1931). On the revision of the interpretation of dreams. In: Ferenczi (1955) *Final Contributions to the Problems and Methods of Psycho-Analysis* (pp. 238–243), M. Balint (Ed.), E. Mosbacher & others (Trans.). London: Hogarth Press, 1955 [reprinted, London: Karnac, 1994].

Ferenczi, S. (1932a). *The Clinical Diary of Sandor Ferenczi*, J. Dupont (Ed.), M. Balint & N. Z. Jackson (Trans.). Cambridge, MA: Harvard University Press, 1988.

Ferenczi, S. (1932b). Notes and fragments (1920 and 1930–1932). In: Ferenczi (1955) *Final Contributions to the Problems and Methods of Psycho-Analysis* (pp. 216–279), M. Balint (Ed.), E. Mosbacher & others (Trans.). London: Hogarth Press, 1955 [reprinted, London: Karnac, 1994].

Ferenczi, S. (1933). Confusion of tongues between adults and the child. In: Ferenczi (1955) *Final Contributions to the Problems and Methods of Psycho-Analysis* (pp. 156–167), M. Balint (Ed.), E. Mosbacher & others (Trans.). London: Hogarth Press, 1955 [reprinted, London: Karnac, 1994].

Ferenczi, S., & Groddeck, G. (1986). *Sandor Ferenczi/Georg Groddeck, Briefwechsel 1921–1933*. Frankfurt: S. Fischer.

Freud, S. (1897). Letter from Freud to Fliess, September 21, 1897. In: J. M. Masson (Ed.), *The Complete Letters of Sigmund Freud to Wilhelm Fliess 1887–1904* (pp. 264–267). Cambridge, MA: Harvard University Press, 1985.

Freud, S. (1940a[1938]). *An Outline of Psycho-Analysis*. S.E., 23: 139–208. London: Hogarth.

Freud, S. (1966). *Pre-Psycho-Analytic Publications and Unpublished Drafts*. S.E., 1: London: Hogarth Press.

Hermann, I. (1933). *A pszichoanalízis mint módszer* [Psychoanalysis as a method]. Budapest: Pantheon.

Hermann, I. (1934). Bevezetés Ferenczi traumáról szóló tanulmányához [Introduction to Ferenczi's paper on trauma]. *Gyógyászat*, 74: 309–310.

Hermann, I. (1943). *Az Ember ősi ösztonei* [Primaeval instincts of Man]. Budapest: Magvető.

Hollós, I. (1934). Emlékezés Ferenczi Sándorra. *Gyógyászat*, 74: 305–309.

Khan, M. (1978). *Le Soi Cache*. Paris: Gallimard.

Laplanche, J., & Pontalis, J.-B. (1973). *The Language of Psychoanalysis*. London: Karnac.

Sterba, R. (1936). Das psychische Trauma und die Handhabung der Übertragung. (Die lezten Arbeiten von S. Ferenczi zur psychoanalytischen Technik). *Internationale Zeitschrift für ärztliche Psychoanalyse*, 22: 40–41.

CHAPTER NINE

Regression post-Ferenczi

Harold Stewart

T he topic of regression in analytic therapy will always be associated with the name of Ferenczi, since he was the first of the
psychoanalytic pioneers to understand and experiment with its
potential as a therapeutic agent and ally. It is a lengthy and controver-
sial issue and only a selection of the issues involved are presented here.

We should first clarify the way the term regression is used, since,
as Michael Balint pointed out in his book of therapeutic regression,
The Basic Fault, the term has four functions, "(1) as a mechanism of
defence (2) as a factor in pathogenesis (3) as a potent form of resistance, and (4) as an essential factor in analytic therapy" (Balint, 1968,
p. 127). Regression refers to a reversion to an earlier state or mode of
functioning, and in therapeutic regression, it is of the formal type
associated with the patient's increasing dependence on the analyst.

Freud had first experimented with the earliest regressive technique, hypnosis, before he discovered its limitations. The aim of the
hypnotherapy had been to achieve emotional abreaction of repressed
traumatic experiences that had given rise to hysterical symptoms.
When he next started to use the technique of free association, which
itself tends to give rise to regression from secondary to primary
process thinking, he still had the same aim but it soon changed from

the exploration of pathogenic traumatic experience to the exploration of the patient's drives and unconscious fantasies. However, it was Ferenczi who persisted in the belief of the importance of early environmental traumata as a result of his own experiences of the analysis of patients.

He was a *conquistador* of analytic technique, always willing to adapt his technique to the patient, and he gained the reputation among analysts of being able to treat apparently hopeless cases, many of which had experienced previous unsuccessful analyses. They would now be described as having a severe borderline pathology. His *Clinical Diary* (Ferenczi, 1932), which he kept during the last nine months of his life, describes his ever-changing techniques and his critical assessments of them. He had first tried the active technique of prohibitions of certain behaviours in an attempt to increase the internal psychic tension, but this had not worked; neither did the encouragement of relaxation to lower the tension; neither did the admission to the patient of his countertransference feelings; and, last, neither did his final experiment of mutual analysis, where patient and analyst took turns in analysing the other.

He based his experimental technique on the firm belief that in the privation and abstinent atmosphere of a typical analysis as recommended by Freud, the patient experienced a replay, a re-enactment, of early traumatic experiences that the patient as a child had undergone at the hands of adults resulting in an under- or over-stimulation of the child, to which the adults had responded by a lack of involvement, implicitly denying responsibility for their share of the trauma. Ferenczi believed that the analyst acted like the adult, in so far as his setting and technique had invited the patient to experience longings and desires, but then responded by interpretations and reconstructions of early life, thereby not accepting any responsibility for the patient's present emotional state. Through his changing techniques, he was looking for ways around this by responding positively to the regressed patient's cravings and "needs".

It was the nature of this positive responding that led to the rift between himself and Freud, but, nevertheless, he clung to his beliefs, having experienced a number of successful analyses in which the regression, to use Balint's later terminology, was of the benign type.

Following Ferenczi's death and the rift with Freud, therapeutic regression was held in great disfavour by the analytic community and it was not until the post-war period that interest in it revived. It happened particularly in the UK, as a result of the interest taken in it by Donald Winnicott and Michael Balint, followed later by Margaret Little, Masud Khan, Christopher Bollas, and Harold Stewart, in developing further understanding of this state.

Let us first turn to Donald Winnicott: his most important paper on this subject was "Metapsychological and clinical aspects of regression within the psycho-analytical set-up" (Winnicott, 1955). He thought that therapeutic regression is a particularly important feature for those patients who have no secure personality structure and space–time unit status, and that they need long periods of management rather than ordinary analytic work. In this group of patients, illness is related to early environmental failure, which has led to the development of a false-self organisation, and that regression meant regression to dependence on the analyst. In the same way that he regarded the mother and baby as an inseparable unit, the baby being dependent on the mother's management, the patient is similarly dependent on the analyst's setting, technique, and responsiveness to the patient. He described the sequence of events in treatment as comprising:

1. The provision of a setting that gives confidence.

2. Regression of the patient to dependence, with due sense of the risk involved.

3. The patient feeling a new sense of self, and the self hitherto hidden becoming surrendered to the total ego. A new progression of the individual processes which had stopped.

4. An unfreezing of an environmental failure situation.

5. From the new position of ego strength, anger related to the early environmental failure, felt in the present and expressed.

6. Return from regression to dependence, in early progress towards independence.

7. Instinctual needs and wishes becoming realizable with genuine vitality and vigour.

All this repeated again and again. (Winnicott, 1955, p. 287)

He also stressed that interpretations of whatever nature that are given during the regressed phase can ruin the development of the emerging processes; the necessary interpretative work is done after emergence from this state. The patient needs to be able to experience the regression without needing or being obliged about anything in the way of insight and understanding coming from the analyst.

The use of regression to dependence and the experience of it should not be confused with that of the correct emotional experience as described by Alexander (1948). He suggested that the corrective emotional experience is a consciously planned regulation of the therapist's own emotional responses to the patient in such a way as to counteract the harmful effects of parental attitudes. This technique is an artificially manipulated experience that might have short-term benefits, but essentially has no place in psychoanalytic technique, where spontaneity and authenticity should be essential features. It is similar to Ferenczi's active techniques, which also had only short-term benefits.

Little (1985, 1987) has written on her own psychoanalysis with Winnicott, in which she described the way he managed her regression. He would increase the length of sessions on a regular basis, would take over the practical management and arrangement of her affairs if necessary, and would hold her head and hands for long periods when he thought it appropriate. A rather artificial aspect of this regression was apparent, since patients had to queue in order to go through this period of regression with him because it was such a taxing experience for the analyst. The patient had to regress in the analyst's time and not in his own. However, the idea that it is the unthought known, to use Bollas's (1987) phrase, the past experience or the fantasy of the past experience that needed to be experienced and thought, is well conveyed.

We shall now turn to Balint and his major contribution to regression. He was the analysand and follower of Ferenczi and was the English translator of all his writings. After Ferenczi's death, he investigated the outcome of Ferenczi's experiments to try to assess their therapeutic results. He noted that although some had relapsed, several had done well, which encouraged him to continue the work. His life's work and thinking on this topic was distilled into his book, *The Basic Fault*, which is subtitled *Therapeutic Aspects of Regression*.

He did not accept Freud's theory of primary narcissism, preferring his own theory of primary object love. In response to the traumatic discovery of frustrations and separations from the infant's primary objects, he believed a basic fault developed in the mind, and this gave rise to two characterological types, *ocnophilia* and *philobatism*, distinguishable by their relationship to objects and the spaces between objects. He noted, as did Ferenczi, that some patients regress to an earlier state in what he termed a benign regression, and this is characterised by:

1. The establishment of a mutually trusting *arglos* state [meaning innocent and guileless] which is reminiscent of the primary relationship towards primary substances.

2. A regression, leading to a true new beginning, and ending in a real new discovery.

3. The regression is for the sake of recognition, in particular, of the patient's internal problems.

4. Only moderately high intensity of the demands, expectations or 'needs'.

5. The absence of signs of severe hysteria in the clinical symptomatology and of genital–orgastic elements in the regressed transference. (Balint, 1968, p. 146)

With this form of regression, which is similar to Winnicott's, the therapist only allows certain gratification of the patient's needs, which, if moderate and infrequent, are therapeutic. Balint included only finger- or hand-holding in the way of physical contact, and in these ways he differed from Winnicott in his technique. In addition to this, he recognised another form of regression, which he called malignant regression, with different characteristics from the benign:

1. Since the mutually trusting relationship is highly precariously balanced, the arglos unsuspecting atmosphere breaks down repeatedly, and frequently symptoms of desperate clinging develop.

2. A malignant form of regression, several unsuccessful attempts at reaching a new beginning, a constant threat of an unending spiral of demands or 'needs', and of development of addiction-like states.

3. The regression is aimed at gratification by external action.

4. Suspiciously high intensity of demands, expectations, or 'needs'.

5. Presence of signs of severe hysteria and of genital–orgastic elements both in the normal and in the regressed form of transference. (ibid., p. 146)

Balint saw that the lack of differentiation of these two types of regression had led to some of the problems with which Ferenczi had been faced. Whereas in the benign type, the regression is aimed at the recognition of the patient's internal state, in the malignant type, the regression is aimed at the gratification of the patient by action from the analyst. These attempts are doomed to failure, since, although there is some improvement in the patient's state of mind, this is short-lived and the demands and "needs" escalate until the analysis breaks down in failure.

Having made this important distinction, Balint suggested various technical recommendations to deal with them. He started from the observation that when patients are regressed to the basic fault level, a transference borderline psychosis, interpretations of all kinds have incomparably reduced power, since words and sentences are no longer experienced as having recognised social meanings but as being persecutory or seductive utterances. He believed that additional therapeutic agents other than interpretations must be considered:

the most important of these is to help the patient to develop a primitive relationship in the analytic situation corresponding to his compulsive pattern and maintained in undisturbed pace till he can discover the possibility of new forms of object relationship, experience them, and experiment with them . . . a necessary task of the treatment is to inactivate the basic fault by creating conditions in which it can heal off. (ibid., p. 166)

Like Winnicott, he also stressed that the interpretative work must be done after the regression.

Balint further suggested that to try to prevent a malignant regression occurring, the analyst should avoid interpreting everything, as transference should avoid appearing to be omnipotent and avoid behaving as a separate object by tolerating some forms of acting-out and accepting the patient's projective identifications of unacceptable aspects of himself for long periods. Like Winnicott, he emphasised the mutual sharing of the experience and the allowing of sufficient space and time in the milieu for facilitating of this experience. He called the stance of the analyst "unobtrusive", and it could also well be described as unintruding.

In his book, Balint gave no clinical case or example of malignant regression, but later workers have done so. Khan (1972) described the analysis of a young woman who had already destroyed two psychotherapies and one psychoanalysis by her violent and destructive behaviour. He dealt with her by setting strict limits to his tolerance of her behaviour by stopping sessions when necessary. He also noted that an important feature of her malignant regression was the destructive envious attacks she made on any achievement and help given by the analyst's skill, and, further, that she had a dread of surrender to dependence on the analyst, which was the outcome of an over-protected infancy and childhood. In addition to this paper, he also wrote a critical and stimulating essay on Balint's theory and technique of regression (Khan, 1969).

In his book *The Shadow of the Object*, Bollas discussed regression to dependence, but selectively, in its benign form. He accepted Balint's distinction between the two forms, and suggested that in this simpler regression,

> it involves the patient's trust in the analyst's capacity to keep the room, the space, the time, and the process going so as to give up certain ego functions (such as integrative thinking, abstracting, observing, reporting, remembering details, attending to the analyst's frame of mind and interpretations, and so on) in order to fall into a state of intense inner self preoccupation . . . This giving up of aspects of the ego to the analyst induces in the analysand earlier memories and experiences. (Bollas, 1987, pp. 269–270)

He also suggests that the processes of musing and evoking are important elements in this self-analytic capacity and in the thinking of the unthought known.

Stewart (1991) also described cases of malignant regression that presented features similar to Khan's patient, particularly of malicious destructive envy and the dread of dependence on the analyst, but their early environment had been under-protected, with unpredictable violence and prolonged separations. He developed his views, particularly on malignant regression, and believed that one of the features of this state is to attack the limits and boundaries of the setting in order to test the firmness and resolve of the analyst to maintain them.

These destructive attacks and their survival by the analyst, according to Winnicott (1969), are important features in the change of the object from being experienced as subjectively conceived to being objectively perceived, real and separate. He goes further than Balint by suggesting that there should be no physical contact with the patient by the analyst. Clinically, it can be observed that in these concretely thinking patients, physical contact can give rise to oversexualisation and hyperexcitement, and lead to severe acting-out or psychotic breakdown. Even the finger-holding might well conceal more than it discloses, as it could well be a form of collusion with a hysterical defensive structure rather than a means of potentiating a growth experience. He set out some of the motivations behind the malignant regression:

1. To obtain gratification of libidinal desires, particularly to fill chronic states of inner emptiness.

2. To spoil and destroy helpful good objects because of excessive envy.

3. To spoil and destroy helpful good objects so as to avoid the anxieties of dependence.

4. To spoil and destroy helpful good objects so as to avoid the anxieties of separation.

5. To test the analyst's ability to maintain limits and boundaries of the analytic setting.

6. To test the analyst's ability to maintain the analytic stance under the most intense provocation without retaliation

7. If one accepts Winnicott's idea that destructive impulses create the reality of objectively perceived objects, this is an unexpected positive motive for the malignant state. (Stewart, 1993, p. 263)

It is in the increased understanding of the psychopathologies and techniques that advances have come in dealing with regression. Ferenczi did not understand the sheer malevolence of severe hysterics, with their borderline or psychotic personalities. He believed in the supreme power of uncovering, reliving, and emotionally understanding traumatic experiences and was convinced that love, sympathy, and understanding would be the therapeutic key. He did not think in terms of envy of the good breast, the good analyst, with the compulsive urge to spoil and destroy the very source of love, sympathy, and understanding. Neither did he realise that when patients apparently responded well, they could well be in a temporary state of idealisation and denial. He also seemed to confuse firmness on the analyst's part with cruelty and neutrality, and, thereby, not realise the need to work with the patient's inevitable near-psychotic response to the analyst. However, Ferenczi, with his exploring and critical mind, might, had he lived, have also come to some similar conclusions to those presented here.

References

Alexander, F. (1948). *Fundamentals of Psychoanalysis*. New York: W. W. Norton.

Balint, M. (1968). *The Basic Fault: Therapeutic Aspects of Regression*. London: Tavistock.

Bollas, C. (1987). *The Shadow of the Object*. London: Free Association Books.

Ferenczi, S. (1932). *The Clinical Diary of Sandor Ferenczi*, J. Dupont (Ed.), M. Balint & N. Z. Jackson (Trans.). Cambridge, MA: Harvard University Press, 1988.

Khan, M. M. R. (1969). On the clinical provision of frustrations, recognitions and failures in the analytic situation. *International Journal of Psycho-Analysis, 50*: 237–248.

Khan, M. M. R. (1972). Dread of surrender to resourceless dependence in the analytic situation. In: *Privacy of the Self*. London: Hogarth Press.

Little, M. I. (1985). Winnicott working in areas where psychotic anxieties predominate: a personal record. *Free Associations, 1D*: 9–42.

Little, M. I. (1987). On the value of regression to dependence. *Free Associations, 1K*: 7–22.

Stewart, H. (1991). *Psychic Experience and Problems of Technique*. London: Routledge.

Stewart, H. (1993). Clinical aspects of malignant regression. In: L. Aron & A. Harris (Eds.), *The Legacy of Sandor Ferenczi* (pp. 249–264). Hillsdale, NJ: Analytic Press.

Winnicott, D. W. (1955). Metapsychological and clinical aspects of regression within the psycho-analytical set-up. In: *Through Paediatrics to Psychoanalysis. Collected Papers* (pp. 278–294). London: Tavistock, 1958.

Winnicott, D. W. (1969). The use of an object. *International Journal of Psychoanalysis, 50*: 711–716.

CHAPTER TEN

Imre Hermann: researching psyche and space

Sára Klaniczay

I mre Hermann was my analyst and trainer for seven years. He died twenty years ago, at the age of ninety-five.

Hermann lived in Hungary and he worked there all his life, even in the years of Nazism and Communism.[1] He played a very important role in the survival of psychoanalysis in Hungary and in preserving the legacy of the Budapest School for the coming generations. He was a doctor of medicine and also a researcher: he observed and described psychological phenomena and searched for their organic basis.

Hermann was a polymath. Besides being an expert in psychology, he was familiar with different natural and social sciences and various branches of the arts. He was very much interested in what we call "talent"; he studied the nature of the process of creation. The most significant step in his career was the discovery and description of the instinct of clinging.

A short summary of Hermann's theory of clinging

Hermann was interested in the behaviour of apes from the very beginning. The inherited clinging reaction of apes has been described by many. It is a well-known fact that apes spend the first months of their lives clinging to their mother's bodies. The essence of Hermann's theory is that the instinctive behaviour of the ape infant, that is, its clinging to the mother, is an existing but inhibited instinctive drive in the human infant as well. Moro, the German paediatrician, described the reflex movement of the arms that can be triggered in the three-month-old infant. This movement resembles the embracing reflex movement of apes and, thus, might have philogenetic origin.

Ferenczi observed similar movements in patients suffering from traumatic neurosis. The reflex-like clinging movement of elderly people suffering from organic injuries is also a well-known phenomenon. Hermann proves the existence of the instinct of clinging in humans by observing infants, studying habits of primitive peoples, and collecting data from the field of cultural history.

The instinct of clinging is frustrated from the very beginning of a human's life, since the mother's body is not hairy and also owing to the process of education, so "it has to go a peculiar way", according to Hermann. As a latent drive, it is effective throughout a human's life. It provides the biological background to the mother–infant relationship. Later, integrated into the libidinal instincts, it gives those instincts their motivational basis. It will be a source of loving relationships, but also a source of aggressive tendencies. The frustrated instinct can revive with amplified strength and be the basis of regression and pathological phenomena and symptoms, particularly after a disappointment or the loss of a loved one.

The instinct of clinging does not come into force by itself. Its opposite is going-in-search: "Going-in-search becomes active when the instinct of clinging is left without an object" of clinging. The aspirations to separate and hide oneself are considered by Hermann to be a manifestation of the instinct of clinging. These are considered to be reaction formations used by the ego as a means of defence. Hermann found that clinging, going-in-search, separation, and hiding are closely connected phenomena; he called them the "clinging syndrome".

In 1943, Hermann described in detail the theory of the instinct of clinging in his book *The Primaeval Instincts of Man*.

In the 1960s, in his experiments with apes, Harlow proved that clinging was a basic instinct, independent from the instinct of eating. He also proved that apes who lacked contact with their mothers did not become sexually mature and had serious problems looking after their offspring, if they had any.

The phenomena observed in apes cannot be applied directly to humans, Hermann emphasises. Study of apes cannot substitute for the study of human behaviour. Regular research studying the human mother–infant relationship started after the Second World War.

Many authors (Bowlby, first of all) have pointed out that lack of security, owing to the absence of the mother, might cause severe somatic and neurotic symptoms in infancy. Spitz described the phenomenon of hospitalisation. György pointed out that even the roots of antisocial development can be found in the disturbances of the early mother–infant relationship.

As I mentioned earlier, different kinds of clinical symptoms can be explained by the frustration of the instinct of clinging. Stuttering is one such symptom—a topic I have been engaged in for about thirty years.

My assumption is that frustrated clinging—for instance, long-lasting separation from the mother between the ages of two and four years old—creates a kind of *basic situation* for the child in which different traumas might cause stuttering. That basic situation is specific to the formation of stuttering, whereas the trigger factors are not necessarily specific ones.

Hermann published a series of case histories of people who reacted to separation traumas by self-destruction: the tearing of their skin, nails, or hair, sometimes even causing bleeding. Biting the nails is also frequent in children. I quote Hermann: "In all these habits a kind of separation is taking place, separation from something that has belonged to the body so far . . ." (Hermann, 2007, p. 43). It involves the motive, emphasised by Freud and Ferenczi, by which our ego strives to relive the trauma (in this case, the separation), but this time without being externally forced. Rather, it happens by our own will and at our own pace.

According to Hermann, the habit of *grooming* among apes is the philogenetic model of self-destructive phenomena. After leaving the mother, a young ape will climb up on to other members of the group, and start grooming their hair. Thereby, the young ape acts out again and again the micro-drama of clinging, going-in-search, and separation. In apes, however, this instinctive act develops into acquiring the skill of social co-operation.

Researching psyche and space

Hermann considered the spatial connections of psychological phenomena very important. The issue of space perception emerges again
and again in his works. *Clinging* and *space* are closely connected
concepts, because it is with the modification of clinging that the basic
phenomenon of space perception—distance—will evolve.

This chapter will consider psyche and space on the basis of
Hermann's oeuvre.

Once upon a time there was a wicked goblin. He created a mirror,
which made things that were nice and good appear small, and evil
things appear large. He wanted to fly up to the sky with his mirror,
but it slipped out of his hands, fell down to the earth among the
people, and broke into millions of pieces. If a small piece of this
mirror, the size of a speck of dust, got into someone's eyes, everything
he saw was distorted . . . This is how Andersen's tale "The Snow
Queen" begins.

A Hungarian professor (Böszörményi, 1959) carried out an experiment in 1959, injecting a volunteer with a certain drug (diethyltrypta-
mine). One and a half hours after receiving the injection, the subject
reported that he perceived the room to be big and spacious, that there
was room for everything and the walls seemed to be far away.
Twenty-three minutes later, he was in a state of euphoria.

Our perception has an influence on our emotions. Hermann studied the interaction between visual space perception and our emotional
life. In order to understand Hermann's thoughts, we have to discuss
some notions that he used.

Topology is a branch of mathematics. From the topological point of
view, an elastic surface remains the same surface after extension,
contraction, or any kind of "continuous deformation". For example,
from the topological point of view, the surface of an empty balloon
does not change after being blown up.

Hermann speaks about the "topological aspect" in the sense that
qualities of things are examined, regardless of their measure. Small
children have a topological way of perception: for example, a big doll
can live well in a small dolls' house.

The notion of *space*, as used by Hermann, also has to be clarified.
Our visual field is three-dimensional. In geometry, there are different
ways of modelling three-dimensional spaces. For example:

- *Euclidean space* has zero deviation. It contains plain surfaces. That is the space we generally see;
- *Spherical space* has a positive deviation, a kind of "narrowing down". It can be demonstrated on the surface of a globe;
- Space with a negative deviation, called *pseudospherical space*, can be demonstrated on the surface of a trumpet or a saddle. It is, in a way, wider than Euclidean space.

The *perception of moving objects* might be different in different kinds of space. The points that seem to be far away in spherical space approach us faster, when moving, than those in Euclidean space. Saddle-like formations are more "spacious": in pseudospherical space, the points that seem to be near us approach us more slowly. Hermann refers to Helmholtz's (1876) experiments, where the illusion of different spaces was created for the subjects by lenses built in their glasses.

Let me also mention the Möbius strip, a well-known phenomenon that had great significance for Hermann. Made by twisting and gluing a strip of paper, it is a "one-sided surface"; there are no directions on it—the notion of orientation of "right" and "left" is meaningless. (If you slide a glove along the surface of the Möbius strip, the thumb starts on the right and is on the left when it comes back.)

In our visual field, Euclidean space is reflected, but not perfectly. For instance, the closer an object is to our eyes, the bigger it seems to be. According to Hermann, the reflection of Euclidean space is the result of the human development process. Curved spaces correspond to lower degrees of development: they are two- or three-dimensional non-Euclidean spaces like that of the Möbius strip or spherical and pseudospherical space. Hermann calls them " ancient topological spaces". Where can we meet spaces like these?

They appear in optical illusions (see Figure 1). In certain circumstances parallels seem to be curved. They also appear in works of art, for instance, in Escher's drawings, where we can see the Möbius strip and other non-Euclidean spaces. Hermann says,

> Artistic works convince us about the existence of ancient topological spaces in our unconscious. It is the demand for measure that prevents them getting into the conscious. However, artistic immersion is able to call them to life just like Greek drama brings the contents of the unconscious to the surface, the Oedipal-conflict for example. (2007, p. 148)

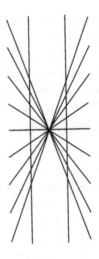

Figure 1.

We can meet non-Euclidean spaces in *pathological cases* as well. In mescalin toxicosis the straight line becomes curved; objects appear as they would in a spherical mirror. People look distorted, as if their hands and feet were close to the lens of a camera. Rooms look bigger than they are, corridors look deeper, and objects far away seem to be near.

Search for congruency is one of Hermann's important methods. To promote the understanding of psychological phenomena, we can examine these phenomena from an entirely different field. There should be a kind of "structural similarity" between the two sets of phenomena, that is, some of their important qualities should correspond. Hermann refers to a method, used in mathematics, named *one-to-one mapping*. A more abstract notion is studied by examining a more concrete, more demonstrative phenomenon. One-to-one mapping, as used in mathematics, is a clearly defined, exact method. Hermann does not apply it to psychology, but uses it as a model in his field.

Hermann searches for congruency between the different topological spaces and certain psychological phenomena. Let us see an example.

According to Binswanger (1933), hypomanic patients seem to move in a broader space. They spend more money, they speak louder, and they perceive objects differently. A sheet of paper that is big for us seems small to them. The social path that is normally broad for other people is too narrow for them.

Hermann thinks that the vivid mood of manic patients can be understood because of their perception of space as being wide, hence "the trouble is far away". They feel that they can avoid everything bad and reach everything good because of their accelerated motor functions. Hermann found congruency between pseudospherical space and hypomanic moods. According to Hermann, the faint-heartedness of depressed people comes from their spatial perception, that is, a bad thing that is far away can happen to them at any moment in the near future because their motor defences are paralysed. So congruency can be found between spherical space and depression. With a depressed patient, the fear of premature death can create a suicidal phantasy. *Ejaculatio praecox*, as a form of "occurrence before time", can be a consequence of depression as well.

The spatial aspects of aggression

Hermann deals profoundly with the question of aggression. History provides the evidence for his research. In 1946, he said, "In the last few years when doing research I have not been able to neglect the question: 'What type of person is this bloodthirsty, brutal man whom my and our fate was to meet on our path?'".

Dealing with this problem, Hermann found different spatial aspects of aggression. Let us see some examples.

1. One of the goals of the *sadist* is *to broaden his space at the expense of others*; for instance, "binding hands and feet" and "cramming people into wagons" is an "extension of power" of the sadist. According to Hermann, sadism can show pesudospherical characteristics. Extension as a consequence of aggression has physiological models. Fónagy (1963) writes that under the influence of anger, due to the swelling of the muscles of the larynx, the glottis becomes narrower and the voice changes.

2. Hatred aims at the removal and annihilation of its object. The spatial expression of this is the expulsion of three-dimensional objects from space by *making them flat or reducing them to a point*. The expressions "to trample someone down" or "to plaster someone on the wall" are very aggressive in their content. One of Hermann's patients had a

dream in which the person of whom she was jealous was thin. In reality, this person was not thin at all: in Hermann's interpretation, the patient's aggression made her appear thin. Kafka writes in one of his short stories: "I would have squashed that student against this wall a long time ago" (1925, p. 48).

3. The way of making something flat or reducing it to a single point involves making the body smaller. *Making small* might mean aggression. A boy saw his father and mother coming from a distance. "Isn't it strange that father is so small while mother is big?" he asked. This boy was just in the Oedipal phase and his emotions tended to diminish his father's value. Ferenczi dealt with the process of "making small" and "enlarging" under the title "Gulliver fantasies" (1964). It is known that Swift was a bitter misanthrope; he was also accused of a cruel assault on a girl. In Swift's case, the connection between spatial change and aggression is plausible.

4. On the basis of his psychoanalytical practice, Hermann supposed that converted left-handedness increases aggression. Roboz's experiments about right/left orientation supported his hypothesis. According to Hermann, converted left-handedness (a kind of torsion) might cause a regressive change in space perception. In the more "ancient space" the ego control is diminished and aggression takes over.

5. *Twisting* is an essential element in sadistic actions; for instance, "twisting one's neck or limbs". Torsion and aggression are closely related, Hermann says. Twisting is congruent with the Möbius surface; it is the space of "orientational disturbances", as I mentioned earlier.

Let me illustrate this with a case from my analytical practice.

The patient was a twelve-year-old boy who had been in hospital for two weeks with disturbances of orientation. Since no organic cause was found, psychotherapy was suggested.

This boy had a strange symptom occurring several times a day, and he himself was scared by it. He put it in the following way: "The world suddenly turns around. The picture changes at once: things which were in the foreground move to the right, everything turns around." I made him explain this symptom many times because I was unable to imagine it.

While telling me about his symptom, he made a repeated movement of his hand, as if he were twisting something in the air. ("The world suddenly turns around: things which were in the foreground move to the right, everything turns around.")

From the anamnesis, it has to be stressed that the boy was afraid of his father. The father used to hit him—not very often, but when he did, it was brutal, using a strap. The boy had a fifteen-year-old brother who liked to bully him. Aggression and defencelessness were frequent subjects of our conversations, but he spoke about them without emotion. When his father hit him with the strap, he felt the pain but thought that it was not to him that it was happening. His mother hit him "only" with her palm. "Nervous atmosphere is worse than being hit," the boy said.

His brother began to take a bigger and bigger part in his stories. He was "very strong" and "as big as a grown-up". The boy spoke about himself as the weakest member in the family.

The boy and his brother slept in a bunkbed. He said his brother often "tortured" him. I asked about the way he did it. The boy gave only one example: his brother wakes him up and makes him bring some water.

The question I put to myself was the following: what happens with the counter-aggression? Where does its energy flow? There was no complaint about the brother's behaviour. I supposed this energy was used up by symptom formation. In the course of the therapy, I tried to bring the repressed aggression to the surface by conversation, play, and dramatisation. I also made the boy bring some water, hoping that the painful experience would enter into the therapy.

It was his movement when he turned off the tap that made me realise the connection. This movement was the same he had made when he explained his symptom. This was the moment when I thought of Hermann and of what he said about the relationship between twisting and aggression. The connection became evident to me; my only problem was how to interpret it for the child. I made him repeat the movement of turning off the tap and asked: "Is this the way the world turns around? I think it is you who makes it turn around. You are so defenceless with your brother that you do not even dare to be angry with him when he hurts you. You cannot return the torture, you cannot 'twist his neck' as you would like to. Instead of returning the insult, you make your own world turn around. Let's speak about your anger openly!"

Following this interpretation, the boy's symptom ceased. Unfortunately, I had no chance to elaborate his aggression because his mother thought that her child was healthy and needed no more therapy. Thus, in spite of my advice, they stopped coming.

Several months later, the headmaster of the boy's school called me on the phone and complained about my patient's behaviour: he had become aggressive and was disturbing the work in class. Thanks to his teacher, the boy returned: this time the therapy was aimed at the elaboration of his aggression. In the course of my work, I confirmed my earlier interpretation that the symptom came from repressed aggression. After the aggression came to the surface, the symptom ceased.

Now let us speak about the spatial aspects of love. "Love and hate, the two basic emotions, are not independent; both come from the instinct of clinging which, if refined, gives impulse for tender love, but if roughened, feeds aggression and hatred," Hermann says (2007, p. 148). Later, he continues with the following:

> The decisive step in the manifestation of love takes place when the tender connection loses the necessity of direct bodily contact and can be present over a distance as well. This step is the feature that can be called 'human'. . . (ibid., p. 147)

According to Hermann, every kind of true love is congruent with pseudospherical space, because "love makes our space broader".

The loving interrelationship can be characterised by an inexhaustible completeness. Shakespeare writes, in Romeo and Juliet,

> My bounty is as boundless as the sea
> My love as deep, the more I give to thee
> The more I have, for those are infinite.

The link between love and completeness can be found in the Bible. Moses declares to his people the law: "Love the Lord thy God with all thy heart and with all thy soul and with all thy might!"

Hermann found the importance of spatial connections in the field of neurophysiology. As we already know, the disturbances of right/left orientation can induce sadistic, aggressive manifestations. Also, aggression can be congruent with a twisted surface. The disturbances of right/left orientation are important from a neurophysiological point of view: they are connected to the functioning of the occipital and parietal lobes. In case of organic or functional disturbances of these lobes, symptoms might occur that can be interpreted with the rotation of space.

Hermann says,

> Examples from neurology support the hypothesis from another angle: the characteristic features of emotions had developed in parallel with ancient spatial qualities and they were mediated by the same part of the brain. The regression of spatial qualities and the pathology of emotions have to be studied together. Every psychiatric and psycho-pathological case has to be examined from the point of view of its rela-tions with ancient topological spaces: there are those the patient desires, those he moves in, those he draws with pleasure, etc. We have to explore the hidden instinctual lives of patients suffering from organic orientational disturbances. This could be a valuable diagnos-tic method and at the same time a new model of interpreting psycho-logical phenomena. (2007, p. 53)

Having mentioned some of Hermann's thoughts about psyche and space, I would like to add my own thoughts about this issue and dedi-cate them to Hermann's memory.

Thoughts on Hermann's themes

There are situations in our lives when we feel that "there is no more space". And there are unforgettable moments when we experience that space expands, like widening circles, almost to infinity.

Many years ago, my son's life was seriously threatened and I could not do anything for him. The proximity of life and death became frighteningly evident: as the Hungarian poet Endre Ady says:

> Life and death are almost the same;
> Great Relations, great Opponents.
> On my two cheeks, just at the same time
> Touched me your hot, debating kiss . . .

I walked up and down the corridor of the clinic. I had no emotions or thoughts, only an unbearable physical feeling that I was unable to localise. I felt an awful lack of space. I put it into words for myself: it was as if I were lying on a stone basement underneath the tightly-joined wooden floor covering it—lying between the two layers. For a long time this picture was my only thought. Later, the following picture emerged: I was running faster and faster in a small cage but there was no space to move forward at all. I was not aware how long it took because my sense of time was not functioning. I could perceive everything happening around me, but I was completely out of it.

At the end of the corridor, a patient was washing the stairs—a very, small old woman in a dressing-gown. "Work-therapy". Suddenly she came up to me and said, "You are in great trouble, aren't you?" "Yes, I am," I answered, "my son . . ." "No need to be afraid!" she said, and gave me a meaningful look as if she knew. I saw that she was mentally ill.

She stood by me, and I, "from under the floorboards", looked up at her. I felt we were close to each other, both of us somewhere on the edge of life, meeting for a moment, a "normal" and a "mentally sick" person. And I thought, "There are no sharp borderlines".

She went back to wash the stairs and I observed the change in myself with increasing curiosity. I stood upright, took a deep breath, and felt that "there was space": I could move, there were people around me. The world seemed to have "opened". And I began to have emotions. I felt touched, a sensation that I put into words: "If mentally sick people are able to love, it is worth living." The fearful thought of "being restricted" was replaced by being part of the "infinite".

This experience reminded me of a playful experiment I had carried out several years earlier. I did not complete it, so it did not reach the level of a scientific experiment, but I will use it to illustrate my thoughts.

I had a patient, a boy of fourteen, who came to therapy because of his stuttering. Once he told me about some trouble he got into during a maths lesson at school. He was called to the blackboard and was told to mark two points and to draw circles so that each should go through both points. He drew one circle, with the two points on the diameter (Figure 2).

The boy could not draw any more circles. The teacher became angry and said that there were an infinite number of circles going through two given points—they had already learnt about this. The boy suddenly had an idea: "There is an infinite number of circles that go through these two points but I cannot draw them on the blackboard for they are in space; this circle has to be rotated around the diameter as an axis!" This was not the answer the teacher had

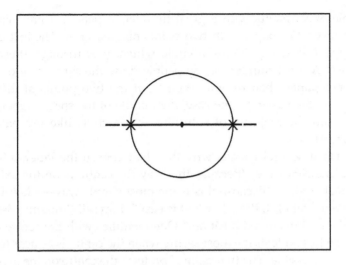

Figure 2.

expected but the boy did not get a bad mark. When the teacher demonstrated the expected solution, the boy exclaimed, "Oh, what a fool I am, I knew this!" (Figure 3).

When he told me the story, he asked in a tempered voice, "Tell me, what is there inside someone that doesn't let things come into his mind? Why does one stick so much to 'that circle'?" (The one with the two points on the axis.) I said, "I don't know. Neither do I know if 'people in general' stick to 'your' circle. We must find out."

The boy's question impressed me very much. I was inclined to think that he had discovered some truth. Later on, I carried out very

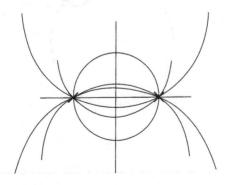

Figure 3.

simple experiments with a great number of people. I gave each of them a sheet of paper with two points marked on it. The instruction was the following: "Draw a circle which goes through these two points!" A great number of the people drew the same type of circle that my patient had drawn. Then I put the two points at different places on the paper. In one case, the middle of the sheet suggests the circle, but the majority of solutions was a circle like my patient's (Figure 4).

I asked several friends why they had chosen the latter solution. Some answers were: "Because this way the centre is on the axis and that feels right"; "Because this is the most simple way—when I have done one half of it, the other half is easy". I myself thought: "Because it is the best defended position." One identifies with the centre of his own circle, and feels the most secure when the centre is as near to both points as possible. The two points "protect" the centre on the axis. The desire for security is so strong that one is willing to disregard aesthetic and rational viewpoints, and, thus, does not use all the available space on the paper.

I share with you these observations, but do not propose to draw any general conclusions.

Later, I carried out a series of experiments with three sheets of paper. The first sheet was the same as before. On the second sheet, the

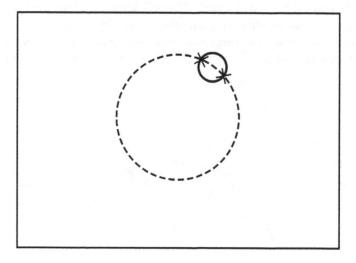

Figure 4.

two points were so close to the side of the paper that it was impossible to draw the type of circle that the majority had drawn in the first experiment: I tried to provoke a different solution. It was interesting to see how people stuck to their former solutions: they drew "potatoes" instead of circles and said, "Let's say this potato is a circle!" (Figure 5).

On the third sheet of paper, I tried to place the points in an extreme position so that the former solution was impossible, even in its symbolic form. I called it the "no-solution situation" (Figure 6).

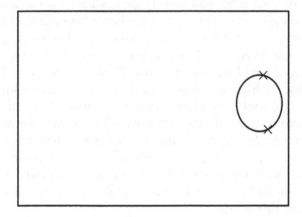

Figure 5.

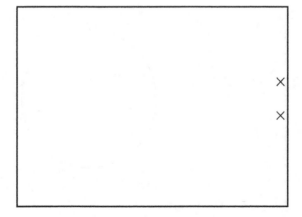

Figure 6.

Some people gave the paper back, saying that the task could not be solved; others smiled, suspecting a trick. Somebody asked, "Do you want to push me off the map?" Then she suddenly clutched her head and drew a long-awaited large circle (Figure 7).

I think this experience carries a kind of general truth that can be described the following way: "In an extremely marginal situation, sometimes one can discover an expanded space."

When Prince Andrej, in Tolstoy's *War and Peace*, fell on the battle-field of Austerlitz with a flag in his hand, he had the following thoughts: "What is this? Am I going to fall? I feel my knees bending beneath me"—and he was already on his back on the ground. He opened his eyes, hoping to see how the battle between the French and the artillery proceeded. He wanted to know whether the ginger-haired artillerist had been killed, and if the cannons had been seized or saved. But he could not see anything. There was nothing above him but the sky, the high sky; it was not cloudless but it was still immeasurably high, and grey clouds floated silently above him. "How silently, calmly, solemnly they float, so different from the way I have run," Prince Andrej thought. "That is not the way this Frenchman and the artillerists are pulling the cannon-stick from each other's hand. The clouds are floating through this infinite sky in quite a different way. How could I not see this infinite, high sky before? How happy I am to know this at last."

I have related my personal experience of the spatial aspects of emotions. I have also reported a playful experiment I carried out

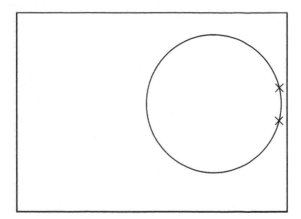

Figure 7.

many years ago. Congruency can be found between the two regarding the "extreme marginal position". A person solving the task of connecting two points to form a circle might discover how much more space can be found on the paper, and the one who has shifted "to the margin of life" might feel that "the world opens" to him/her.

Note

1.   Editors' note: Imre Hermann was Ferenczi's student and colleague. Hermann's obituary of Ferenczi can be found in Chapter Three.

References

Binswanger, L. (1933). *Über Ideenflucht* [*On the Escape of Ideas*]. Zürich: Niehaus.
Böszörményi, Z. (1959). *Megfigyelések egy új révületkeltő anyag hatására* [Observations on the influence of a new halucinogenic substance]. *Orvosi Hetilap, Vol. 100.*
Ferenczi, S. (1964). *Gulliver-Phantasien* [Gulliver fantasies]. *Bausteine für Psychoanalyse, III.* Bern: Hans Huber.
Fónagy, I. (1963). *Érzelmek kifejező mozgása a gége szintjén* [Expressive movements of emotions on the level of the larynx]. *Magyar Pszichológiai Szemle, No. 2.*
Helmholtz, H. (1876). The origin and meaning of geometrical axioms. *Mind, 3*(July): 21.
Hermann, I. (1943). *Az Ember ősi ösztonei* [Primaeval Instincts of Man]. Budapest: Magvetö.
Hermann, I. (2007). Néhány lelki jelenség térvonatkozása. In: *Magyar nyelvü cikkek és tanulmányok 1934–1971.* Budapest: Animula.
Kafka, F. (1925). *The Trial.* London: Penguin Modern Classics, 1994.

CHAPTER ELEVEN

Physics, metaphysics, and psychoanalysis

Tom Keve

Niels Bohr, the famous Danish physicist, owned a wooden cottage in the country where he liked to invite his physics colleagues for long and deep discussions. One day, a distinguished visitor was surprised to see a horseshoe hanging on the doorframe. "Is it possible, that you, of all people, believe this will bring you luck?" he asked. To which Bohr replied, "Of course not—but I understand it works whether or not you believe."

This chapter is about coincidences of history and coincidences of ideas. You do not have to believe, but I am told it works anyway.

In 1909, the triad of Ferenczi, Freud, and Jung travelled together to the USA, Freud and Jung as invited speakers at the Clark University 20th anniversary celebrations, and Ferenczi as Freud's intellectual "assistant". All three of them thought of this as a very significant event in their lives. Freud always considered that his international acceptance started with this conference. It was also the first exposure of Jung as an analytical expert in his own right and, in Jung's view at least, it was on this trip that the seeds of his break with Freud were planted.

Given how significant the event was in the history of psychoanalysis, it would be reasonable to conclude that Freud, or Freud and Jung, were the stars of the academic celebration. However, this was not the case. The *really* famous people invited to talk at Clark were not the analysts, but the physicists Ernest Rutherford and A. A. Michelson.[1] Both had very recently won Nobel Prizes: Michelson for Physics two years earlier and Rutherford for Chemistry in the previous year. And it is curious to reflect on the fact that just as twentieth-century psychoanalysis flowed from Freud, Jung, and Ferenczi, twentieth-century physics flowed from the work of the other two men. Michelson had shown experimentally that—unexpectedly—the motion of the earth through the ether did not affect the speed of light; that is to say, the speed of light was always constant. It was in order to explain this result that Einstein developed the theory of relativity, one of the two great pillars of modern physics. The other pillar, atomic physics and, later, quantum theory, flowed directly from the work, heritage, and school of Lord Rutherford.

The Clark celebration was a small event with few speakers, so almost certainly these five men, analysts and physicists, would have met one another. In a sense, this presentation is about what the five of them started and the kind of discussion they might enjoy, should they meet today.

Jung's interest in metaphysics is well known. Also quite well known is his connection with the great quantum physicist, Wolfgang Pauli, who was patient, friend, and collaborator on the physics–psychology interface (Meyer, 2001). Jung analysed hundreds of Pauli's dreams (Bair, 2003) and published a great many of them (Jung, 1968a–d).

Ferenczi's interest in both physics and metaphysics—and their relationship to the psyche—is less well known, yet he preceded Jung. In fact, it is quite likely that Jung's interest in such matters was ignited, or at least had its fires fanned, by Ferenczi. You will recall that Freud wrote to Ferenczi on 11 May 1911 on the subject of Jung's and Ferenczi's interest in mysticism: "I see that both of you can't be restrained. You should at least proceed in harmony with each other; these are dangerous expeditions, and I can't go along there" (Brabant, Falzeder, & Giampieri-Deutsch, 1993, p. 274).

Unfortunately, Ferenczi wrote very little on the subject of physics and metaphysics and their relationship to the psyche, compared with Jung's volumes. but Ferenczi was, arguably, more sophisticated in his views than Jung, and might even have been the deeper thinker of the two.

In 1899, when he was only twenty-six, Ferenczi published a paper entitled "Spiritism" (Ferenczi, 1899). There, he first expressed his views on the relationship between physics, metaphysics, and what would later be called psychoanalysis.

He wrote, "the following is beyond any doubt; that within each cognisant human being, there exists, flourishes and continuously operates a certain sensitivity toward things transcendental", and, later on,

> The majority so called of "civilised" society imbibes ideas of atomistic materialism during formal education. The world is but an endless collection of indivisible particles of various sizes, which, through their vibrating motion bring about light, heat, electricity, and so on, – and human self-awareness itself, is only an extraction of the constituent particles of the brain. What an easy task our school physics teacher had . . . who could lecture on these topics with the force of conviction. How simple it all was from his viewpoint! 60 to 70 types of atom (since then another ten elements have been discovered!), 8 or 10 sorts of vibrations of the ether, this is the essence of the Universe. Only fools spoke of the unity of all things, of the soul, of metaphysics. (p. 169)

But Ferenczi predicts that this is about to change. He writes,

> This rigid materialistic paradigm . . . today rules the roost with the large majority of educated medical men and natural scientists . . . we may be witnessing . . . a drastic change of paradigm . . . in the field of fundamental concepts. (ibid.)

In other words, Ferenczi predicted that a new scientific paradigm was about to be born. He prophesied a move from reductionist to holistic, from atomistic to an integral view of the world. Remember, this was 1899! He was writing about the unity of all things twenty to thirty years before Jung—about a holistic approach to physics twenty-five years before quantum theory.

In the same article, he continues, "Physics insists that metaphysics does not exist. Yet is it not the case that materialism is founded on unprovable dogma—matter and force—just as monotheism is, with its faith in God?" (ibid.).

In the Introduction to *Thalassa*, published in 1924, though Ferenczi stated that he had already formulated these ideas in 1915 and earlier, he writes,

... the conviction grew in me, that an interpretation into psychology of concepts belonging to the field of natural science, and into the natural sciences of psychological concepts, was inevitable and might be extremely fruitful.

The physicist is able to make the phenomena of his science comprehensible only when he compares them to "forces", "attraction", "repulsion", to "resistance", "inertia" and the like which are simply things with which we are acquainted from the mental side alone. (Ferenczi, 1924, p. 3)

In 1918, Ferenczi wrote an article in *Nyugat*, a literary journal whose editor, Ignotus, was a founder member of the Hungarian Psychoanalytic Society. The article was entitled "Spiritual development and the history of mechanics—a critique of Ernst Mach's 'Kultur und Mechanik'"; in fact, this was a critique of the introduction to the book, not of the book itself.

Before discussing what Ferenczi wrote, a few words about Ernst Mach, in order to illustrate the intricate web of personal contacts that is very much part of this story. Mach was, of course, a great physicist and very influential philosopher. Einstein stated that Mach was the single greatest influence on his work on relativity. We all know of Mach 1, Mach 2, etc. But here are some facts, which perhaps you do not all know. He was a friend and colleague of Joseph Breuer—the same Joseph Breuer who, as Freud declared at Clark University, "brought psychoanalysis into being". It was Mach who proposed Breuer for membership of the Imperial Academy of Sciences. When Ernst Mach, a professor of physics in Prague, was enticed to move to Vienna, one of his conditions was that he could name his chair to reflect his interests; he did so, and became Professor of the History and Theory of the Inductive Sciences at the University of Vienna. The person doing the enticing, and funding Mach's chair, was Theodore Gomperz. His wife, Elise Gomperz, was a grateful patient of Freud's, and it was she who eventually got Freud's professorship for him (with great difficulty, and only *extraordinarius*).

Mach was the guiding light of what became the Vienna Circle of philosophers. He was also a close personal friend and collaborator of William James, the philosopher and psychologist, who came to Clark in 1909 to hear Freud, and who was the one man Freud wanted to impress there. Incidentally, Jung wrote very positively of *his* meeting with James at Clark (Jung, 1949): "I was interested in parapsychology and my discussions with William James were chiefly about this subject and about the psychology of religious experience".

In addition, Mach was the godfather and mentor of the great quantum physicist I mentioned earlier in connection with Jung, Wolfgang Pauli. If that is not enough, I can add that Mach even wrote a book on the interpretation of dreams: *Analyse der Empfindungen* (1886). But then Freud and Mach's mutual friend Josef Popper-Lynkeus, physicist and philosopher, also wrote a book on dream interpretation (Popper-Lynkeus, 1899). These authors were only following a trend started by Mach's benefactor, Theodore Gomperz, who was the first of the Viennese scientist–philosophers to treat the subject in *Traumdeutung und Zauberie*, or Dream Interpretation and Magic (1866).

Freud was closely acquainted with all the above thinkers, and, I am told, also wrote a book on the interpretation of dreams (1900a).

So, what did Ferenczi write in the article entitled "Spiritual development and the history of mechanics—critical remarks on a work by Ernst Mach"?

He wrote (Ferenczi, 1918),

> My objective is to highlight the rich source of insights our scientists deprive themselves of by ignoring the results of psychoanalysis. Our dearest wish as psychoanalysts, is to work together with practicians of the exact sciences, just as Mach demands. We ask in return that the exact scientists make use of our techniques of psychological analysis and that they should not treat the psychological problems which interest them in isolation from the remaining psychic content. (p. 191)

Ferenczi goes on to make a plea for some kind of synthesis between psychoanalysis and physics . . .

> How long will it be before the physicist (who can even find soul in a mechanism) will offer his hand to the psychoanalyst (who in his turn perceives mechanics in the soul), so that they can combine forces to build up a view of the world which is not one sided, or "ideal". (ibid.)

In 1921, Ferenczi made a set of notes, hardly more than headings, which were published posthumously as the paper "Mathematics" (Ferenczi, 1955). These notes are full of the most insightful and sometimes provocative observations—I shall quote only a few:

... armed with the tools of psychoanalysis, we must try to increase our understanding of one special talent—mathematics.

The brain is a counting machine.

Mathematical genius is self-observation.

Mathematics is self-observation for the metapsychological processes of thought and action. Mathematics = self-observation of one's own conscious function.

The pure logician is the mathematician among psychologists.

The mathematician appears to have a fine self-observation for the metapsychic processes, finds formulas for the operation in the mind ... projects them onto the external world and believes that he has learnt through external experience. (p. 186)

And last ... "Query: Is mathematics abstraction from external experience? Or *a priori* knowledge? In other words is mathematics internal or external perception?" (ibid., p. 192).

It is clear from the above that Ferenczi recognised the need for a synthesis between physics–mathematics–logic on the one hand, and man's internal world on the other. It is hardly surprising that he did not achieve such a synthesis himself as, arguably, nobody has. Yet.

What was Ferenczi's connection with physics and mathematics? Well, he attended high school in Miskolc, where his teacher for these subjects (and also the school principal) was György Csorba (Moreau-Ricaud & Mádai, 1991), who is still remembered today as the most advanced and innovative teacher of mathematics and physics in Hungary at the time. At university in Vienna, Ferenczi was not registered for courses in either subject,[2] although he did overlap for one year with Ernst Mach's professorship, and might have attended his lectures. (It is most unlikely, given Mach's fame and Ferenczi's interests, that Ferenczi did not attend Mach's lectures.) But, in any case, the source or the link we should look for is elsewhere.

Let me digress and talk about John von Neumann, known to Hungarians as margittai Neumann János. Few experts would deny the status of von Neumann as the greatest mathematician of the twentieth century. Von Neumann did not win a Nobel Prize, because there is no Nobel Prize for Mathematics. He would have been a candidate for a Nobel Prize for Economics, but this award did not exist in von Neumann's lifetime. Von Neumann's achievements are legion: he laid the mathematical basis of quantum theory; he launched mathematical economics; he invented game theory; in the Manhattan project, he came up with the implosion technique that made the atom bomb possible; and he was the father of modern computers in theory and in practice: even today, every PC and mainframe computer is built according to what is known as the von Neumann architecture.

The von Neumann computer, affectionately known as JONIAC, only knew the letters A to E, though, of course, it was familiar with all the digits. When the programme crashed, the following error message was printed out

E2 A B1DE5 10

This gibberish was not immediately recognised by everyone as an expression of frustration by the computer's programmer, von Neumann's second wife, Klári. Hungarians who defocus a little will recognise the hidden meaning in the above – EZ A BIDES LÓ (literally "This stinking horse!" or, more colloquially, "That rotten beast!"). Apart from the humour, E2 A B1DE5 10 is of interest as an example of several meanings: in this case, at least three, (1) gibberish, (2) this stinking horse, and (3) this programme has just crashed, within the same set of symbols; a phenomenon very common in mystical or kabbalistic texts.

It turns out that John von Neumann was part of Ferenczi's extended family, with whom he had much contact, and it is also known that von Neumann's father consulted Ferenczi a number of times regarding John's education. Though it is unlikely, it may even be that John von Neumann was Ferenczi's famous "Little chanticleer", the boy who identified with a cockerel. It is certainly clear that the young John had a cockerel as his totem animal. This information is to be found, together with photographs of a representation of the totem cockerel, on the wall and in a stained-glass window of the von Neumann's second home in Buda (Nagy, 1987).

Ferenczi's brother in-law (Gizella's brother) was Ágoston Alcsuti (Altschul). Alcsuti's best friend was Miksa Neumann. These two men, Alcsuti and Neumann, married sisters, Lili Kann and Margit Kann. Miksa and Margit were the parents of John von Neumann. So, John von Neumann's uncle was Ferenczi's brother-in-law. But the link is much closer than that implies.

The Alcsutis and the Neumanns lived in the same building; they had one floor each at 62 Bajcsy-Zsilinsky út in Budapest. The whole edifice belonged to grandfather Kann, who lived on the top floor. All the children were brought up together as if in a large clan. There is even a published photo of John von Neumann, aged twelve, doing his homework with his cousin Lili Alcsuti, who was a few years younger (see below).

Lili Alcsuti (later Pedroni) was named after her aunt Lili Kann, John's mother. Her other aunt was, of course, Gizella Ferenczi. The Ferenczis lived close by and, according to the memoirs of John's younger brother Nicholas Vonneuman (1988), "Ferenczi was a close relative and member of the family circle. As a result, discussions about Freud and psychoanalysis were among the subjects frequently encountered around the dinner table" (p. 11).

This is a second example of the intricate network of personal relationships, which, I believe, have a very important role in how ideas form, spread, and cross-fertilise one another. For instance, Ferenczi was closely acquainted with the eminent mathematician Lipót Fejér and the physicist Rudolf Ortvay—the latter wanted to change professions and become a psychoanalyst instead of a physicist, but Ferenczi dissuaded him. Ferenczi was also very close to the Polányi family

The Ferenczis' niece, Lili Alcsuti, with her cousin, John von Neumann.

(mentioned several times in the Freud–Ferenczi correspondence, sometimes as Pollacsek or Pollatschek). Through the Galileo Circle, an intellectual student forum in which the Polányis had a leading role and where Ferenczi gave several talks on psychoanalysis, Ferenczi would also have been acquainted with the mathematician György Pólya, with Theodore von Kármán, and even with Mátyás Rákosi and George Lukács.

These types of contact were endless and quite often amazing. I have written about them in my book, *Triad* (Keve, 2000). Below are a few other examples of interrelationships that may be of interest.

Leo Szilárd, inventor of the nuclear chain reaction, and author of the "Einstein" letter to President Roosevelt, which started the Manhattan project to build the atom bomb, was closely connected to Ferenczi's circle. Ferenczi arranged a villa for Freud to spend his summer vacation in 1918 at Csorba Tó. The villa belonged to the Vidors (Regina and Emil).[3] Regina was a Freund, the sister of Toni, Emil Freund, and of Kata, Lajos Lévy's wife. Leo Szilárd was a nephew of Emil Vidor; Emil's sister, Tekla Vidor, was Leo Szilárd's mother. And Szilárd had confessed that, as a young man, "the love of his life" was Lajos Lévy's sister-in-law Mici (Emil Freund's wife) (Lanouette, 1992).

Theodor von Kármán has been described as the father of aerodynamics. He founded the famous Jet Propulsion Laboratory in California and was very much involved in military flying. In fact, in the 1930s, Göring invited him to come back to Germany to work on aircraft design for the Luftwaffe. "But I am a Jew," von Kármán protested; to which Göring replied, "*I* decide who is a Jew and who is not."

In 1918, von Kármán was Professor of Physics at Budapest, but when the Communists came to power he was replaced by Hevesy and von Kármán became Deputy Commissar for Culture. In that function he signed (together with George Lukács, the Commissar) Ferenczi's appointment as professor of psychoanalysis.[4] The point of this digression is that von Kármán was a first cousin of Lajos Lévy.[5]

Lajos Lévy was a very close personal friend and physician to both Ferenczi and Freud, and his brother-in-law, Toni Freund, was the great financial benefactor of psychoanalysis and also a close friend of Ferenczi and Freud. To complete the circle, we should recall that Toni Freund's sister, Regina, was Leo Szilárd's aunt.

I would like to give one last example of interrelationships. John von Neumann, together with Kurt Gödel and Paul Bernays, created what is known as axiomatic set theory, an important but highly technical sector of modern mathematics. Gödel was a patient in Wagner-Jauregg's clinic when Anna Freud was an assistant there, and Paul Bernays was Freud's "nephew". In fact, Bernays was Anna Freud's second cousin and the only man, according to Elisabeth Young-Bruehl, to have been kissed by Anna in a less than (or more than?) Platonic way (Young-Bruehl, 1998). We even know, from Andreas Salomé's letter to Freud, that Anna "stirred up quite a storm of passion in him, but nevertheless returned home [from a party where Paul took her] totally unseared by these flames".

The last work von Neumann wrote before he died in 1957 (in fact, written on his deathbed) was entitled *The Computer and the Brain* (von Neumann, 1958). The title puts one in mind of Ferenczi's remark forty years earlier in "Mathematics", that "the brain is a counting machine".

Although John von Neumann starts his book with the apology, "I am neither a neurologist nor a psychiatrist, but a mathematician", he concludes, "I suspect that a deeper mathematical study of the nervous system will affect the understanding of the aspects of mathematics itself. In fact it may alter the way in which we look upon mathematics and logics proper" (p. 1).

And this not from a mystic, but from the greatest mathematician of the century. One might think that his words could have come straight from Ferenczi's paper, "Mathematics", and, in a profound sense, they did.

John von Neumann's closest friend at school in Budapest (the Fasori Gimnázium), and a close friend and colleague for the rest of his life, was Eugene Wigner, a world famous quantum physicist and Nobel Prize winner. Wigner is famous for many great achievements, and also for his philosophical ideas, published in a paper entitled The unreasonable effectiveness of mathematics in the natural sciences" (Wigner, 1960) and elsewhere. How odd that the universe follows mathematical rules instead of being just chaotic, he wrote. And how *extremely* odd that these rules are simple enough to be understood by a high-school student! I should add that Hungarian high schools such as the Fasori Gimnázium were and are of an exceptional quality, but the sentiment remains true, nevertheless.

The quality of Hungarian high schools is very relevant to our story. John von Neumann (father of the digital computer), Eugene Wigner (winner of the Nobel Prize for physics), John Harsányi (winner of the

Nobel Prize for economics), and Theodore Herzl (the Father of Zionism), all attended the same high school—Fasori Gimnázium.

This is about par for the course. The Piarist Gimnázium, about a mile east of the Fasori, also produced two Nobel Prize Winners, George Olah and George Hevesy, both in Chemistry. The Minta Gimnázium, founded by Mór Kármán and located about a half-mile from each of the other two, produced not only the founder's son, Theodore von Kármán, but also the physicist Edward Teller (the so-called "father of the hydrogen bomb"), Michael Polányi and Nicholas Kurti (both Fellows of the Royal Society), and two Lords of the Realm, economists Lord Thomas Balogh and Lord Michael Káldor (Marx, 1997).

Marx also wrote,

> There are phenomena which physics cannot yet describe. For example it cannot describe life, emotion or consciousness. This situation is like not taking gravitation into account would be. But gravitation exists and life exists. I am here, I feel joy and desire. It used to be said that man is subdued by the laws of physics, and his emotions are irrelevant. I cannot accept that! I am convinced that the sequence of events is influenced by my consciousness in a similar way as it is influenced by the force of gravity. (1997, p. 194)

I hope I am not the only one who can see the effect of Ferenczi in these words.

There is no doubt that Wigner would have known Ferenczi, both via von Neumann and also via Ortvay, just as there is little doubt that Ferenczi had John von Neumann (and, to a lesser extent, John's mentor Lipót Fejér) in mind when he wrote "Mathematics". When Ferenczi wrote this paper, John von Neumann was only eighteen years old, but was already recognised as a mathematical genius and registered for a doctorate in mathematics at the University of Budapest.

So far, I have concentrated on Ferenczi and the Hungarian connection, for obvious reasons, but the ideas are not restricted to that sector. Certainly, the interaction of Jung and Pauli are very significant, and also much better known than the Ferenczi-centred ones. But these two complexes are not independent of one another. The early link between Ferenczi and Jung is well known and needs little elaboration. There was an intense professional relationship between von Neumann and

Pauli in the field of physics, as well as a strong personal bond between them: for instance, von Neumann was entrusted with Pauli's financial transactions in the USA, von Neumann and Wigner were in constant communication by letter with Ortvay, some Ortvay–Ferenczi correspondence survives, and Ortvay was a patient of Pauli's father, a professor of medicine. There are so many cross-links at the personal level that the total result looks like some intricate spider's web.

Now I would like to move to more general ideas. Searching for links between the psyche, the material world, and metaphysics is not new—in fact, it is an ancient pursuit. It is what primitive people were doing; it is what the alchemists were doing. Incidentally, there is an interesting link back to Ferenczi; his famous "mutual analysand", Elisabeth Severn, was a member of the Alchemical Society, wrote papers on alchemy, and described herself professionally as a "metaphysician".

The links between psychoanalysis and mysticism in general (and Kabbalah in particular) have been written about by Bakan (1965), by Berke (1996), and by Jung himself in many works.

It is said that in the sixteenth to the eighteenth centuries, every Jewish home had a copy of two books. One was Dream Interpretation, or *Pitron Calmot*, by a sage called Sol Almoli, and the other was the *Zohar*, or Book of Splendour, written in the thirteenth century by a Spanish Kabbalist, Moses de Leon. The *Zohar* was described by a twentieth-century commentator as a psychoanalysis of God. And since Moses de Leon, like most of us, knew nothing of God but knew a little about himself, the book can better be described as a psychoanalysis of Man.

Gershom Scholem wrote of the Zohar,

> . . . the chief interest of the Kabbalah for us [lies] in the light it throws on the 'historical psychology' of the Jews. Here each individual was the totality. And this is the source of the fascination which the great symbols of the Kabbalah possess for a historian, no less than a psychologist. (1988, p. 239)

Incidentally, Scholem was the foremost academic scholar of Kabbalah. He was Professor of Kabbalah at the Hebrew University in Jerusalem, later Dean of that university, and President of the Israeli Academy of Sciences. In his youth, he was a close friend of Sigmund's niece, Toni

Freud (Scholem, 1997), and he later married a Freud, Fanya. In the 1950s, he was close to Jung and to the physicist Wolfgang Pauli; he was also a frequent lecturer at Jung's Eranos conferences.

Kabbalah, in part, is also about numbers: there is an aspect of Kabbalah, called *Gematria*, which can be described as number mysticism. It has to do with special numbers, magic numbers, integers, the numerical value of words, and the verbal equivalents of numbers. In Hebrew, numerals are denoted by letters, so that a set of letters can code for one word, or (because vowels are omitted) for several words, or for a number. Equally, any number will also code for words. This leads to a rich possibility of hidden meanings which, in a believer's view, are divinely inspired.

As an example, the Gematria value of the Hebrew word Kabbalah is 137. This number, or something very close to it, also turns out to be "the magic number of physics" (the inverse fine structure constant, which has a value of about 137.036).

I would like now to talk about the links between physics and mysticism and between physics and the psyche. To do this, I have to say just a few words about quantum physics.

Quantum physics is about the way small things behave. It has the distinction of being the most successful, most accurate, and most thoroughly checked scientific theory there has ever been. It is not esoteric, in that it is an everyday phenomenon. We are confronted with it constantly in our lives in the modern world. Yet, quantum physics is counter-intuitive. It is *not* causal or deterministic.

The observer and the observed are intimately connected. According to quantum physics, "everything" is discontinuous: the universe has a quantised or grainy structure, and changes occur in discrete steps, which can be counted, hence the rule of the integer.

The "knowability" of the universe is limited, not by lack of accurate enough instruments, or even by limitations of the human intellect, but, intrinsically, by its very nature.

These are the results of observation and of mathematics. Yet, they sound as if they were straight out of the Kabbalah or some other mystical work, a point that did not escape the physicists in the 1930s. They jokingly, or perhaps not jokingly, referred to the Physics Institute in Munich under Sommerfeld (a non-Jew) as the Institute of Number Mysticism, and described the properties of the lines in optical spectra as kabbalistic. And the greatest mystery of physics was deemed to be (and perhaps still is) discovering why the inverse of the fine structure constant has a value very close to the integer 137, the magic number of physics.

There are deep connections between quantum physics and mathematics on one side, and psyche or psychoanalysis on the other.

There is a famous issue in quantum physics called the measurement problem. This refers to the fact that, in a quantum physical observation, the observer and the observed are one total system: hence, the observer affects the observed and vice versa, so that, in a sense, one never knows what "really" happened or would have happened if the observation had not been made.

Furthermore, it is the act of observation that makes an event "real". It is the act of observation that changes situations from quantum potentialities into concrete actualities: this postulate is due to none other than von Neumann.

And it was Wigner who proposed that it is consciousness that creates the actual world.

Thus, quantum physics teaches us that the material world and the world of consciousness are linked at the most fundamental level, and that the observer and the observed can only be understood as one total system, because of the effect they have on each other.

Intriguingly, and probably not coincidentally, this situation in physics, where the observer intrinsically affects the observed and vice versa (and, therefore, both observer and observed must be analysed as a single system) is exactly Ferenczi's mutual analysis. In mutual analysis, the observer and the observed (the analyst and the analysand) mutually affect one another and the only hope of disentangling the two is by analysing the total, analyst and analysand, as one system.

Can it be a coincidence that the protagonists of the very same idea, in physics and in psychoanalysis, are so closely related?

This parallel between the measurement problem and psychoanalysis was not lost on the physicists. Niels Bohr, the father of quantum physics, wrote in 1932, ". . . the necessity of considering the interaction between the measuring instruments and the object under investigation in atomic physics exhibits a close analogy to the peculiar difficulties in psychological analysis" (p. 458).

I would like to digress and mention briefly the great nineteenth-century mathematician Cantor, who founded the mathematics of infinity. He studied infinities—in the plural, for he discovered that there are various orders of infinities, or trans-finite numbers. Cantor considered this study of infinities a divine search, an investigation into the nature of God (see, for instance, Aczel (2000)). He was also something of a kabbalist. The symbol he gave to his infinities—a symbol that is used universally even today—was the Aleph, the first letter of the Hebrew alphabet, a letter which also signifies the numeral 1 and which, in Kabbalah, stands for infinite nature and the oneness of God. Unfortunately, Cantor, largely unrecognised in his lifetime but now considered one of the greatest of all mathematicians, suffered from chronic depression and died in a mental institution.

As if all the problems of quantum physics were not enough, Gödel, whom I mentioned in connection with von Neumann, proved in the 1930s that *all* mathematical systems are either incomplete or inconsistent. So even mathematics is not on an absolutely firm foundation. Gödel's proof is straight out of the Kabbalah: his technique is now called Gödel numbering. Just as in a Kabbalistic text, where Hebrew letters could stand for words and numbers at the same time, so that two "messages" could be encoded or decoded in the same "text", Gödel used numbers as shorthand for mathematical symbols as well as representing themselves, so that two "statements" could be created simultaneously with the same set of symbols. In this way, he could construct a mathematical "sentence" that simultaneously stated one thing and its opposite. Gödel was Einstein's closest friend for the last twenty years of the former's life. He (Gödel) was described by John von Neumann as the greatest logician since Aristotle. He was undoubtedly a mystic and, like Cantor, he, too, succumbed to mental illness, became psychotic, and died in a psychiatric institution.

Let us return to Wigner. Karl Pribram, Professor of Psychology and Cognitive Science, wrote (Pribram, 2003),

> Once, Eugene Wigner remarked that in quantum physics we no longer have observables, only observations. Tongue in cheek I asked whether that meant that quantum physics is really psychology, expecting a gruff reply to my sassiness. Instead, Wigner beamed a happy smile of understanding and replied, yes, yes, that's exactly correct. If indeed one wants to take the reductive path, one ends up with psychology, not particles. In fact, it is mathematics, a psychological process that is the language of physics. (p. 82)

To paraphrase: *physics is psychology*, because physics is mathematics and mathematics is psychology.

As I said earlier, Wigner pointed out that the universe follows mathematical rules, which even a high-school student could understand. But then, the next question is, what is mathematics? If mathematics is a creation of the human mind, why does the universe bother to follow it? If mathematics is not a creation of the human mind, then what is it? Is it perhaps some kind of reflection of the universe *in* the human mind? But *that* sounds like nothing more or less than mysticism . . .

And did not Ferenczi pose the same question, much more pertinently, in his paper "Mathematics", asking, "Is mathematics internal or external perception?"

Ferenczi gave his own answer to the ancient question, "What is real?" In "Mathematics", he wrote, "Proof for the reality of the external world: The introspectively acquired (a priori) mathematical laws prove also to be valid in the 'external world'" (1955, p. 191).

And here we come to the physics–psyche issue of our time. Modern physics ends up in mathematics—"just" equations. When a theory, such as quantum theory, works, there is no dispute about the equations. They are not contradicted by experience. They work, they predict, they are useful. You can build things with them—atom bombs and transistors, compact disc players and television sets. But there are deep disputes, not unlike religious disputes, about what these equations "mean", if anything; what reality is like, or even if reality has any meaning. These are like religious arguments—they are certainly spiritual arguments and, like religion, they are engendered by a psychological need in their human protagonists.

Human beings need to put pictures to the equations. And where do such pictures come from once we have gone beyond the everyday world? They can only come from within; archaic, archetypal, spiritual, transcendental, numinous, mystical. Of course, some say (Bohr was one) that there is no need for such pictures, that the only reality is the equation, that there is no sense in talking about what "really" happens.

But, for most humans, this is a psychologically untenable situation. They need a picture. They need "reality". Einstein was one of these. Famously, he talked about the *Alte* (God) not playing dice, and he maintained that the *Alte* might be mysterious but He is not vicious.

Einstein could not accept that below quantum theory there was not another layer waiting to be discovered. He had no evidence for this except what he felt within. He could not accept, again on spiritual grounds rather than physical, that there can be indeterminacy in the universe. He had a famous and long-running debate with Bohr, not about the equations of quantum physics, but about their meaning. In a very famous paper written in 1935 (usually referred to as EPR), Einstein proposed a thought experiment concerning two electrons obeying quantum theory, which led to such an "obviously" ridiculous result that, as Einstein wrote, "no reasonable definition of reality could be expected to permit this" (Einstein, Podolsky, & Rosen, 1935, p. 777).

You might be bemused by the phrase *no reasonable definition of reality*, especially when I tell you that about thirty years ago, Einstein was proved unequivocally wrong both experimentally and theoretically. From which, one may conclude that we inhabit a world that is outside of any *reasonable definition of reality*.

Or, as the science writer and Professor of Mathematics, Amir Aczel, put it, "God *does* play dice, and why not?—after all He knows the result of the throw beforehand" (2002, p. 106).

It was during Ferenczi's life that the great change occurred, that physics was reduced to mathematics and "understanding" became a psychological problem. As Ferenczi describes in "Mathematics", the explanations beyond equations which we demand come from a mirroring of the inner world; from beliefs, Jungian archetypes, remnants of religious images, metaphysical prejudices, and spiritual preconceptions.

Yet again, Ferenczi foresaw this when he wrote, in "Mathematics",

> The mathematician appears to have a fine self-observation for the metapsychic processes, he finds formulas for the operation in the mind . . . projects them onto the external world and believes that he has learnt through external experience. (1955, p. 195)

There is a very deep psychological need in most of us, especially the non-religious, that something, even if it is just a single concept, be permanent, fundamental, and unchanging in the universe. Physicists constantly seek such concepts, ones that are simple and sympathetic to the needs of the human psyche. And yes, one may argue that such a quest is a surrogate for religion.

One such fundamental truth is the belief in the law of conservation of energy. Physicists cling to this as religious zealots do to their "truths". Every now and then, theories are proposed counter to it, but such "heretical" proposals invariably raise an enormous degree of opposition (psychologically driven) and so far have always been shot down. One such proposal was in the 1930s, when it was Pauli who saved the day, and the law of conservation of energy, through his postulate of the existence of a new particle, the neutrino. This was an almost kabbalistic proposal: a particle with no mass and no charge, yet "real", nevertheless. The neutrino remained only a postulate for thirty years, but was found through experiments in the 1950s.

So far, the law of conservation of energy is safe. But the so-called constants of nature—numbers that supposedly are fixed for all space and all time, like the gravitational constant—are in grave danger. We live in an age of physics when the constancy of the constants of nature is regularly called into question. We have accepted for a hundred years that the speed of light is constant: Michelson, the other speaker at Clark University, demonstrated this fact with a classical experiment. Accepting his result that the speed of light is constant has led to all kinds of complications, which we call relativity, but, because of his experiment, because relativity theory predicts things which can be measured, and because it is deeply satisfying to have such a firm, fundamental constant, we accept the constancy of the speed of light and the resulting complications. But beware! In the last couple of years, observations by the Hubble Space telescope seem to show that the inverse fine structure constant—137—the magic number of physics, might have had a different value in the past. Which would probably mean that the speed of light has changed since the early days of the universe.[6]

People are now scrambling to find reasons why this is, after all, not the case. The history of physics is full of such episodes, when tremendous ingenuity had to be exercised to save various conservation laws.

But, sometimes, new information gives us no choice except to give up such semi-religious beliefs. And when we are forced to do this, when these inner images are shown, after all, to be incorrect, we pay a high psychological price.

Symmetry is such a semi-religious area. Our souls demand it. Most of fundamental research in physics has one way or another been a search for symmetry. There is a need in us to believe that symmetry is fundamental.

One type of symmetry is called parity. The theoretical basis for it—the law of conservation of parity—was formulated by none other than our friend Eugene Wigner in the 1930s. Parity is a very fundamental, but very simple, symmetry. It says that, as far as the universe is concerned, left and right are equivalent. This is a deeply satisfying result. Which is why it caused such consternation when it was proved experimentally that this symmetry is not fundamental and is sometimes broken. Pauli, for one, was very profoundly affected; some say he was devastated by the psychological impact. The very last letter he wrote to Jung was about this cataclysmic event.[7] "I shall now attempt to explain to you about mirror symmetry, a curious mixture of physics and psychology", he wrote to Jung. It was also in this letter that Pauli coined a phrase, later to become famous: "It is now clear that God is a weak left-hander after all".

Pauli died six months later, having had no further contact with Jung. On his deathbed, Pauli said he wished he could talk to Jung just one more time. Although a young man of fifty-seven, Pauli knew that he would not leave his hospital room alive. How? He pointed out to a visitor that his hospital room was number 137, the famous, mystical, magic number of physics, which he took to be a sign from within.

Given that the title of my chapter was "Physics, metaphysics, and psychoanalysis", I should like to finish with the three quotes, which I included on the dustcover of my book.

First, from the physicist: "I have some doubts whether Jewish mysticism is fundamentally different from the non-Jewish—I am interested in mysticism in general" (Pauli, quoted in Keve, 2000, p. 257).

From the metaphysicist: "the Kabbalistic way consists of an amalgamation in the soul of man of the principles of mathematical and natural science . . . (Abulafila, quoted in Scholem, 1988, p. 153).

And from the psychoanalyst: "importation into psychology concepts belonging to the field of natural science, and into the natural sciences of psychological concepts is inevitable and might prove extremely useful" (Ferenczi, 1924, p. 3).

Notes

1. Rutherford's paper at Clark was entitled "History of the alpha rays from radio-active substances"; Michelson's paper was a description of his new engine for ruling diffraction gratings.
2. Letter from Pillinger Elfriede to Michael Balint, 10 March 1967—with thanks to Dr Judith Dupont.
3. See letters from Sigmund Freud to Sandor Ferenczi, August 8 1917, and September 10 1918. In: Falzeder and Brabant (1996), pp. 230–232 and pp. 292–293.
4. The document was part of the special Ferenczi Exhibition at the London Freud Museum, curated by the Sandor Ferenczi Society of Budapest in conjunction with the Ferenczi conference, 2004. Kármán's signature is easily legible.
5. Lajos Lévy's mother was née Kármán. Mór Kármán, founder of the Minta Gimnázium and father of Theodor, was her brother.
6. If the fine structure constant has changed, then one or more of h, c, or e must have changed (these being Planck's constant, the speed of light, and the charge on an electron). Theoreticians believe that a change in c is more "likely" than in the other two.
7. Letter 76P dated 5 August 1957, in Meyer (2001).

References

Aczel, A. D. (2000). *The Mystery of the Aleph*. New York: Four Walls Eight Windows.

Aczel, A. D. (2002). *Entanglement, the Greatest Mystery in Physics*. New York: Four Walls Eight Windows.

Bair, D. (2003). *Jung: A Biography*. New York: Little, Brown.

Bakan, D. (1965). *Sigmund Freud and the Jewish Mystical Tradition*. New York: Schocken Books [reprinted, London: Free Association Books, 1991].

Berke, J. H. (1996). Psychoanalysis and Kabbalah. *Psychoanalytic Review*, 83: 849–863.

Bohr, N. (1932). Light and life. Presented at the International Congress on Light Therapy, Copenhagen, 15 August 1932, also in *Nature*, 131: 458, 1933.

Brabant, E., Falzeder, E., & Giampieri-Deutsch, P. (1993). *The Correspondence of Sigmund Freud and Sandor Ferenczi, Volume 1, 1908–1914*. Cambridge, MA: Harvard University Press.

Einstein, A., Podolsky, B., & Rosen, N. (1935). Can quantum-mechanical description of reality be considered Ccmplete? *Physical Review, 47*: 777.

Falzeder, E., & Brabant, E. (Eds.) (1996). *The Correspondence of Sigmund Freud and Sandor Ferenczi, Volume 2, 1914–1919*. Cambridge, MA: Harvard University Press.

Ferenczi, S. (1899). Spiritism. In: T. Keve (Trans.) (2000), *Triad: The Physicists, the Analysts, the Kabbalists* (pp. 168–172). London: Rosenberger & Krausz.

Ferenczi, S. (1918). Spiritual development and the history of mechanics— critical remarks on a work by Ernst Mach. In: T. Keve (Trans.) (2000), *Triad: The Physicists, the Analysts, the Kabbalists* (pp. 188–191). London: Rosenberger & Krausz.

Ferenczi, S. (1924). *Thalassa*, published in English as *Thalassa, a Theory of Genitality*. London: Maresfield Library, 1989.

Ferenczi, S. (1955). Mathematics [c. 1920]. In: M. Balint (Ed.), *Final Contributions to the Problems and Methods of Psycho-Analysis* (pp. 183–196). London: Hogarth Press [reprinted, London: Karnac, 1994].

Freud, S. (1900a). *The Interpretation of Dreams. S.E., 4–5*. London: Hogarth.

Gomperz, T. (1866). *Traumdeutung und Zauberie*. Vienna: Vortrag.

Jung, C. G. (1949). C. G. Jung letter to Virginia Payne, July 23, 1949, http://des.emory.edu/mfp/jamesjung.html

Jung, C. G. (1968a). Individual dream symbolism in relation to alchemy. In: *Collected Works of C. G. Jung, Vol. 12* (2nd edn) (pp. 39–46). New Haven, NJ: Princeton University Press.

Jung, C. G. (1968b). Dream 26, *ibid.*, p. 172.

Jung, C. G. (1968c). Dream 17, *ibid.*, p. 138.

Jung, C. G. (1968d). Psychology and Religion. In: *Collected Works of C. G. Jung, Vol. 11* (2nd edn) (p. 24). New Haven, NJ: Princeton University Press.

Keve, T. (2000). *Triad: The Physicists, the Analysts, the Kabbalists*. London: Rosenberger & Krausz.

Lanouette, W. (1992). *Genius in the Shadows, a Biography of Leo Szilárd, the Man Behind the Bomb*. New York: Maxwell Macmillan International.

Mach, E. (1886). *Analyse der Empfindungen*. Jena: Verlag Gustav Fischer.

Marx, G. (1997). *The Voice of the Martians*. Budapest: Akademiai Kiado.

Meyer, C. A. (Ed.) (2001). *Atom and Archetype—The Pauli/Jung Letters 1932–1958*. New Haven, NJ: Princeton University Press.

Moreau-Ricaud, M., & Mádai, G. (1991). Sandor Ferenczi les années de lycée (1882–1890) [Sandor Ferenczi, the high-school years]. *Revue Internationale d'Histoire de la Psychanalyse, 4*: 659–669.

Nagy, F. (Ed.) (1987). *Neumann János és a "magyar titok" a dokumentumok Tükrében* [John (von) Neumann and the "Hungarian secret" as mirrored by documents]. Budapest: Országos Műszaki Információs Központ és Könyvtár.

Popper-Lynkeus, J. (1899). *Die Phantasien eines Realisten* [A Realist's Fantasies]. Dresden: Carl Reissner.

Pribram, K. (2003). Proceedings of the Conference Towards a Science of Consciousness, Prague, 6–10 July 2003.

Scholem, G. (1977). *Von Berlin nach Jerusalem*. Frankfurt am Main: Suhrkamp. English edition: H. Zohn (Trans.), *From Berlin to Jerusalem: Memories of My Youth*. New York: Schocken, 1980].

Scholem, G. (1988). *Major Trends in Jewish Mysticism*. New York: Schoken Books.

Von Neumann, J. (1958). *The Computer and the Brain*. New Haven, CT: Yale University Press.

Vonneuman, N. (1988). *John von Neumann as Seen by His Brother*. Washington, DC: Library of Congress.

Wigner, E. (1960). The unreasonable effectiveness of mathematics in the natural sciences. *Communications in Pure and Applied Mathematics, 13*: 1–14.

Young-Bruehl, E. (1998). *Anna Freud*. New York: Macmillan.

INDEX

abuse, 65
  child, 65, 121–122
  sexual, 59, 64–65
Aczel, A. D., 171, 173, 176
affect, 71–72, 81, 119, 170
aggression, 59, 65–66, 70, 75, 117–119, 140, 145–148 *see also*: sexual
Alchemical Society, 168
Alcsuti, A., 106, 163–164
Alexander, F., xxi, 132, 137
ambivalence, 13, 22, 35, 47, 49, 70
American Psychoanalytic Association, 60
Andreas-Salomé, L., xiii, 34, 87, 94, 166
anti-Semitism, 45, 48, 51, 55, 103–105
anxiety, 18–19, 26, 62, 72, 76, 79, 113, 116, 119, 136
  castration, 116
  hidden, 18
  neurotic, 116
  separation, 116, 136

attachment, 18, 64, 70, 76
  theory, 82
Auschwitz, 66, 107
Az Est, 1

Baczoni, M., 2, 7, 11
Bair, D., 158, 176
Bakan, D., 168, 176
Balint, A., xxi, xxiv, 78, 82, 87, 124–125
Balint, G., 47, 52
Balint, M., xiii–xviii, xxi–xxii, xxiv, 2, 14–15, 21, 28, 46, 52, 64, 73, 77–78, 81–82, 87, 90, 92, 94, 114, 125, 129–137, 176
behaviour, 18–19, 65, 104, 118, 122, 125, 130, 134–135, 139, 141, 147–148
  hypocritical, 19
  instinctive, 140
  peer, 62
Berke, J. H., 168, 176

Bible, The, 148
Binswanger, L., 144, 155
Bion, W. R., 71, 80, 82
    vertex, 71
Bohr, N., xviii, 157, 170, 172–173, 176
Bollas, C., 131–132, 135, 137
Bolsheviks, 9
Böszörményi, Z., 142, 155
Bowlby, J., 64, 66, 141
Brabant, E., 108, 158, 176
British Psychoanalytical Society, xiii, xxiii, 23, 25, 28
Budapest Congress, 15, 23, 44
Budapest Hírlap, 2
Budapest Medical Association, xvii, 45
Buddhism, 103

Catholic, 103, 105
Christianity, 103
Clark University, xviii, 157, 160, 174
Cohen, J., 121, 126
Communism, 43–45, 48–50, 139, 165
conscious(ness), 16–17, 32, 47, 51, 60, 89, 114, 117, 120–121, 123, 132, 143, 162, 167, 170 *see also*: self, unconscious(ness)
    sub-, 9
countertransference, xxii, 61, 63, 130
    see also: transference
Crossman, R., 49, 53

Domes, M., 122, 126

ego, 14, 46, 56–58, 63–64, 71–73, 77, 116, 119–120, 131, 135, 140–146
Einstein, A., xv, 5, 37, 158, 160, 171–173, 177
    theory of relativity, xv, xviii, 5, 9, 158, 160, 174
ELTE Eötvös Loránd University, 97
Erős, F., 22, 26, 28

Fairbairn, W. R. D., 64, 66
Falzeder, E., 108, 158, 176

fantasy, 20, 61, 65, 71, 75, 81, 116, 119–123, 132, 146 *see also*: unconscious(ness)
Farkasrét Jewish Cemetery, 2
Fascism, 40, 44, 48–50
Federn, P., 2, 43
Ferenczi, S. cited works, 11, 28, 32–34, 37, 43, 45–46, 53, 61–62, 64–65, 67, 69, 71–73, 79, 81–83, 89–90, 93–95, 106, 108, 111–115, 117–120, 122–124, 126–127, 130, 137, 146, 155, 159–162, 172–173, 175, 177
Fónagy, I., 145, 155
Frank, A., 19
free association, 15–16, 19, 129
Freud, S., xv–xviii, xxi, 1, 3–5, 8–13, 15–17, 20, 22, 24–27, 33–35, 37, 39, 41–42, 44–53, 55–64, 66–67, 69–77, 79, 81–84, 88–91, 93–95, 98–108, 111–112, 114–119, 121–122, 124, 126–127, 129–130, 132, 141, 157–158, 160–161, 164–166, 169, 176–177
    Anna O, xiv, 17
    Rat Man, 81
Fromm, E., xvii, 44, 46, 48–49, 53, 56, 60, 64
Füstöss, L., 98, 107–108

Galileo Circle, 42–43, 47, 165
Giampieri-Deutsch, P., 108, 158, 176
Gomperz, T., 160–161, 177
Gribinski, M., 88, 95
Groddeck, G., 113, 127
Grunberger, B., 72, 84
guilt, 26, 65, 74, 103, 114, 119
Gyógyászat, 90–91, 112

Hajdu, L., 50–51, 125
Haynal, A., xvii–xviii, 58, 67, 73, 84, 88, 91–92, 95, 115
Heisenberg, W., 98, 107
Helmholtz, H., 143, 155
Hermann, I., xiii–xvi, xviii, xxi, xxiv, 2, 22, 32, 37, 44, 48, 50–52, 82,

114–115, 119, 124, 127, 139–149, 155
Hevesy, G., 97–98, 107, 165, 167
Hitler, A., 9, 51, 57
Hoffer, A., 63, 67
Hollós, I., xxi, 91, 114, 124, 127
Holocaust, 65–66
Hungarian Psychoanalytic Society, 31, 114, 160
Hungarian Psychoanalytical Association, xiv, 1–2, 41–42, 50–51

Ignotus, xiv–xvi, 2–3, 10, 28, 31, 37, 41–42, 53, 91–92, 160
Imperial Academy of Sciences, 160
International Psychoanalytical Association (IPA), xxi, xxiv, 2, 58
intervention, 16–17, 62–63, 121

Jászi, O., 43–44, 53
Jew, 2, 9, 41, 45, 50–51, 90, 103, 107, 165, 168–169, 175
Jones, E., xiii–xvi, xxi–xxii, 4, 21–22, 25–26, 28, 35–37, 58–59
Journal of the Psychical Society, 26
Jung, C. G., xviii, 34, 57, 92, 101, 103–104, 157–161, 167–169, 173, 175, 177

Kabbalah, xix, 168–169, 171
Kafka, F., 146, 155
Karinthy, F., xiv, 10–11, 28–29, 31, 37, 42, 92–93
Keve, T., xiii–xiv, xvi–xix, 165, 175, 177
Khan, M. M. R., 116–117, 127, 131, 135, 137
King, P., 26, 29
Kinston, W., 121, 126
Klein, M., xiii, xvi, xxi–xxii, xxiv, 27, 56, 58, 71, 73, 75–76, 84
Kosztolányi, D., 10, 29, 31, 37, 42, 87–88, 92–95
Kurtzweil, E., 58, 67

Lanouette, W., 165, 189
Lanouzière, J., 75, 84

Laplanche, J., xviii, 74, 84, 118, 127
Lister, J., 36
Little, M. I., 131–132, 137
Lorin, C., 88, 90–91, 95
Lukács, G., 50–53, 88, 92, 165

Mach, E., 160–162, 177
Mádai, G., 89–90, 96, 162, 177
Magyar Hírlap, 2
Márai, S., xiv, xvi–xvii, 6–7, 10, 29, 93
Marcuse, H., xvii, 43, 53
Marx, G., 47, 49, 52, 167, 177
Marxism, xvii, 44, 47–52, 56
Masson, J. M. M., 72, 84, 116
Meyer, C. A., 158, 176–177
Michelson, A. A., xviii, 158, 174, 176
Möbius strip, 143
Moreau, M., 87, 95
Moreau-Ricaud, M., xvii–xviii, 42, 53, 88–91, 94–96, 162, 177
mother, xvi, 7, 19, 33, 61–63, 70, 74–75, 113, 117–119, 122, 125, 131, 140–141, 146–147, 188
body, 5
–infant relationship, 46, 117, 122, 140–141
Musil, R., 40, 53

Nagy, F., 107–108, 163, 178
National Institute of Mental and Nervous Diseases, 50
National Library of Budapest, 90
Nazi, 40, 51, 139
New York Psychoanalytic Institute, 59
New York Psychoanalytic Society, 59
Nobel Prize, 158, 162, 166–167

object, 3, 133–134, 136, 140
good, 136
love, 64, 132
primary, 133
relations, 46, 52, 73, 82, 90, 134
Oedipal ideas, 19, 74–76, 84, 116, 143, 146

Ortvay, R., xviii, 97–102, 104–108, 164, 167–168

parent(s), 33, 62–64, 75, 80, 106, 132, 163
Pauli, W., xix, 98, 107, 158, 161, 167–169, 174–175
Pfeifer, Z., 32, 48
Podolsky, B., 173, 177
Pontalis, J. B., 88, 95, 118, 127
Popper-Lynkeus, J., 161, 178
Pribram, K., 171, 178

Radó, S., xv, xxi, 4, 32, 44, 91
regression, xviii, 73, 115, 129–136, 140, 149
  mental, xv, 24
  therapeutic, 125, 129–131
repression, xvii, 9–10, 36, 42–44, 47, 80, 103, 106, 108, 111, 116, 118–119, 121, 129, 147–148
Revolutionary Council Republic, 32
Rickman, J., xiii–xiv, xvi, xxi–xxiii, 25–26, 29
Roazen, P., 77, 84
Robinson, K., vii, 22, 26, 28
Róheim, G., xvi, xxi, 27, 32, 44, 48, 87
Rosen, N., 173, 177
Rutherford, E., xviii, 158, 176

sadism, xvii, 46, 93, 145–146, 148
Schächter, M., 90–91, 112
Scholem, G., 168–169, 175, 178
Second International Conference, 22
seduction, xviii, 70–72, 74–76, 79, 82, 114–116, 121
self, xiv, 56, 80, 82, 117, 124, 131, 135
  -analysis, 34, 39, 76, 104, 135
  -aware(ness), 159
  -conscious(ness), 9
  -control, 63
  -critical, 59
  -denial, 103
  -destructive, 93, 141
  -effacement, 33
  -esteem, 62

false-, 131
  -image, 112
  -knowledge, 13
  -observation, 162, 173
  -preservation, 118
  -questioning, 80
  -regard, 117
sexual, 5, 64–65, 70, 72–74, 76, 104–105, 114–116, 118, 136, 141
  see also: abuse
  aggression, 104
  development, 65
  symbolism, 105
sexuality, 65, 71, 74, 76, 79, 104, 107, 112
  bi-, 106
  child, 75
  homo-, 24, 106, 112
Shakespeare, W., 148
Sterba, R., 123, 127
Stern, D. N., 72, 84
Stewart, H., xvii–xviii, 131, 135–137
Strenger, C., 78, 84
subject(s), 4, 20, 118, 142–143
subjectivity, 24, 81, 111, 113, 126, 136
  inter-, 81
Szalai, S., 52–53
Szalay, K., 11, 29
Szekacs-Weisz, J., 22, 26, 28
Szilárd, L., 165
Szőke, G., 51, 54

Tariska, I., 50–51, 54
Tóth, V., 98, 108–109
transference, xvi, xxii, 17, 47, 63, 71, 78, 112, 125, 133–134 see also: countertransference
trauma, xv, xviii, xxii, 5, 12, 18, 45, 61, 65, 70–72, 74, 79–80, 82, 111–125, 129–130, 132, 136, 140–141

unconscious(ness), xvi, 19, 39, 51, 55, 57–60, 65–66, 72, 76, 103–104, 107, 112–114, 117, 120–121, 143
  see also: conscious(ness)

fantasies, 116, 130
University of Vienna, 160

Vas, I., 47–48, 54
Veigelsberg, H. *see*: Ignotus
von Kármán, T., 97, 165, 167
Von Neumann, J., 97–98, 106–107,
    162–168, 170–171, 178
Vonneuman, N., 106, 109, 164, 178

War, 15, 22–23, 31, 48, 50–51, 58, 107,
    131
  Cold, 49, 51
  First World, xvii, 41–45, 47
  Second World, 6, 56, 60, 107, 141

Wednesday Society, xv, 57
Wiener, P., 91, 95
Wigner, E., 97–98, 107, 166–168,
    170–172, 175, 178
William Alanson White Institute, 60
Winnicott, D. W., 64, 67, 70, 73, 76,
    85, 131–134, 136–137
world, 70, 74, 80, 111, 170
  external, 26–27, 118, 122, 162,
    172–173
  internal, xviii, 75, 162, 173

Young-Bruehl, E., 166, 178

Zsigmond, J., 98, 109